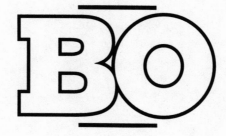

BO SCHEMBECHLER & MITCH ALBOM

WARNER BOOKS

A Warner Communications Company

Warner Books, Inc., 666 Fifth Avenue, New York, NY 10103

w A Warner Communications Company

Printed in the United States of America
First printing: September 1989
10 9
Library of Congress Cataloging in Publication Data

Schembechler, Bo.
  Bo / Bo Schembechler, Mitch Albom.
    p.   cm.
  ISBN 0–446–51536–1
      1. Schembechler, Bo. 2. Football—United States—Coaches—
Biography. 3. University of Michigan—Football—History.
I. Albom, Mich, 1958-   II. Title.
GV939.S33A3   1989
796.332′092—dc20   89-40032
[B]   CPI

Book design: H. Roberts

For Millie, my sons, my mother, and all the young men who have played for me.

—*Bo Schembechler*

For my Uncle Ed, the greatest tough guy on earth.

—*Mitch Albom*

Acknowledgments

For their help in putting this book together and jogging Bo's memory banks, the authors wish to thank:

Jim Betts, Denny Franklin, Dan Dierdorf, Reggie McKenzie, Jim Mandich, Glenn Doughty, Calvin O'Neal, John Wangler, Joe Hayden, Betty Schembechler, Alex Agase, Jim Harbaugh, Jack Harbaugh, Ernie Kellerman, Larry Smith, Ara Parseghian, Jim Young, Bill McCartney, Dick Calderazzo, Jeff Cohen, Tom Coyle, Tom Dohring, Mike Husar, John Kolesar, Matt McCoy, T.J. Osman, Marc Ramirez, Greg Skrepenak, Scott Smykowski, Trey Walker, Brent White, Tim Williams, John Anderson, John Arbeznik, Greg Bartnick, Gene Bell, Jim Bolden, David Brown, Andy Cannavino, Anthony Carter, John Ceddia, Gil Chapman, Jeff Cohen, Jim Brandstatter, Dana Coin, Don Coleman, Garvie Craw, Thom Darden, Russell Davis, Mark DeSantis, Bill Dufek, Don Dufek, Stan Edwards, Bruce Elliott, Curtis Greer, Frank Gusich, John Hennessy, Rich Hewlett, Mike Hoban, Derek Howard, Harlan Huckelby, Mike Jolly, Mike Keller, Mike Kenn, Mike Lantry, George

Acknowledgments

Lilja, Rob Lytle, Larry Kellog, Gil Marchman, Lindsay McClain, Jerry Meter, Don Moorhead, Greg Morton, Pete Newell, Mel Owens, Jim Pickens, Monte Robbins, Tom Seabron, Paul Seymour, Phil Seymour, Ron Simpkins, Tom Slade, Neal Hiller, Tubby Raymond, Bruce Matte, Steve Smith Strinko, Jerry Zuver, Frank Strocha, Dave Young, James L. Jones.

Much appreciation to Lynn Koch, Mary Passink, Linda Beard, Ken Droz, and Mike Stone. Special thanks to Ken Clover, Bill Diem, and Chris Kucharski of *The Detroit Free Press* for their assistance and patience. And special thanks to Adam Schefter, who got a real Bo education.

(P.S. I want to personally thank Mitch Albom; the poor son of a bitch had no idea what he was getting into. *Bo Schembechler*)

Contents

Contents

Foreword

"Goddamn it," he said, sitting behind the steering wheel, "you'd better be good, because *I'm not saying a single thing that's worthwhile.*"

You want to know what it was like to write a book with Bo Schembechler? That is what it was like. Sitting in a car in the middle of a snowstorm being told that nothing he'd said after talking for three hours was worthwhile.

Not that I knew it would be like that when we started. Not that I had the slightest idea what putting together this project would involve. Had I known, I might have opted for some other activity, say, chasing wild animals in the Yukon.

Instead, I spent countless hours listening to a man who can be described in a single sentence, provided that sentence contains the following words: *explosive, warm, intelligent, opinionated, stubborn, emotional, hysterical, sympathetic, old-fashioned, grumpy, short-tempered, quick,* and *loud.* Very loud. **VERY LOUD.**

And honest. As honest as the day is long. Here was the only agreement Bo and I had before diving into his life:

ME: "Bo, you know I'm a sports columnist. You can't expect me to go easy on you in the newspaper just because we're doing this book."

BO: "Fine. And don't expect me to treat you any better than I treat any other sportswriter."

ME: "Like dirt, right?"

BO: "Heh-heh."

You get the picture.

In the eight months it took to put this book together, I've had the chance to see Bo in a wide range of moods and places. I've seen his eyes light up when a former player drops into his office. And I've seen him lost in thought over an upcoming game.

I've seen him march into training table, joking and singing—then snapping at some lineman to "take that hat off, son," spinning to another to say, "You'd better get to math class."

I've seen him in the car on the way to make a speech, moping and moaning about how he hates these things, hates talking to groups, hates being the celebrity, and I've seen him make that speech and have the audience rolling, riveted, on the edge of their seats. I've seen him on the last days of recruiting season, frustrated, fed up, sweet-talking on the phone to prospective players around the country, then hanging up and shaking his head. "Can you believe I have to do this at my age?"

I've seen him relaxing in his easy chair at home, staring at a picture of his father, saying, "Yep. That's the old man." I've seen him on an airplane, reading the chapter about Woody Hayes, a man he loved, hated, fought, and admired, finishing that chapter and wiping tears from his eyes. I've seen him stand before a group of Navy cadets and bellow, "YOU MEN WILL NEVER ACHIEVE SUCCESS UNTIL YOU BEAT

ARMY!" And I've seen him trying to hide at the NCAA basketball championships, when an overzealous group of Michigan fans began to chant *"BO IS GOD! BO IS GOD!"*

I have seen him lose his temper and frighten visitors. I have seen him so sweet to strangers, they want to invite him home. I've sat with him on the veranda of his hotel room a few days before the Rose Bowl, as he worried about the opponent, shaking his head. And I found him all alone in the coaches' locker room after Michigan won that Rose Bowl, when he pulled out a cigar and sniffed it as if he were in heaven.

I have spoken with countless former players who refer to him as if he were royalty, and countless fellow coaches who worship the ground he walks on. He has been around the world, to the heights of athletic glory. And yet my favorite moment with him involved . . . a hamburger.

Really. We took a trip to Annapolis, Maryland, where he was to address the Naval academy in an evening banquet. After hours of shaking hands, we were finally driven back to our hotel by Elliot Uzelac, the Navy coach, for one hour's rest before the affair. We pulled into the parking lot. Across the street was a well-known hamburger restaurant.

"I love those things," Bo sighed, looking at the sign.

"Now, Bo, you got a banquet tonight," Elliot reminded him. "Steak and everything. You can't eat any hamburgers."

"Yeah, yeah, I know."

"I'm serious."

"I know. I won't eat anything."

"Good."

Elliot left. I was hot, grimy, tired, and hungry. I wasn't about to wait several hours for dinner.

"I don't know about you, Bo," I said, "but I'm going across the street. The hell with the steak."

His eyes lit up.

"You *dawg!*" he yelled.

"You with me?"

"AFFIRMATIVE!"

We marched over, slammed down an order, and when I tell you that watching him eat that hamburger was like watching a toddler play with his first Christmas present, I am not exaggerating. Here is a man who has won countless college championships, been named the best in his business, been profiled by every major newspaper and sports magazine, is recognized around the country, knows presidents, movie stars, billionaires.

A hamburger.

"Outstanding!" he said, over and over. "This is the best idea you ever had. Outstanding!"

A hamburger.

But that tells you something—maybe everything—you need to know about Bo Schembechler. He is a thousand things on the outside, and deep down, he is a very simple man. He truly does not think of himself as anything more than a football coach, and he doesn't need anything more than a field, decent kids to work with, and a good hamburger now and then. He has dedicated his life to molding young men, giving them a purpose and an experience that they will treasure for a lifetime. I was struck in the interviews with his former players by how many said Michigan football was the best time of their lives, and by how many couldn't stop smiling—I mean literally, ear-to-ear, all teeth, head-shaking, God-the-guy-was-unbelievable smiles—whenever his name was mentioned.

If the measure of a coach is how much he affects his players, then there is no doubt in my mind that Bo is amongst the greatest ever. His effect, I believe, is close to everlasting. Some of that comes through yelling, some through fear, some through intimidation, but most of it comes through a genuine concern, a fatherly kind of thing, a piece of the heart you can bank on, like a gold coin, to be there years from now. Wherever you are, you can always call Bo.

They do.

* * *

We had our share of arguments in putting this book together. And I must say, the man's memory, at times, can be as porous as a prevent defense. It took a long while to get him to remember certain events, and yet he did remember, eventually, gradually, richly, as if the memories were deserving of a slow return, a simmer rather than a boil.

Those memories are here in this book, as are his thoughts on his own reputation, which makes him laugh pretty hard sometimes. I can't say I blame him. I've heard more lies about Bo Schembechler than probably any man this side of Elvis Presley. When you live in Michigan, everyone has a Bo story; most of them, like fish stories, grow more impressive with the retelling.

My favorite part of the book is the final section, "Straight Talk," because here you see Bo at his best, explaining the game he loves, what's gone wrong with it, who's ruining it, and what can be done to save it. It is biting, hard-hitting, and very serious, yet it is swathed in a cloth of concern, love, if you can use that word with football, a real love for what the game should be. It is important reading, I think, and I sure hope the right people read it.

And then, of course, there are all the stories: his days with Woody Hayes, the first year at Michigan, the famous 1969 upset of Ohio State, the Rose Bowls. Personal memories of names like Carter, Harbaugh, Dierdorf, Lytle. Moments on the sidelines. Moments on the airplanes. Moments in his office.

The guy can tell a story.

Dan Dierdorf once told me that "few people have walked the earth the likes of Bo Schembechler." I'd like to go along with that. Oh, this is not a perfect man. He is stubborn, grizzled, old-fashioned, and a little bit the male chauvinist. I learned that. I also learned that he is not always sure of himself, that he has his foul-ups, that he doubts himself as a father.

I also learned that he takes a nap every day. Really. For about twenty minutes. When you call his office, they'll tell you he is in a meeting. But one day, his secretary whispered, "You know, he's sleeping."

Sorry, Bo. I had to reveal at least one secret.

For all the long hours and arguments we've had in putting this book together, I'll bet there are times in the years to come that I will miss talking to him—the clarity, the laughter, the volume. Whether he was telling stories or making a point about the college game, he was always emphatic and true to himself. I doubt many of us are truly in touch with our emotions; Bo isn't only in touch, he has them, as they say, by the short hairs.

So I close this little foreword by saying that, after being allowed to get closer to Bo Schembechler than almost anyone these last eight months, I believe with all my heart that this is an exceptional story, and that what lies between these covers is the story of a good man, an opinionated man, a man who is wise and funny and outspoken in his chosen field of excellence.

And I can't help thinking back to that car ride in that snowstorm. *"You better be good . . ."*

Here's what I figure: I didn't have to be good, Bo.

You were.

—Mitch Albom, May 1, 1989

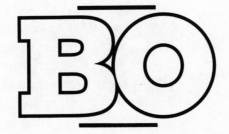

Why a Book?

FELT a pain in my chest. I began to sweat. "This isn't happening," I told myself. "This *can't* be happening." I lay back in the hospital bed and felt weak. It was early, around 6 A.M. I was dressed in my jogging suit, ready to go home. Suddenly, I wasn't going anywhere. The pain tightened around my lungs, a gripping, queasy pain that made me a prisoner of my own body. I dropped the newspaper I had been reading and looked at my wife, Millie, who had come to drive me back to the office.

"Get the doctor," I said.

"Bo, what's wr—"

"I'm having a heart attack."

Now, I am no stranger to medical emergency. I suffered my first heart attack when I was forty years old, on the morning of the Rose Bowl. I had the playsheets in my hands as the doctors pushed me down on the table. "Mr. Schembechler," they said, "we have to sedate you . . ."

I didn't want to believe it then. I didn't want to believe

it now. I popped two nitroglycerin tablets onto my tongue. The doctors arrived. They undressed me and smeared my chest with goop and slapped on the EKG machine. Suddenly, my life was a blip on the screen.

"Bo," the doctor said, "we need to operate."

"How soon?"

"Now."

So this is how fast you can go, I thought to myself. Ten minutes earlier, I had been ready to return to my team. We had the Hall of Fame Bowl in a few weeks. Recruiting season was under way. And here were these doctors, sticking needles in my arms, preparing me for open-heart surgery. *Now?* Did he say *now?* I was only supposed to be here for tests!

My skin had lost its color. My face was sweaty. Millie came over and stood beside me. She knew we were in trouble this time, that at my age, this could be it. I suddenly realized I might never see my wife or sons again. I asked the doctors for a moment alone.

"Millie . . ." I began. And I didn't know what to say. When am I ever at a loss for words? I have coached thousands of college football players, scared them, inspired them, broken them down and built them back up. I've become famous for screaming, for temper tantrums, for never failing to have an opinion.

And now, in this sterile hospital room, I could think of nothing comforting to tell my wife. "I love you," I whispered. "I'll come through this all right. And if I don't, you and the kids are taken care of . . ."

She was crying. Inside, I was crying too. They wheeled me out and pushed me towards surgery. It would be the second time they would slice open my chest and try to clear a path to my heart—and I would be helpless to do anything about it. Funny. At Michigan, during practice, if one of my players accidentally knocked me down, I always made sure to pop up, laughing, never letting them see the pain. "You think that hurt?" I would say. "You better hit a lot harder on Saturday, son."

There would be no popping up here. I was no longer Bo, the football coach. I was just another fifty-eight-year-old man at the mercy of my own flesh.

I was scared to death.

"Hey, put me out," I whispered to the doctor. "I don't even want to think about this."

"OK," he said.

His face was the last thing I saw. As my world darkened, I had two haunting thoughts:

Please, Lord, let me live.

And if I live, what will I do without football?

You are about to read the story of a man who probably doesn't deserve to have his life in a book. Books are for exceptional people: scholars, generals, historians, presidents. I am a football coach. Nothing more, nothing less. For the last twenty years, I've coached the same college team, the Michigan Wolverines, and when you stay in one place that long people start to get a fix on you:

"Oh, that Bo, he's a grumpy old man who yells and screams at the referees."

"Oh, that Bo, he's the coach who wins all those Big Ten championships, then blows the Rose Bowl."

"Oh, that Bo, he's the athletic director who took so long to hire that basketball coach, Steve Fisher."

Looking back, I've heard so many opinions about myself, nothing surprises me anymore. I get letters telling me I shouldn't scream so much on television. I get letters saying I'll never win a national championship if I refuse to cheat in recruiting. I get letters complaining I don't pass enough. I get letters asking why the Wolverines still wear those ugly black football shoes.

And on it goes. For a long time, I felt I never owed

anybody an explanation. In fact, in my earlier years of coaching, I was rough on anyone who interrupted my concentration—particularly sportswriters. "Hey listen," I would tell my assistants, "I don't need them if I win, and they can't help me if I lose." I only wanted to be left alone with my football team, free to do what I did best: coach the hell out of those young men.

That began to change in the recovery room of that hospital. I didn't know how long I'd been unconscious, but I knew how I felt when I finally awoke: like I'd been run over by a truck. There were eleven tubes coming from my body. Tubes from my throat, from my chest, tubes to the respirator. I could only blink my eyelids and wiggle my fingers.

"Well, I'm alive," I moaned to myself. Now the hard part would begin. Life as I knew it would be finished, I was sure of that. No more football. No more riding my players' shoulders after a championship.

I lay on that ice mattress, my body limp, my skin tight around my face. I would later learn that the doctors had taken internal mammary arteries and used them to keep my heart pumping. It had been a long, tedious operation. Quadruple bypass. If I hadn't been at the hospital when the attack happened, I'd probably be dead.

I stared at the white tiles of the ceiling. Would I walk again? Could I still be a decent husband to Millie? Finally, my surgeon, Dr. Otto Gago, came in. I braced myself.

"Well, Bo," he said from beneath his mask, "I just got back from speaking to the press."

I saw a chalk and slate nearby. Dr. Gago handed it over. *"What . . . did . . . you . . . tell . . . them?"* I scribbled.

"Believe it or not," he said, reading, "I told them you could coach again."

Now, I have heard some sweet words in my time. None of those compared to this. *I told them you could coach again.*

I stared at that doctor.

And I wept.

* * *

Ever since that day, I've given a lot of thought to the career I've had and the people who taught me about football and life. Men like Woody Hayes. Bear Bryant. They're gone now. And so is their style of coaching: brash, loud, get down in the mud and fight with your players. Today's coach is more often a "face man." He looks good on TV, speaks nicely to alumni, plays in the celebrity golf tournaments—and stands on the sidelines with his arms crossed during a game!

Which makes me a Neanderthal, I guess: the old way of thinking stuck in the new era of coaching. I can't stand with my arms crossed—not during a game, nor during a practice. I feel a little discouraged when I see these young guys looking pretty for the cameras, jumping from job to job, and ignoring the recruiting, academic, and drug scandals that are soiling our sport. The game has exploded. It's big money. It's big presure. It's out of control.

But it's still football, and as long as I'm here I'll coach it my way, thank you. I'll still scream at a freshman who fumbles the ball during practice. I'll still suspend a kid who misses classes. And I'll still defend what I think is the most important element: not championships, not TV contracts, but that every kid come out of the program with a diploma and a feeling he was a part of something special.

And the knowledge that his coach—who may have yelled and kicked and busted his ass—is now a friend forever.

That's the way it was for me. I pray that's the way it was for 640 Wolverines who have heard me blow my whistle. I am a football coach. And I never thought that was all that important, until my heart tried to take it away from me two years ago.

I have put together this book because I want people to know some of the things I've learned, some of the things I've seen, and why I said and did what I did in my thirty-seven years of coaching. I wrote it now, frankly, because I don't know how much longer I'll be around. It's not Shakespeare. I realize that. But it's my story.

Go ahead. Turn the page.

Now.

☆ ☆ ☆

A MICHIGAN MAN, AND HOW I GOT THIS WAY

☆ ☆ ☆

Growing Up Bo

WE were sitting inside our two-story wood house, my two sisters, my mother, and I. Suddenly, we heard the fire engine racing past.

"Let's go!" I yelled, dropping my baseball glove. "Come on! That's Dad!"

We ran outside, jumped in the car, and drove through the streets of Barberton, Ohio, turning left, turning right, chasing the sirens.

"That way!" I yelled, my head out the window.

"OK, OK," said my mother.

"No, that way!" said my sister.

"OK, OK!"

Such was life for a fireman's family. Some kids go to Dad's office; we rode to his fires. On this particular day, a local rubber plant was burning. Clouds of dark smoke billowed, and the smell was wicked. We got out of the car, and I gazed through the flames for my father's familiar figure. "Hey, Dad! Hey, Dad!"

Maybe that's where I first developed a sense for the sidelines, in Barberton, where a fire was as well-attended as a football game. The town had lots of manufacturing plants; that seemed to mean lots of blazes. There was even a place called the Diamond Match Factory, and one night, believe it or not, *it* caught fire. Zoom! Went right up.

The kids would sit on nearby curbs, or on car hoods, watching the flames lick into the sky. Sometimes the towns-people would bring sandwiches and hamburgers for the fire-men, to keep their strength up in between shifts.

"That's my dad," I would say, to whomever would listen.

"Yeah, we know," they would answer.

My childhood was small-town life, small-town values. I was a stocky kid with corduroy knickers, a striped shirt, and a crew cut. Had a lot of friends, a baseball field right near my house; what more could you want? My only beef was being the youngest of three children, the other two of whom were girls. My sisters, Marge and Virginia, teased me to no end. It was Marge who gave me my nickname. As a baby, she was trying to say "brother" but she could only say "Bobo . . . Bobo."

I've been Bo ever since.

A lot of habits I have today were formed in that old house on Baird Avenue. My temper, for one. Having two older sisters gave me plenty of excuses to lose it. We fought about food, we fought about the radio, we fought about who got to use the one bicycle that we owned. The arguments I have today with referees are nothing compared to some of the tussles we had in that living room.

I was also taught never to lie, and as a result, I developed into a very bad liar. I felt so guilty whenever I tried it—my father, a highly principled man, would not accept lies—that finally I just quit. I told the truth and took the consequences. To this day, I marvel at kids who lie so beautifully, they think they're telling the truth.

My love of sports was the theme of my childhood. I played all sports, all the time, I listened to every baseball game that came over the radio. I knew all the players—by name, number, and statistic. My dream back then was not to be a football player but a baseball star, a pitcher, on the mound during the seventh game of the World Series. *Schembechler sets, he delivers . . . STRIKE THREE! THE BALL GAME IS OVER! . . .*

One night we were all sitting in the living room. I was maybe ten years old. The phone rang and my dad picked it up. I could hear him saying, "No, no . . . no . . . never!" By the time he hung up, tears were coming down his face.

"Shem, what's the matter?" my mother said.

"Those bastards," he mumbled. "Those bastards."

"What? What?"

"That was the guys from the club. They want me to come down there. They want to give me a cheater's copy of the civil service exam."

"Why?"

He looked at her with a mixture of anger and shock.

"Because the *other guy* has one."

The "other guy," it turned out, was my father's rival for a promotion to fire chief. It was a job my father wanted. He was qualified; he was a captain. But you had to take these civil service exams, and somehow, the other guy had gotten hold of the questions. My father's friends found this out and got a copy, too. They were offering him a chance to cheat before he got cheated.

"It's only fair," they told him.

Not to my father, it wasn't. He never went down to that club. He refused to look at the questions beforehand. He took the test cleanly, scored high, maybe a ninety-seven. And the other guy beat him by a point.

So they made the other guy fire chief. My dad walked up to him, looked him square in the eye, and said, "You son of a bitch. I know how you got that score. And I am not working for you."

And he didn't. He took an inspector's position. Drove a red car around town, checking buildings for fire hazards.

He died doing that job.

I learned more from that night than any single lesson of my childhood. Do not bend your principles. Even if it costs you. Even if everyone else is doing it. I remind myself of that, and my dad, all the time as a football coach.

Especially during recruiting season.

Most of the characteristics football fans associate with me—temper, energy, stubbornness—I get from my mother, Betty. If you think *I'm* straightforward, you should meet her.

Ask her about my social life, she'll say: "Bo never had a date in high school."

Ask her about my sports prowess, she'll say: "Bo was never much of an athlete."

She would have made a good football coach.

Lucky for me, Mom understood my passion for sports. Once, during a football game, someone smashed my nose against the side of my face. She took me to this doctor who must have been ninety years old.

"My goodness," he said, "this nose is broken."

Oh, really?

"There will be no more football for this boy."

I gave my mother a look. She understood. To hell with him; I played the rest of the season with an old face-mask helmet. Good thing, too. Or I might be a toothbrush salesman today.

Mom was the force in our family, and I was absolutely crazy about her. She worked in the bank and, during the war, at the rubber factory. She cooked wonderful, ample meals—chicken, beef, potato salad—that always made me feel we were far better off than middle class. Mom was also the real sports fan of the house. On Ladies Day, she would take us to Cleveland Stadium to see the Indians. And does she know football? After our Rose Bowl victory last year, when we came back from a 14–3 halftime deficit to beat USC, her first words to me were: "What the heck were you doing in the first half?"

I still remember the night in 1957 when I was working as an assistant coach for Woody Hayes at Ohio State. The phone rang. It was my mother.

"Bo," she said, her voice quivering.

"What is it, Mom?"

"It's Dad . . . He had a stroke. He's dead."

And from that day on, my mother has been independent. As this book is being written, she is eighty-six years old, still living in Barberton—and she won't leave, because she is on her second or third set of friends. I guess she spoiled me a bit, as I was her youngest child and only boy. But if she did, it's only because she wanted to.

I don't think anyone has ever talked Mom into anything.

I was a teenager when World War II broke out. I got a job at the Nye Rubber Company, helping out as a stock boy. One of my jobs was to unload cases of lye, and if one fell and broke open, my eyes would burn for hours.

"This is awful," I said to myself, wiping the tears off my face. I think I realized then that factory life was not for me.

Girls? I was never much with girls, not in grade school, not in high school. I missed the junior prom. Missed the senior prom. Spent Friday nights at home listening to the Cleveland Indians games on the radio. Hey, I was a gym rat, a jock. What do you want?

By my sophomore year, I was a wingback on my high school football team. One day I watched the incoming freshmen work out, and I saw that they were all faster than me. Never one to warm the bench, I went straight to my coach, Karl Harter.

"Coach," I said, "where do you need help the most?"

"Offensive guard," he said. "Why?"

"I want to switch to offensive guard."

And I'm lucky I did. I never would have earned a college scholarship at tailback.

Now it hurts me to say this, but my dream back then was to play college football for Notre Dame. Fortunately for both of us, Notre Dame wasn't interested in me. I wasn't very big (maybe five foot ten, 193 pounds.) And I wasn't very good. I like to think of myself back then as, shall we say . . . a master technician?

One day, during senior year, Sid Gillman, the coach at Miami of Ohio, came to our high school. He was a big guy, well built, and he had come to recruit a teammate and me. He took us into an office near the gym. He pulled out a brochure which listed all his school's fees for tuition, room, board, and so on. Then he drew a line through each one.

"If you come to Miami," he said, "your scholarship will pay for this . . ."

"Uh-huh," we said.

"And this . . ."

"Uh-huh."

"And this . . .

"Uh-huh."

By the time he was done, the only thing left was books. Maybe twenty-five dollars.

"Now how about that?" he said.

I went to Miami.

Oh, if recruiting were only that easy today!

Big Man on Campus

I N my junior year of college, my life changed forever.

Woody Hayes took over as coach.

I never met anyone like him. I never will. He was the greatest teacher I have ever seen, the greatest motivator I have ever met, and quite possibly the best coach in the history of college football. Over the years, he would humble me, anger me, befriend me, and inspire me, and to this day, I miss him, I honestly do.

But back then, I despised him. Most of us did. He had just been announced as our new football coach—much to our surprise—and he was tough and nasty. He looked like a naval officer, with perfect posture and broad shoulders. He wore white shirts with ties, his dark hair slicked back. And he began that season by throwing out all the offensive innovations we had learned under Gillman, and replacing them with old-fashioned blocking, tackling, and physical torture.

"YOU'RE NOT TRYING HARD ENOUGH!"

"NO MISTAKES!"

"HARDER! WE WILL WORK HARDER!"

Who was this guy? We certainly didn't ask for him. Gillman had recruited us. But Gillman was now coaching Cincinnati, our arch rival. And he'd stolen half our team: Danny McKeever, our starting halfback; Gene Rossi, the quarterback; Jim Driscoll, a tackle. The rest of us were left with Hayes, who was making life miserable.

"Can you believe him?" we whispered, as we limped home after practice.

"He's so mean! And he never lets up."

Nobody could scream like Woody. One time, on a punting drill, my friend Al Maccioli was playing left end. He got beat, and his man blocked the punt.

In two seconds, Woody was in Al's face.

"WHAT THE HELL WERE YOU DOING?" He grabbed Al's jersey and yanked him so close he could smell his breath. "WHAT THE HELL WERE YOU DOING? WHY DIDN'T YOU STOP THAT MAN?"

We were stunned. No coach had ever grabbed a guy like that. "Coach," Al said, "I gave him a hard arm."

"A HARD ARM? WHAT THE HELL IS A HARD ARM? IF YOU CAN'T BLOCK THEN WE DON'T NEED YOU, YOU UNDERSTAND THAT?"

The whole field was silent. I watched Al walk away, his head down, as Woody stood there glaring. God, I hated him.

All that fall, we lived in fear of making a mistake. Woody had an expression, "No back is worth two fumbles." And he meant it. You fumbled once, you were in trouble. You fumbled twice, you'd be lucky to still have your uniform.

"But, Woody," a player would plead, "the guy popped me from behind!"

"IT WAS YOUR FAULT!" he would holler. "YOU DID NOT CARRY THAT BALL WITH PROPER LEVERAGE! YOU MUST LEVERAGE THE BALL WITH BOTH HANDS! IT WAS YOUR FAULT!"

Pretty soon, you would *never* see our running backs

without both hands on the ball. It may have looked old-fashioned, and maybe some of the other teams made fun of us, but we were more scared of Woody than of any of our opponents.

We finished that first season 5–4. It was a bad performance, and we bitched and moaned all season long. Of course, we blamed Woody, although in truth, the loss of talent and the adjustment to a new system were more responsible.

The following year, 1950, we began to see the results of a year's worth of torture. With hard hitting, crushing running, and of course, as few mistakes as possible, we suffered only one loss. We ripped through everybody and won the Mid-American Conference. Our defense was sharp, we had a good quarterback in Nobby Wirkowski, and a big guy named "Boxcar" Jim Bailey—the only black player on our team—a strapping fullback who could run the 100 yard dash in 9.5 seconds.

As per tradition back then, we were scheduled to play Cincinnati in the final game of the season. The newspapers made a big deal out of it. Gillman against Hayes. The former Miami coach versus the current Miami coach. For added intrigue, the Ohio State coaching job had opened, and most people figured the new coach would be—who else?—Gillman or Hayes. Talk about a showdown!

The game was played in frozen weather. Snow was falling all day. "Men," Woody had said to us, "a bigger prize is at stake here." And it was. Revenge. When I lined up, Driscoll was across from me. When our defense lined up, Gene Rossi was the opposing quarterback; Danny McKeever was the halfback. My God. It was like an old intra-squad scrimmage!

"Let's show them what they left behind," the Miami guys whispered to one another.

And it was no contest. In the first half, we scored four

times. I had maybe the best game of my college career, knocking people down as if they owed me money. We completely dominated. And once the second half started, the weather was so bad, nobody could do anything. We shut them out, 28–0, and Woody had finally beaten Sid. We celebrated like kids, throwing snow on each other, laughing, falling down. All that work and suffering—it was finally worth it!

In the newsletter that he put out for recruits, Woody wrote up that game. And in his account, he said, "Bo Schembechler, our offensive tackle, draped the snow-covered field with Cincinnati defenders . . ."

I thought I'd died and gone to heaven.

By that point, Woody had loosened up enough to show us another side. On the field, he was still terrifying. But off the field, he was a marvelous conversationalist, and we began to stop by his apartment just to talk, first one or two of us, then five or six. He would ramble on about military history, his favorite subject. He was so passionate when he spoke. You watched his eyes, and you were just mesmerized. Of course, winning the conference helped his popularity with us. We felt sort of like Marines, I guess, who had survived basic training and become proud soldiers.

In December, we flew out to play Arizona State in the Salad Bowl and won, completing our successful season. On the flight back, we got caught in a heavy storm and had to land in Nashville, Tennessee, around 2 A.M. It was late, and we were hungry.

Woody went to the man in charge of the airport cafeteria. "We've got to get these guys something to eat," he said.

The guy looked at our team. Then he pointed to Boxcar Bailey, who, as I mentioned, was our only black player.

"That guy isn't going to eat here," he said.

Woody stared at him. "What do you mean, he isn't?"

"We don't serve his kind."

"That guy don't eat here, none of us eat here."

"Well, he can't eat right here," the man stammered. "He'll have to eat upstairs."

"Fine. Then we'll *all eat upstairs.*"

"There's not enough room up there for all of you."

"Then Boxcar and I," Woody said slowly, clenching his teeth, "will eat . . . upstairs . . . together!"

And that's what happened. Woody and Boxcar ate in that little room while we all ate down below. A white coach. A black player. In the middle of a Southern airport.

We fell in love with Woody that night, this same guy we had hated so much during his first few days. We realized then he might kill you, break your spirit, scream until your ears were bleeding, but Woody Hayes was always for his players, rich, poor, black, or white. All the time.

Weeks later, I remember, he phoned and told me to come down and play racquet ball with him. Right in the middle of the game, he stopped and said "Who do you think should be the next coach at Ohio State?"

I said, "You, of course."

"Why do you say that?"

"Because you're the best man for the job. You proved it. You beat Gillman with the guys he left behind."

He looked at me.

Then we just went on playing.

A few weeks later, he got the job.

When college ended, I spent one year as a graduate assistant to Woody in Columbus. Here, after being just another grunt on his team, I was suddenly allowed inside all those mysterious staff meetings and film sessions, listening to the great coach teach his secrets, hearing him explain the variations on the off-tackle play.

He affected me in every imaginable way—and some unimaginable. I swear I heard his voice in my *sleep.* One of my responsibilities that year was to help coach the junior varsity, and early in the season, we took a road trip to play Wittenberg

College. It was a Saturday night, and the game was close. Late in the third quarter, we had a fourth-and-two at our own thirty-yard line.

"All right, punting team!" I said. "Get in there."

Just then I felt a hand clamp down on my shoulder. "GOD DAMN IT, BO! SHOW THEM YOU'VE GOT SOME GUTS!"

I spun around. It was Woody. What was he doing here?

"SHOW THEM YOU'VE GOT SOME GUTS, BO!"

"You mean . . . run the fullback?" I said. "On fourth-down at our own thirty?"

"YOU'RE GOD DAMN RIGHT."

"Well . . . OK."

We ran the fullback. He gained one yard. Wittenberg took possession, and scored the winning touchdown.

By the time I looked up, Woody was gone.

Such was Woody's mystique. It had already captured me. But the Buckeye players needed more time. They lost to Michigan State, tied Wisconsin, lost to Indiana, and tied Illinois. The fans in Columbus began to grumble. "What's with this Hayes? Why can't he win?"

In the final game of the season, Ohio State went to play Michigan. We took the train, sleeping overnight in Toledo and arriving in Ann Arbor the following morning. We walked to the stadium from the railroad station, got dressed, and we were awful. Got beat 7–0, with an offense that couldn't even crawl.

And the following day, Woody called us in for the last meeting. Someone turned on the projector and we began to watch film of the defeat.

After ten minutes, Woody got up, walked over, grabbed the projector and heaved it across the room with a crash.

"I WILL NOT SUBJECT THE PEOPLE OF COLUMBUS TO THAT KIND OF FOOTBALL," he said.

End of meeting.

It was hard for me to see Woody so frustrated. Believe it or not, many Buckeye fans back then wanted him fired. Including some of the boosters.

"Woody," a man once told him, "some of the local businesses are thinking of pulling out of the jobs program for your players."

"They are?" he said. "Well, let me ask you something. If I resigned, do you think they might change their minds?"

"I think so, yes."

Woody's face turned red. He spoke slowly, through gritted teeth, steam coming out of his nostrils. "Screw them. I'll mortgage my house and pay the players *myself*!"

The man left and never came back.

And I believe Woody would have done it.

The following summer, the army called. I said goodbye to Woody. Private Schembechler, reporting for duty. It was 1951. I was stationed in Camp Rucker, Alabama, the kind of place you want to leave the minute you arrive. Hot weather. Snakes. There was, however, football. Each regiment had its own team. And ours, the 135th, seemed to attract some top guys. We even had a running back from the Chicago Bears named Brad Roland, who is still a friend of mine.

I coached the defense and played middle linebacker—a position I was never good enough to play in college. I had a blast. Of course the games were not exactly Michigan Stadium. We played on dimly lit fields with maybe a dozen people watching. I'll never forget the championship game. They tried to dress up the opening ceremony by dropping the football from a helicopter. I was captain of our team, so I stood out there at mid-field along with the opposing captain. And this helicopter dropped in, with its propeller whirring and making us deaf. The wind was kicking up from the blades, and they dropped this football that we were supposed to catch. All we did was jump away from it and let it ricochet off the ground. I mean, it was like a bomb coming out of there.

"Awright, kick off!" somebody yelled.

So much for army ceremony.

The next ten years would see me coaching at five different schools. And much of what I am today comes from the lessons I learned during that decade. Footballwise, of course, I would get the most from Ara Parseghian at Northwestern, Doyt Perry at Bowling Green, and Woody at Ohio State. But for sheer fun, adventure, and pleasure, the best job I ever had was the one year I spent at Presbyterian College in Clinton, South Carolina, in 1954.

Now, I had never been to South Carolina in my life, let alone Clinton, a small town of about ten thousand. The Presbyterian coach, Bill Crutchfield, had hired me over the phone—in August, no less—to help coach his defense.

"Can you pick up this recruit in Pittsburgh on your way down?" he asked.

"Sure, no problem," I said.

"Good. See ya when you get here."

I picked the kid up and we rode down South together— you did that kind of thing back in those days—cruising along with the windows open and the radio on. When we reached Clinton, I dropped him on campus, and then began looking for a place to live.

After a few days of asking around, I learned that the Bailey family, which owned the big cotton mill, had traditionally taken in one faculty boarder each year. I called and made an appointment.

When I got out there, I couldn't believe my eyes. The most beautiful little Southern plantation home, with rows of boxwood trees and colorful gardens. Mrs. Bailey was an elderly woman whose husband was deceased. She had a daughter named Mrs. Marshall, whose husband was also deceased, and *she* had a daughter named Miss Marshall, who was away most of the time at boarding school. The three women lived there together, with a staff of servants and cooks and gardeners. I mean, this was right out of *Gone With the Wind*.

We sat in the parlor and had tea, and then they showed me the room, which was very large, with a porch and a balcony overlooking the gardens. Gardens? When I tell you that you could whack a 5-iron into those gardens and still not hit the road, I am dead serious.

"This is a lovely room," I said to Mrs. Bailey. "I'm very interested. I should, however, get back to a couple of people I had promised to speak with . . ."

"Mr. Schembechler," she said, "we normally ask for thirty dollars a month for this room. If you want it, you can have it for twenty-five."

I was no fool. I took it. My first night, I came home from work and there was a note taped to my door: *"Chicken sandwich and milk is in the refrigerator. Help yourself."*

When I came downstairs the next morning, the cook greeted me. "What would you like for breakfast?" he said.

"Uh . . . eggs over easy?"

"Very good, sir."

Mrs. Bailey and Mrs. Marshall were already sitting in the dining room. "Your seat is right there at the head of the table," Mrs. Bailey said. "Would you mind reading the Bible a little in the morning for us? Just pick out a couple of passages."

And that's the way it went the entire season. Breakfast in the morning, sandwiches at midnight, cooks and laundry and shoes shined. I was treated like some sort of Rhett Butler, which is pretty unusual for a football coach. Especially one who is only twenty-five years old. On top of that, after the first month, I tried to give Mrs. Bailey my rent check, but she tore it up.

"Now, Mr. Schembechler, we just enjoy having you here," she said, "We won't be needing any more of these checks."

Can you believe it?

I was making thirty-two hundred dollars a year for coaching football, baseball, and helping out with basketball. In those days, a coach did everything: lined the fields, taped the ankles. I hardly minded. We won some games and the students began to get excited. Then came the big showdown with our rival, Wofford College. We drove up on Saturday with great anticipation.

God, what a night! It was like parachuting into enemy territory. They made us dress in a cinder-block locker room a hundred yards from the field. We tried to give our guys a pep talk. "Okay, men, you know what this means. We're going out and take on Wofford. Let's *go get 'em!*" We fired up and came charging out of the locker room.

Unfortunately, there was only one long, thin path up to the football field, and we had to go single file. And on both sides of that path were the Wofford freshmen, all wearing their beanies, hollering the official death chant:

"Terrier meat! Terrier meat! Dog food, dog food!"

"Terrier meat! Terrier meat! Dog food, dog food!"

They were right on top of us. You couldn't help but see their taunting faces. By the time we reached the field, our locker room speech had evaporated.

"Terrier meat! Terrier meat! Dog food, dog food!"

The game was a disaster. By the fourth quarter. Wofford was winning 19 to 6, and they were driving again. Crutchfield and I were mad as hell.

"Hey," he said, "let's just pull the first team out of there; throw the second team in. See if they can do any better."

Wouldn't you know it? The second team stopped Wofford on the goal line. Then, on our very first offensive play, the fullback broke free for ninety-nine yards and a touchdown. We kicked the extra point and the score was 19 to 13, with about three minutes left.

The crowd was now down around the field, standing right behind the end zones and the sidelines. You could almost feel their breath. We short-kicked Wofford and—surprise!—we recovered the ball.

"We're gonna pull this out!" I told Crutchfield.

Sure enough, we drove down to the goal line. Less than a minute left. Fourth-down and inches. The Wofford fans by now were literally on the lip of the end zone, leaving almost no room for players to move. They screamed "HOLD 'EM! HOLD EM! HOLD EM!"

We took the snap, and our quarterback sneaked into a pile. The whistles blew and the referee dove in for the ball.

"He made it! He made it!" I screamed.

The bodies were peeled away. The crowd was chanting "NO! NO! NO! NO!" And soon it was just the referee standing there with the ball. Normally, he would look to the linesman to see where to mark the forward progress. But for some reason, the linesman had his back turned, and all the referee saw was a sea of Wofford fans.

"NO! NO! NO!"

That poor guy. Probably fearing for his life, he put the ball down on *the one-yard line*.

"First down, Wofford!" he said.

I went crazy. They had to hold me back.

"ARE YOU NUTS? ARE YOU OUT OF YOUR MIND? WHY, YOU NO GOOD—"

I mean, I was hot.

So it's not just Big Ten officials I have problems with.

Anyhow, we ended up 6–3 at Presbyterian, which was a fine record for that school, and after the season, I got a call from Doyt Perry, who had been an assistant coach at Ohio State and who had just taken over at Bowling Green. He offered me a job and I took it.

Good-bye, chicken sandwiches.

"Oh, Bo," said Mrs. Bailey, as I packed up to leave. "We're gonna miss you. We were hoping to introduce you to some proper ladies, and maybe get you married."

"Well, gee, Mrs. Bailey. Thanks, but I've got to go. You know this football."

"Yes," she said, "football."

Before I knew it, I was back in Ohio. Little did I know, I would never leave the Midwest again.

Working for Doyt was an experience. He reminded me of Barry Fitzgerald, the actor who played the friendly priest with Bing Crosby in *Going My Way*. In the mornings, he would get up, put his hat on, light up his pipe—and *then* shave. I know this, because we all lived together that year— Doyt, me, and Bill Gunlock, a former Miami teammate (naturally) whom Doyt hired to coach the defense—in a place called Ridge Cottage. It had no kitchen. Just a lot of bunk beds. Whenever a recruit came to visit the campus, he would stay with us. Just give him a spare bunk bed.

You did that kind of thing back in those days.

Speaking of recruiting, that year was really my introduction to the whole crazy process. I learned how to make the trips, how to make the speeches—and how to prepare for aggravation. One time Gunlock and I went to Cleveland to recruit a halfback named Bob Ramlow. He was working at a gas station.

"Hey, Bob," I said, "how's it going?"

"Good, coach," he said, "but I can't really talk right now. My boss is watching. I gotta grease this car."

"That's OK," I said, "we'll talk while you work."

Now, you have to picture this. I was wearing one of the two suits I owned. Ramlow was in his overalls. The car was up on the lift, and he was squirting it with the grease gun.

"We'd love to have you at Bowling Green," I said, reciting my lines.

"Uh-huh," said Ramlow. Squirt, squirt.

"Play a little football, you know."

"Uh-huh." Squirt, squirt.

"We're really turning things around up there."

"Uh-huh." Squirt, squirt.

When I was finished, I said good-bye and got back in the car. "Look at you," Gunlock said, stifling a laugh.

"What?" I looked down—my suit was covered in grease. "God damn it, if that kid doesn't end up coming to Miami, I'm gonna kill him."

In thirty-five years, recruiting has not gotten any better.

Anyhow, Doyt did a whale of a job coaching that season. About the only thing he didn't turn around was the wind. The stadium at Bowling Green was built east-west, which is strange, because, as any football coach knows, in the autumn, that's the direction the winds blow. That's why most football stadiums are built north-south. Throw in that flat Ohio landscape, and the wind got ridiculous. In one game against Toledo we kicked off, the ball bounced at their twenty-five–yard line, and blew back so far our *kicker* recovered it.

"How'd we do that?" Doyt asked.

"Wind," we said.

"Oh."

And thirty minutes later, it happened again!

"Wind again?" Doyt asked.

"Yep."

Under Doyt's gentle-yet-firm style, the players clicked, and we went 7–1–1 that year. We actually played for the championship against Miami (which at that time was coached by Ara Parseghian). The week of the game, our starting quarterback, Jim Bryant, got hurt, and we had to go with this skinny backup kid named Don Nehlen. He threw three interceptions. We lost 7–0.

Today Nehlen is head coach at West Virginia. Last year his team played for the national championship. Good thing the coach wasn't quarterbacking.

Just kidding, Don.

The following year, Ara went to Northwestern and offered me a job there. It was a chance to move up to Big Ten football, and as close as I was to Doyt, I felt I had to take it. Ara was an intense guy, with those dark eyebrows and dark eyes, but he was well known as a brilliant coach, and I was anxious to learn from him.

It was also at Northwestern that I met Alex Agase, who coached the defense. He would become a lifelong friend.

Here's the only story you need to know about Alex. He was stronger than me—he had been a great linebacker for the Cleveland Browns—but I would always argue that in line play, it was technique that mattered, not strength.

"You old, fat, All-American," I would tease him. "I could knock you on your fanny."

"Oh yeah?" he said one day. "I'll tell you what. Let's try it this afternoon."

"You're on."

We met on the field. I dropped into the most beautiful three-point stance you ever saw. Ready . . . go! I fired out, he fired out—and he knocked me four yards backwards.

"Aw, lemme try it again," I said.

"Fine," he said.

Same stance. Same technique. Pow! Same result. I was flat on my behind.

"Just remember," Alex said, walking away, "*sometimes* strength beats technique."

Gotcha.

The Northwestern experience was interesting because here we were, working under one of the greatest minds in college football, Ara Parseghian, and yet in 1957, my second year there, we lost every game we played. *Every single game.* We were 0–9, the only losing team I've ever coached. How did it happen? The talent wasn't there. And we had no leadership amongst the seniors.

And yet, as weird as this sounds, that might have been Ara's finest year of coaching—only because, through all those defeats, he never cracked, he never made his coaches feel inferior, and he never stopped trying new things. We used to take the demo teams on Monday afternoons to a practice field we called "The Laboratory." There Ara set up a mock defense of the team we were playing that week, and tried all sorts of offensive twists to see if they might work. Reverses, traps, counters, blocking assignments. I never met anyone with that kind of football imagination.

During meetings, after each loss, Ara would say to us, "Listen, I know this isn't a great year. But you guys are not to blame. We'll get through this. We will turn it around."

He was great. He kept his sense of humor. Sometimes we'd work until 2 A.M., and then Ara, as down as he was, would walk out with Alex. They'd get into their cars, drive to the traffic light, and gun their motors.

"Come on!" Ara would yell, the competitive juices still flowing.

"You got it!" Alex would answer.

And they'd drag-race down Central Avenue.

What truly inspired me about Ara, more than any single incident, was the time the athletic director, Stu Holcomb, wanted his son to play quarterback. We had only recruited this kid because Holcomb told us he might be an asset. Suddenly, in the midst of that terrible 1957 season, he began to put the pressure on Ara.

"I want you to put him in there," Holcomb said. "Come on. Let him play. What are you waiting for?"

Every week, Ara got this. "Come on, I want him in." A lot of coaches would have done it. Especially when they were losing and knew their job was on the line.

Ara never cracked. He never used that kid as quarterback. "I'll do things my way, or no way," he told me. I'll never forget that. It's largely why today I never let outside influences affect my football program.

Of course, we continued to lose, and in the final game of the season, Illinois clobbered us 27–0, with Ray Nitschke breaking a seventy yard touchdown run right in front of our sideline. As he lumbered past—and Nitschke was *not* fast—I watched him, Alex watched him, Ara watched him.

"Jesus," Ara said, shaking his head.

That about summed up the season.

Not long after, Woody called me up. He finally had an opening on his staff.

"Come on down here and coach with me," he said.

"Gee, Woody, you know I'd love to. That's something I've always wanted to do."

"So?"

"Well, how can I leave here? We were 0–9. I'd feel like I was bailing out."

"Damn it, Bo. I don't have these openings all the time. Now, they'll understand. I want you down here with me."

"OK, Woody. Let me just think about it, OK?"

I took a few days and talked it over. Ara was disappointed, but he knew Ohio State was a golden opportunity. Still, after the meeting, I thought, "Forget it. I'm staying. He's too good a guy to abandon like this."

The last person left to talk to was Alex. I told him my dilemma. He was quick with his advice.

"Go to Ohio State."

"But, Ags, I feel like I'm—"

"Never mind that deserting business. Everyone knows

you're not doing that. And everyone knows that you don't pass up a chance to coach under Woody."

"You sure?"

Alex looked at me, the same way he had just before he plowed me over in our blocking drill. "Bo," he said, "you take that damn job or I'm gonna hit you in the mouth."

Ohio State, here I come.

Woody And Me

I LOVED Woody Hayes. I am not ashamed to say it. In the thirty-seven years I knew him, he coached me, humbled me, employed me, angered me, and taught me more about the game than anyone could. I guess I was about as close to him as anyone, but to the day he died, I never considered myself his equal.

Certainly not in the late 1950s, when I was working for him at Ohio State. Back then, he was the very essence of discipline. He wore white shirts with ties, all the time, except at practice, where he wore one gray T-shirt and no jacket. When November came, and it was freezing cold, maybe he would put on *two* gray T-shirts. Maybe.

"Woody, you'll catch pneumonia," I used to tell him.

"Bo," he said, "if the players see you don't think it's cold, then *they* won't think it's cold."

He was right. But by the time he came in from those practices, his skin was frozen. He'd take a shower and stand under the hot water for a long time, just thawing out, until his skin turned lobster red. I can still see him now, his whole body almost glowing under the water.

Believe me, none of us ever complained about the cold.

Not that you would complain too much to Woody about anything. At least not to his face. His temper was legendary. He would scream at coaches, officials, players, his arms flailing, his face turning crimson. But however tough he was on others, Woody was toughest on himself. There are accounts of him biting his hand so hard it would bleed. He would yank off his hat and rip it in half.

Once, I saw him punch himself in the face. We had a terrible scrimmage, and he got so mad he punched himself in the eye and split his eye open. The next morning I picked up the newspaper and read where Woody "was so excited at the scrimmage that his whistle flew up and cut him in the eye." That, folks, is not what happened.

When Woody talked, it was best to sit and listen. I learned that in my first Ohio State staff meeting, when he was outlining a play on the blackboard.

"Woody, I don't think that's right," I said.

He turned. "What the hell do you mean, you don't think it's right?"

"Well, I don't think you should block it that way. My experience has been that you take this guy and you hit him in there and you bounce on him and you . . ."

I went on and on about this technique. Now you have to remember, Woody was just coming off a successful Rose Bowl season. And I was fresh in from Northwestern, where we went 0–9. Woody stood there as I talked and the other staff members looked at the walls, trying to hide their grins.

Finally Woody said, "Let me ask you one question, Bo."

I said, "What's that?"

"How many goddamn games did you win last year?"

And I said, "Well, none."

"Then sit down."

When I look back on it, I should have been thankful that was all he said. When Woody was ticked, there was no telling what he'd do. Once, before a game, he put his fist smack through a blackboard. Really. He had written the word *DESIRE* on the board. Then he wrote the word *EXECUTION*. The letters got bigger and bigger because he was getting madder and madder and finally, he got so mad that boom! He punched a hole right through it. Had a hard time getting his hand out. He sort of dragged the blackboard across the locker room, and sent the team out to play.

It was inspiring, I'll tell you that.

I guess I was as much Woody's friend back then as I was his assistant. He loved to wake me up first thing in the morning with some request, or call me late at night to watch film. Sometimes he'd send me to the airport, or out to find a player. Sometimes I would pick up the phone and hear him bark: "YOU MEET ME AT THE RACQUETBALL COURT IN HALF AN HOUR, BO. AND IF YOU'RE NOT THERE, IT'S BECAUSE YOU CAN'T TAKE IT."

I never minded. During those years at Ohio State, I'd have done anything for him. Want proof? How about my very first night? I had just driven in from Chicago. We were monitoring study table when, suddenly, Woody yelled, "Hey, where's that damn Jim Marshall?"

You may remember Jim Marshall. Very big guy? Became an All-Pro lineman with the Minnesota Vikings?

"I hate to tell you this, coach," one of the assistants said, "He's up at French Field House. He's throwing the shot put in an intramural track meet."

"WHAT?" Woody screamed. "And missing study table? Goddamn it, Bo, you go up and get him, and you get him down here *now!*"

I didn't know Marshall. I'd never seen Marshall. I hadn't even unpacked my bags yet. But I wandered into the track meet. There he was.

"Uh, Jim," I said. "Come here a minute, will you?"

He stepped out of the ring.

"Jim, I'm Bo Schembechler. I'm the new coach here."

"Oh, yeah? How you doing?"

"Well, I want you to know I just left Woody. You're supposed to be in study table, and he's ticked off. So you're going to come with me now. OK?"

"Goddamn son of a bitch!" he screamed. And he slammed down the shot put and made a scene in front of all these people. Remember, I've just been on the job two hours. Everyone was staring. We left together, and Marshall didn't say a word to me the entire way. I dropped him with Woody, who grabbed him, took him in a room—and began to tutor him. Not yell at him. *Tutor* him.

That was Woody.

People ask me all the time about our fights. First of all, they were arguments, not fights. As the years went on, and I became more and more bold, they got pretty heated, sure, but Woody never really hit me and I never hit him. I wouldn't dare. We did argue over just about everything. And we did take some of our frustrations out on the furniture.

Chairs, for instance. We had this argument once in the staff room, and we were kicking chairs around left and right. I would scream something and kick a chair at him. He would scream something and kick a chair at me.

"YOU'RE OUT OF YOUR &%$# MIND!"

"I AM NOT!"

"YES YOU ARE!"

And then he fired me.

Just like that.

Now, he had threatened to do that plenty of times. He'd say "If you don't do this right I'm going to fire your butt!" But he'd never gone through with it before.

So I stormed out, marched up and down the halls, and then I went to the bathroom. Man, I was hot. And suddenly, he came marching in. I don't think he was looking for me. I think he just had to use the bathroom. Anyhow, he saw me in there, and he said "OK, you can come back."

And I did.

Oh, don't worry. I would have gone back anyhow. You don't let a little thing like getting fired keep you from a meeting. The funny thing is, I can't for the life of me remember what Woody and I were fighting about. It was football, I'm sure of that. It always was.

And he won every argument.

Just like I win every one at Michigan.

They call that "Being the Head Coach."

Still, we had some great moments together in Columbus. Coaching a game with Woody was an adventure. Once, in 1961, against Michigan, we went into the second half and our phone system broke. I was yelling "Hey! Woody! Hello! Hello?" but there was no response. We desperately tried to get the things fixed, but Woody couldn't wait. He just ripped the headphones off and called the plays himself from the sidelines. We won 50–20. I just sat there and watched.

Another time we were playing Iowa in Iowa City. It was one of these games where they score, we score, they score, we score. So in the fourth quarter, the score was 28–28, and we drove all the way down this muddy field to the one-yard line. Fourth down.

"Let's go for it, Woody!" I urged over the headphone. "Let's go for the touchdown!"

"I'm going for the *field goal!*"

"No, Woody, let's get the touchdown!"

"I am going for the *field goal!*"

We kicked the field goal and went up, 31–28. Iowa got the ball and began to drive and I figured they were going to score. I was wrong. They threw an interception; we took it in and beat them 38–28.

In the locker room after the game. Woody found me and gave me a slap to the stomach.

"I *told* you I was going for the field goal!"

And he walked away.

There was plenty to criticize about Woody Hayes. His methods were tough, his temper was, at times, unforgivable. And, unless you knew him or played for him, it is hard to explain why you *liked* being around the guy. But you didn't just like it, you loved it. He was simply fascinating.

Think about all the great players he recruited for Ohio State. How do you think he did it? Simple. In the home, there was no one more charming, polite, or intriguing than Woody Hayes. Parents would say, "I'll never let my son play for Woody Hayes. I don't approve of his methods."

Then, sooner or later, Woody would pay them a visit. He would spin stories about football, about their home town, maybe he'd tell them some history they never knew about where they lived. He'd have some pie the player's mother had cooked and say it was "the most delicious thing I've ever eaten"—and mean it. And the next day, the parents would be telling friends, "You know, that man is not at all like they say. He's well-mannered and very intelligent; people have him all wrong . . ."

The kid usually ended up at Ohio State, too.

Woody was always nonmaterialistic. He seemed to revel in having as few possessions as possible. I remember him once turning down a Cadillac that someone had offered. "I'm not driving any Cadillac," he said. "We'll take that money and put it in a fund to send our coaches' children to school."

Clothes didn't interest him. Furniture didn't interest him. Military history? That interested him. He knew about battles that I'd never heard of. The Roman Empire. The Punic Wars. Napoleon. He spoke of them all as if he had been there. Woody never believed football was all you needed to know.

He did, however, make sure you knew football. For the six years I coached under him, our first play on offense was always 26–27, the fullback off-tackle. Simple. Basic. Yet I swear he would go to that blackboard and draw it up with the enthusiasm of a man who'd just discovered the greatest innovation in the history of football. It was marvelous. We'd just sit there and gaze. "This is what I learned last year about this play that we can improve on," he'd say, "If we move this tackle out one foot . . ."

When he took that play before the squad he'd have the players so inspired they'd be gasping, "Oh my God." The simple off-tackle play! We'd run it over and over, block, run, block, run, practice after practice, with Woody egging us on, so that when that play was finally called in a game, it was like saying "Shoot, this is it, man. We're gonna knock their ass out of here." Critics all laughed. But when you're standing on the other side and that play is coming at you, let me tell you, it preys on your mind. "We can't stop the fullback," you say. "We can't stop the goddamn fullback . . ."

Now, *that* was Woody Hayes.

Temper? That was his middle name. I've seen him chew out officials. I've seen him take apart assistant coaches. I even saw him storm into a campus meeting once and grab the microphone to defend the Ohio State president. But the maddest I ever saw Woody—and the most brilliant—was at the end of my next-to-last season with him, 1961. We had just won the Big Ten championship with an 8–0–1 record, and we were looking forward to playing UCLA in the Rose Bowl.

Woody and I were in a hotel suite in Cleveland, waiting for an alumni banquet to begin. He was the guest speaker.

The phone rang. Woody picked it up. It was Dick Larkins, the Ohio State athletic director. In a highly political and very dubious vote, the Ohio State Athletic Board of Control had suddenly voted to decline the Rose Bowl, saying that, since Ohio State had already defeated UCLA earlier in the season, the trip was somehow unjustified.

"Woody," Larkins said glumly, "we're not going. Minnesota, the runner-up, will go instead."

Woody was so mortified, he could barely speak. He slammed down the phone. The room was full of people. "GODDAMN!" he screamed. "BO, COME HERE! WE'RE LEAVING NOW! GODDAMN!!"

We marched out of that hotel and into the night and not a word was said. It was freezing outside and Woody's breath came in spurts of cold smoke. The streets were deserted. The stores were all closed. Woody just kept walking in the darkness, with me a half step behind. Now and then he'd turn and mumble, "Goddamn people . . . they don't know what they're doing . . ."

We walked for an hour, maybe longer. I never spoke. All this time, remember, there's this banquet that is waiting for Woody to speak. Finally he turned to me. His eyes were steady. His voice was calm.

"We're going back," he whispered.

"What are you going to tell them?"

He paused. "Just come and listen."

By the time we returned to the hotel, the word had spread. The ballroom was buzzing. When we walked through the door the people rose and gave Woody a thunderous ovation.

"These people," he said, his voice trembling, "who have voted this decision today, have never *played* in a Rose Bowl! They cannot *comprehend* the pride and the confidence and the lifelong memories that a game like this gives the young men who play college football. To deny those men this precious chance is the *worst judgment they could possibly exercise* . . ."

He had those people spellbound. I can hear still his voice today, ringing with anger. Someone had crossed his players and his heart literally exploded with rage. That's when you knew where Woody Hayes really stood on things. At moments like that. God, he was good.

The following year, Johnny Pont left Miami of Ohio, my alma mater. They were looking for a new coach. I went to Woody and told him I wanted that job. I'd been in the system for ten years, and I thought I was ready.

"You can't leave," Woody said, banging his fist on the desk.

"What do you mean, I can't leave?"

"You can't leave," he said, "because you're going to be the next head coach here at Ohio State."

"Woody," I said, "how much longer are you going to coach?"

"Three to five years. No longer."

I didn't believe that. I don't think he did either.

"Gee, Woody," I said, apologetically, "I'm ready to go now. I shouldn't wait around."

It was a good thing I didn't. He stayed there another sixteen years. As I drove away from Columbus, I knew I would never work for Woody Hayes again. But I had a feeling he was not out of my life. And, man, was I right about that.

Go ... Miami!

W ORK.
Work harder.
Work harder than that.
This was my approach to my first head coaching job. I was back at Miami of Ohio, my alma mater, and I dug in for six years, and I swear to you, I never came up for air. Never took a vacation. Almost never went out socially. You think I'm intense now? Heaven *forbid* you were there back in Oxford.

This was the first thing I did as new coach of the Miami Redskins: I moved into the dormitory. Not some faculty dormitory. The dormitory where my players lived. I took the ground floor room closest to the door. And I slept with my door open. And if any of those players were even thinking about sneaking in past curfew—ha!

"Bo," the athletic director said to me during a visit to the cafeteria on my first day there, "I want you to meet Ernie Kellermann. Ernie was quarterback of the team last year."

I looked at this kid, small and skinny, and I grabbed his

arm. "THIS IS MY QUARTERBACK! HOW CAN YOU EVEN THROW WITH ARMS LIKE THESE?"

That was about as social as I got those first months at Oxford. I was determined to establish myself as a coach. You have to remember, I learned from a guy who was obsessed with the game. Naturally, I figured to be good you must be the same way. I did my best. I watched film for hours, until I fell asleep by the projector. I went over formations and game plans until my eyes were bloodshot. "No one will out-work me," Woody had always said. I could hear his voice echo in my ears, and I was determined to say the same.

Our practices that first season were unforgiving. Even for me. I made them work two-a-days in the summer heat. We practiced at night, moving back across Park Street, which ran through the campus, so we could work under the street lights. I screamed. I kicked players in the butt. When some-one screwed up, he was sent off for laps. Around the field. And around again. Keep going until I stop you. One time, I sent a kid out there and flat-out forgot about him. I think he was running for two hours before someone said to me, "Hey Bo, he's still out there."

"Oh, geez. Well, call him in."

Carry him in might have been a better word.

We began the season with a loss, then a tie, then two wins, then two losses. It wasn't good enough for me. "WE ARE NOT WORKING HARD ENOUGH," I would holler. "WE ARE MAKING TOO MANY MISTAKES."

The truth was, it was largely my fault. I was concen-trating too much on offense and not enough on defense. Having previously been an offensive line coach, maybe it was natural. But it was quickly becoming clear to me that out-scoring the opponent was not the way to go.

The turning point of that first season came with our game against Bowling Green. They had the best team in the league. Nobody gave us a chance. But we went up there and played with an intensity that I had not seen before. We employed a shifted defense, and Dave Mallory, our middle linebacker and captain—and one of the toughest guys we ever had—was keying on their fullback all day. He made every hit. Any time the fullback had the ball, he was all over him. Bam. Boom.

The funny thing about Mallory was that his brother, Bill, was an assistant coach for Bowling Green. He was over on their sidelines. At one point, a Bowling Green player was knocked out of bounds, he was clearly down, and Dave—who was jacked—came charging over and speared the guy anyhow. A vicious hit. Bill, his brother, began screaming for a penalty.

"LATE HIT! LATE HIT!" Bill yelled. "COME ON REF! LATE HIT!"

Dave rose from the ground and stuck his helmet right in his brother's face. "Eat shit," he said.

They didn't call a penalty.

We won that game, and the rest of our games that season. I was on my way as a coach. I eventually moved out of the dormitory and rented a house. But most of my coaches lived with me, so I wasn't exactly moving out of football. Our house had more *film* in it than furniture.

Of course, being the head coach had its privileges. There was only one bathroom, for example. And guess who had first rights? I would generally shower and shave between 7 and 7:30 A.M. I wanted everyone at the office working by 8. They had two choices: get up before me or rush like mad after me.

Success had only made me more brash, and my temper was at full boil. Especially on game day. In 1965, we played the season opener at Purdue in the worst heat wave I can ever remember. It must have been over a hundred degrees.

I had a thirty-eight-man traveling squad. Purdue dressed

more than twice as many. By halftime, our guys were dropping like flies. I was scrambling. "You, offensive tackle, you play defensive end from now on. You, wide receiver, you play defensive back . . ."

We were getting killed. It was Band Day, and all these marching bands were sprawled out across the grass, panting and wheezing, suffering from heat stroke. Finally, the officials decided to shave three minutes off of every quarter to end it quicker. To me, that was too much like surrender. "WE CAN MAKE IT!" I screamed. "DON'T YOU CUT THIS GAME SHORT!"

They did it anyhow. The final score was 38–0.

In the locker room afterwards, the players were huddled together, gasping for breath. I stood in front of them, hopping mad, and screamed "WE WILL NEVER GET HUMILIATED LIKE THIS AGAIN! WE WILL NEVER LET IT HAPPEN!" There was a water bucket nearby, and I was so upset, I went to kick it. And as I did, my other foot went out from under me and I whiffed and fell flat on my butt. I jumped back up and kept right on talking.

They never laughed; they didn't even blink.

They were either too scared, or too tired.

We had quite a cast of players come through Miami in my six years there. I was tough on every one of them. And probably too unforgiving. One time, I was making them run the mile. I had a rule. Backs and receivers had to finish in under six minutes, everyone else in under seven. We had this backup quarterback named Joe Minotti. He came charging around the final turn, trying desperately to make it under six. And he fell about ten yeards from the line.

"Five fifty-eight," I said, looking at my stopwatch, "five fifty-nine . . ."

He was crawling on his hands and knees. He scraped across the line.

"Six minutes, one second," I said. "Too slow. You come

back and do it again tomorrow. For now, get up and give me four 440s. GET GOING!"

Sometimes, however, a player got the better of me. We had this one linebacker who was out of control. He put a bag over his head one night and ran naked through the girls' dormitory. He got bored at study table one night and leaped out a *two-story window*. His home was in a rural area in Ohio, and one summer, he sneaked into an Amish village, stole a horse and buggy, and was racing them up and down the roads when the police got him.

"What the hell were you doing?" I asked him when he got back to school.

"I dunno, just having fun," he said.

I learned a lot about damage control with that kid.

And then there was my quarterback, Bruce Matte. He was the younger brother of Tom Matte, from Baltimore Colts fame, and he was enormously talented. For a while there, he was my only quarterback. I made him do everything. Run all the drills, even the option plays. He'd be halfway downfield, and he'd have to run back and start the next play.

"Come on, Matte. Let's go, Matte."

"I'm coming, coach. I'm coming."

This kid was talented. He was also wild. I knew he wouldn't be able to concentrate on football the way I really wanted or needed him to as my only quarterback. Especially with a whole summer to himself. So I did something that really wasn't allowed. Between his junior and senior years, Bruce moved in with me at the house.

Every morning we would get up and go over drills. Passing and more passing and more passing. Then I would go to work and he would go fishing.

"Meet me back at the field at four o'clock," I said. And at four o'clock, we resumed our drills. Matte threw so much that summer, he had calluses on every one of his fingers. But he improved. He concentrated. And he was a great kid to have around. We ate together. We talked about life. I knew his mother and father extremely well, and it was only with their permission that he lived with me. But I still shouldn't have done it. That's how obsessed I was back then.

We won two championships with Matte at the helm. Before each game, we'd have a last-minute meeting with the quarterbacks. On the way out, he never failed to throw his arm around me.

"So, you ready for this one, coach?"

"I'm ready, Mats. How about you?"

"Oh, yeah. I'm always ready. Let's give 'em a little dance, OK?"

And he would break into this little wiggle that always cracked me up.

God, if they were all like that . . .

. . . I'd probably be dead by now.

In the summer of 1968, I did something that surprised even myself. I got married. Millie and I met, fell in love, and were wed within three amazing months—she likes to tell me that I only moved that quickly because fall practice was coming up. And who knows? The way I was back then, she may be right.

Anyhow, by the time we opened against Xavier that September, I had a new wife, and three new kids (hers by a previous marriage.) I was no longer coming home to assistant coaches and empty refrigerators. The story of how that all came about I will tell in a later chapter. Suffice it to say that for four glorious months, Millie, the kids, and I were the picture of marital bliss.

And then everything exploded.

I had a lot of job offers during those years at Miami. The school was known for being a springboard to coaching careers, and of course, Woody, Ara, and Johnny Pont had coached there before me. I actually interviewed with Pitt (was offered the job but turned it down), with Tulane (was offered the job, turned it down), with Wisconsin (was not interested and was not offered it), and with North Carolina (was interested but was never offered it).

Then came Michigan.

At first, they wanted bigger names than me. But at the time the program was down, and men like Joe Paterno, whom they coveted, were not really interested. Eventually, they got around to me. I flew up for an interview on a Sunday, checked into a hotel under an assumed name, met all day with Don Canham, the athletic director, then flew back home.

Sure enough, I was offered the job. I was in the office of my friend Joe Hayden when I officially accepted. I hung up and said, "Well, Joe, that's it. I'm going to Ann Arbor. Back to the Big Ten."

"Great. How much are they paying you?"

I looked at him and laughed.

"I have no idea," I said.

Those Who Stayed
Were Champions

WE loaded up the cars and took one last look at Ohio. "All right, men, follow me," I yelled to my assistant coaches, "and damn it, don't get lost!" We rolled onto the highway, headed for Michigan, like some Wild West football gang.

Thus began the best year of the best job of my life. The first year at Michigan. I guess if you want to understand why football means so much to me, why I've stayed in it so long, then you have to understand 1969.

When I was a kid, my family drove through Ann Arbor on a vacation. I begged my father to stop at the football field.

"That's where the Michigan Wolverines play," I said.

He walked me to the gate. I peeked inside. And there they were, in their dark blue jerseys and leather helmets. I saw Lenny Ford, the great end, and coach Fritz Crisler and the rest. They seemed so big, I almost lost my breath. I ducked away, afraid of being spotted. But in the car ride home to Ohio, I babbled on and on about my wonderful secret. I had seen the great Michigan Wolverines.

Now, at age thirty-nine, I was their new head coach. That field would be my field. Those uniforms would be mine to issue. With me were most of my assistants from Miami: Jim Young, Larry Smith, Chuck Stobart, Gary Moeller, Jerry Hanlon, Dick Hunter. We were a brash young group of football fanatics, rolling down the highway, filled with dreams of how we'd turn Michigan into the best program in the country . . .

And we got lost. OK. *I* got lost. I couldn't find the darn school. I pulled into Ann Arbor, passed one street, then another, then another. Finally, I stopped at a hotel, ran to a pay phone, and called the football office.

"Yeah, hi, this is Bo Schembechler . . . the new coach . . . uh . . . where *are* you?"

That's how I began at Michigan. To be honest, there were probably a few people who wished I'd stayed lost. Ann Arbor was not necessarily ready for the changes I was about to make. It was a highly academic and politically active campus—football was not the number one priority. One look at the facilities told you that. In the beginning, believe it or not, we coaches slept in the clubhouse on the golf course. We walked across the greens to get to work. I remember entering our dressing room at Yost Field House and seeing nothing but a wooden two-by-four, bolted to the wall, with a couple of nails sticking out. The nails were our lockers.

"Men," I said, seeing the looks on my coaches' faces, "we are going to make a few changes here."

This was Michigan in 1969: campus unrest, student protests, long hair, rock music, anti–Viet-Nam. They were taking over the president's office. Students. Just marched in and took it.

And this was me in 1969: short hair, small-town values, a whistle, and no clout. I had uprooted my kids, my wife (who was now pregnant), and my staff, to take on the Michigan tradition. People insisted my conservative approach would never fly in Ann Arbor.

We would see about that. I was either going to make it or I was going to leave, but I wasn't going to bend. I had inherited a good bunch of athletes. On the first day of practice, I lined them up, blacks next to whites, long hair next to short hair. I marched in front of them, looking them over.

"Now, you listen to *me*! All of you. I do not care if your are white or black or Irish or Italian or Catholic or Jewish or liberal or conservative. From this point, I will treat you all exactly the same—like dogs!"

They snapped to attention.

Let the season begin.

Spring practice in Michigan had traditionally been a time of light workouts, off on weekends, just stay in decent shape. Not anymore. Under my system, we practiced twice a day, all week. On Sundays I made them run. After final exams, when the rest of the student body went home, I made them come back and practice again. I marched up and down that field in their midst, grabbing them, urging them on, screaming, yelling, cursing, never letting up. I would yank their face masks. Slap them in the butt. Kick them in the shins. Drag them downfield.

Nobody got special treatment. Ask Dan Dierdorf. You probably know him as the analyst on "Monday Night Football." Well, back in 1969, he was just another Michigan lineman that I had inherited. Oh, he was talented. We had tried to recruit him at Miami of Ohio. I sent Jerry Hanlon to his high school to talk to him, but Dierdorf (who wasn't interested in Miami) sneaked out the back door.

Now the tables were turned. Now I was his head coach. I passed him in the hallway, and he quickly offered his hand.

"Hello, Coach Schembechler," he said, very politely. "I'm Dan Dierdorf."

I stared at him, went right past his hand to his waist, and grabbed a fistful. "YOU ARE FAT!" I said.

And I walked away.

What a spring that was! Our drills were at full speed. Our scrimmages were furious. I threw those guys into the weight room, made them run, had them wrestle each other on mats. If a guy messed up, I was in his face. If he messed up twice? Off the field. It was Woody all over again, I guess. If a running back fumbled, I'd toss him out.

"Give me another running back," I'd yell.

If *he* fumbled, I'd toss *him* out.

"Get me another running back."

Weeks passed. Guys were complaining. We did so many wind sprints, Dierdorf once told a reporter, "The track team runs less than us. And their coach isn't as mean."

But I would not let up. I wanted to see what kind of football players I had, winners or quitters. To do what we had hoped to do—win a Big Ten championship in our first year—I would need every drop of sweat, every pound of courage.

"I want a slogan," I said to my staff one day.

"A slogan?"

"Yeah. Something the team can rally around."

We came up with "Those Who Stay Will Be Champions."

I liked it. I spent $150—which was a lot of money in those days—to have a sign painted with those words. "Those Who Stay Will Be Champions."

We hung it above the locker room door, so they would see it every day. "Those Who Stay Will Be Champions."

We pointed to it for inspiration. "Those Who Stay Will Be Champions."

Of course, not everyone stayed. Many quit. One morning I came in, looked up at the sign, and underneath "Those Who Stay Will Be Champions," someone had written in blue magic marker, *"And those who quit will be doctors, lawyers, and captains of industry."*

And I cracked up.

Hey. I knew what I was doing wasn't for everybody. I'm

sure many of those guys who dropped out are indeed, today, very successful. Take the guy who wrote it, John Prusiecki, a former lineman. He's a lawyer.

Didn't think I knew, did you, John?

You owe me $150.

The guys who did stay, however, were the greatest. Jim Mandich, the tight end. Don Moorhead, the quarterback. Garvie Craw and Glenn Doughty, the running backs. Dierdorf. Billy Taylor. Reggie McKenzie. The funny thing is, none of those guys was my recruit. They had all been brought to Michigan by the previous coach, Bump Elliott, who had retired the year before. Of all the Wolverines I've ever had, they had the most right to resent me; after all, they didn't pick me, they got stuck with me. And I killed them. I ran them ragged. I made them suffer every day of that first maddening season.

Somehow, they believed in me. They stayed.

And I intended to live up to my slogan.

Right from the start, I set a single goal for those men. Beat Ohio State. The Buckeyes were the most dominant team in the conference. In fact, they were the most dominant team in the country. They were the defending national champions. People were calling them "The Greatest College Football Team of the Century." There was already a strong Michigan–Ohio State rivalry, and I knew we played them in the final game of the season. We could never be champions until we beat them. So they became our obsession. Our ghosts. Our dreams. If we gunned for them, I figured, the hunger just might carry us through the first nine games.

Besides, I had an advantage. I had worked at Ohio State for six years under Woody. I had played for Woody before that. I knew the way Woody worked, the way Woody taught, and I molded Michigan after his example—with one twist: his goal was to beat everybody.

Our goal was to beat him.

When September came, we set out to make it happen. In our first game, we crushed Vanderbilt, 42–14. We gained over three hundred and sixty yards rushing. The following week we beat Washington, 45–7. That was the week my son, Shemy, was born.

It was a crazy time. I was running in circles from home to hospital to the football field. I was up at dawn and can't remember when I found time to eat. I suddenly felt like I had two new families: Millie, our three sons, the child I had fathered—and the young men who had begun to believe in me as their leader.

God, they were a great bunch, that team. Funny—and gutsy. People think I was just this bully of a coach, but those guys didn't always take my guff. At the start of the season, I remember, I got them new white socks with a thick blue border.

"We don't like them," they said.

"Why not?" I said.

"They look like crap," they said.

OK. We'd get different socks. But I wanted haircuts. And the mustaches had to go.

"Wait a minute, Bo . . ." said Jimmy Betts.

Jimmy Betts was one of our black players, a fine back with a good sense of humor. He had this big Afro and a peanut head. I used to tease him. "Betts, nothing could look worse than that combination. You're a handsome guy, but people can't even see your face."

He would always laugh me off. But when this mustache thing came up, he got serious. He came to my office. "Coach," he said, "you have to understand about mustaches for us black players. They're part of our heritage. If you ask us to shave them off, you're asking us to give up a part of our heritage."

I looked at him and made a face. "Are you for real?" I said.

"Oh, I'm very serious, coach. Speaking for the other

black players on the team, I'm asking that you let us keep our mustaches as part of our heritage."

Now, maybe I believed him and maybe I didn't. But in the end I went before the team. "Men," I said, "it has come to my attention that mustaches are part of the black players' heritage. Therefore, the black players will be allowed to keep them."

Pause.

"You white players, however, have no heritage—so shave them off!"

Hey. It was good for a laugh, anyhow. And the black players liked it. We never had any racial problems, by the way, despite the civil rights upheaval that was going on around the country. Now and then, the more militant blacks on campus would come to our black players and say, "You got to boycott practice. The coach is white. Make a statement."

And our guys would tell them, "No. This is not the place. There is no problem here."

That made me feel good. I may have treated them all like dogs. But *equal* dogs.

In our third game of 1969, we faced Missouri, a nationally ranked team. We fumbled the ball away four times and allowed seven sacks. They beat us soundly, 40–17. It was the most lopsided defeat I have *ever* had at Michigan. No team has scored 40 on us since. I was mad. I moped. I kicked things. I stayed up all night.

One of the key plays in that game was a blocked punt. I vowed we would never have a punt blocked again. We practiced that week with painstaking attention. One time we lined up, and Jim Brandstatter, a young, beefy, freshman lineman, failed to block his man effectively—or so I thought—and the guy blocked the punt. I took off downfield after Brandstatter, and when I caught up with him, I kicked him so hard in the butt he went flying.

"YOU STUPID BLEEP! HOW COULD YOU LET THAT MAN IN THERE?"

"But . . . but . . ."

"YOU ARE THE WORST LINEMAN IN THE HISTORY OF INTERCOLLEGIATE FOOTBALL."

"But . . . but . . ."

"GET OFF THIS FIELD. YOU ARE THROUGH AT MICHIGAN. YOU WILL NEVER PLAY HERE! NEVER!"

He waddled off the field and into the tunnel. It wasn't until later that one of my assistants took me aside.

"Hey, Bo," he whispered. "It wasn't Brandstatter."

"It wasn't?"

"Uh-uh."

"You sure?"

"Uh-huh."

"Aw, shoot. Well, go get him back then."

The next day, Brandstatter was reinstated. A few days later, I passed him at the training table. I wasn't really big on apologies back then.

"I guess you think I was wrong for yelling at you the other day, huh?" I said.

"Uh-huh," he answered, mustering his courage. "It wasn't me. I made my block."

"Oh yeah?" I said. "Well you probably did something *else* wrong that I didn't catch. So you *deserved it anyway*."

And I walked away.

Fortunately for both Brandstatter and me, Michigan came back the following Saturday and beat Purdue, 31–20, in a beautifully played game. We intercepted Mike Phipps four times. My mood improved considerably. After all, Purdue and Ohio State were the top two teams in the conference.

One down.

I could see we had the makings of a terrific football team. Billy Taylor was an excellent rusher, always dangerous, and Moorhead was the kind of leader you needed in a quarterback. Dierdorf was ferocious, and, on the defensive side, Tom

Curtis and Thom Darden were top-notch defensive backs. The elements for success were all there.

And then we stumbled. We went to East Lansing and lost to Michigan State, 23–12. Fumbled. Made stupid mistakes. Just played terrible. We were not prepared defensively. They were rolling up yardage as if we were a lace curtain.

I marched over to Jim Young, my defensive coordinator, and began screaming. "JIM, WHAT THE HELL IS GOING ON OUT THERE? THEY'RE KILLING US!"

He looked at me—and he fainted dead away. Right before my eyes, just went down. Ker–plop.

"Hey, wait a minute," I said.

We carried him to the bench and eventually revived him. "Hey, Jim," I said, "I don't mind you bailing out on me. BUT FOR PETE'S SAKE, WAIT UNTIL WE'RE AHEAD!"

That may be funny now, twenty years later, but back then, I was not amused. I was really hot after that game. I screamed. Threw a fit. The typical behavior. But I remember coming home late Saturday night, and Millie and the three boys were still out. I sent the babysitter home, stripped down to my undershirt, and walked over to Shemy's crib. Here was this little child who knew nothing about football, knew nothing about my obsession with Ohio State, knew nothing about my fear of failure now that I was finally the head coach I had waited my whole life to be. I picked him up and held him close to my chest, and I lay back on the reclining chair, just for a minute.

I must have been more exhausted than I thought, because I fell asleep holding him, and Millie came home to find the two of us asleep in that chair. She says it was the most peaceful night's sleep I ever had after a loss. I can thank Shemy for that.

By Monday, however, I was back in a crummy mood. No Brandstatter antics this time; our drills were tougher than ever. We lined up defensive backs, let them charge at each other, and threw a football in the middle—the winner was whoever came away with it. Minnesota was our next opponent, and even with this increased intensity, I was not satisfied. Many of our players seemed to complain about little aches and pains. Finally, on Thursday night, I called a team meeting.

"Now you listen to me good," I told them, walking up and down the aisles. "I don't like what I'm seeing out there. I don't care how important any of you think you are. I am not taking anyone to Minnesota that isn't ready to play. If you are not 100 percent in my opinion, I will leave you home!"

And that is what I did. Left half the team in Ann Arbor. "You sure you want to do this?" my assistants asked, as we boarded the bus.

"The hell with it," I said. "We'll win with the guys we've got or we'll go down trying."

It was a gamble. I had only one wingback. If something happened to him, I might have to suit up myself. We went up to Minnesota and at halftime we trailed, 9 to 7.

That wasn't the worst part. Moorhead, my quarterback, suffered a hip pointer. He could barely move. I went to Dr. Gerald O'Connor and said, "Can he play?"

The doctor shrugged. Moorhead was standing next to him. "I'll play," he said. "I promise you. I will play."

We gathered together in that cramped locker room. "OK, men," I said, "this is it." They all knew that a loss here would pretty much kill our dreams of a championship. Ohio State hadn't lost a game yet, and we were already one behind them. What could I say? Here we were, half a team, with an injured quarterback, trailing on the road. If it got any worse, I didn't want to know about it.

"What the hell," I mumbled and led us out for the second half. And wouldn't you know it? We kicked the living daylights out of Minnesota. Didn't let them score another point. Billy Taylor ran like a wild man. Scored three touchdowns. Moorhead was fantastic. And we won 35–9.

In the locker room afterwards, you could feel the tide had just come in. We had overcome adversity. We had proven our character. From that point on there would be no stopping us. We clobbered Wisconsin, 35 to 7, at home, then went to Champaign and destroyed Illinois 57–0. Only Iowa stood between us and our showdown with Ohio State. We went down there, took the ball on our first drive, and marched seventy-seven yards for a touchdown.

We never looked back. By the final gun, it was Michigan 51, Iowa 6. An awesome display of football. "Your guys knocked the tar out of us," Iowa coach Ray Nagel told me.

He should have seen what went on in the locker room afterwards. Not a single player took off his uniform. A chant began from the back of that tiny room, and it grew and grew until my ears were ringing. "BEAT THE BUCKS! BEAT THE BUCKS! BEAT THE BUCKS!"

I swear, there was saliva dripping in there. You could not catch your breath. "BEAT THE BUCKS!" I could not calm them down. I didn't try. I joined in the cheer, as eager to defeat my old coach as they were to defeat their arch rivals. "BEAT THE BUCKS! BEAT THE BUCKS!" They were pounding on the walls and slamming the chairs. "BEAT THE BUCKS!"

"Look at this!" I screamed to Jerry Hanlon over the raucous noise. "I'll tell you something. That bleeping Ohio State better be good—*or we'll kill them.*"

The next seven days were an explosion of energy and impatience. The game couldn't come fast enough. The whole school was into it, hippies and crew cuts alike. *Do you think they can do it? No way they can do it—can they?* Only we knew. But we still had to get through practice. The weather was terrible. Cold. Dreary. On Tuesday, it snowed so badly, the entire field was covered.

"All right, everybody inside the football building except

freshmen and coaches," I said, rubbing my hands together. I turned to those guys and told them to get some shovels from maintenance.

"We are gonna clean this field."

Less than an hour later, we were practicing. Hey. A tornado wouldn't have stopped us. We were just days away from our dream. BEAT THE BUCKS! Our defense already knew as much about Ohio State as was possible. Our offense was already patterned after theirs. Every drill was like running against them. We were, in essence, about to face our shadow. Only this time our shadow had arms and legs and a twenty-two–game winning streak. *The Greatest Team of the Century.*"

"Gentlemen," I said, during that week, marching amongst them, "Ohio State has the All-American Rex Kern at quarterback. Moorhead, are you prepared to play better than Rex Kern this Saturday?"

"Yes, coach!"

"And, gentlemen, Ohio State has the great Jim Otis at fullback. Craw. Are you ready to play a better game than the great Jim Otis?"

"Yes, coach!"

I had photos of the Ohio State players taped to each of my players' lockers. I wanted them to see their rivals every day. Usually, you can only ask a player to outplay the man he is facing. But to win on this Saturday—to pull off the upset of the decade in college football—each of us had to perform beyond his Buckeye parallel as well.

"Ohio State has the mean and nasty Jack Tatum, the All-American, at defensive back. Thom Darden, are you prepared to outplay Mr. Tatum?"

"Yes, coach!"

Of course, I really didn't need to ask this of my juniors and seniors. Most of those guys—Mandich, Dierdorf, Moorhead, Craw, Curtis, Barry Pierson, Cecil Pryor—had been humiliated the year before by Ohio State. The Buckeyes had been way ahead, and their last touchdown gave them a 48–14 lead. They went for the two-point conversion for an even 50.

Football players don't forget that sort of thing. If they did, I was going to remind them. I had "50–14" taped to every player's uniform.

They wore that humiliation all week.

By Friday, we could see scarlet and gray in our sleep. The mood was electric. We had stayed away from interviews. We had kept outside distractions to a minimum. Ohio State was favored by 17 points, and around the country, nobody gave us a chance. The network wasn't even sending its first-string crew. Why bother? It was a foregone conclusion that we would lose: not only lose, but be blown out.

We went to the hotel that night, and right in the middle of bed check, the power went out. No heat. No lights. I had to run from room to room, throwing blankets on all my players, trying to urge them to sleep.

"Forget the cold," I said. "We know what we have to do. Let's get some rest now and tomorrow we'll do it."

No heat? No lights? Was this some kind of omen? Around 3 A.M., I finally settled into bed. My eyes were wide open. What I hadn't told anybody was how nervous I was, facing my old coach for the first time. Was I capable of beating Woody Hayes? The man who had tortured me the way I was torturing my team? The man who had taught me everything about football, motivation and success? I had given each of my players a shadow to out-perform; mine was the man with the square shoulders and the slicked-back hair. Woody Hayes. My god. I was about to fight my football father.

The room was black and silent. I closed my eyes.

Hurry, morning.

Game day. The parking lot was mobbed with fans. Maize and blue was everywhere. We dressed in a businesslike fashion, allowing the energy to build, slowly, gradually, because we would need all of it. I motioned for the players to follow me through the tunnel for our pre-game drills, and the first thing we saw when we hit the sunlight was the old man himself. Boom. He was standing there, in his traditional white shirt and tie, hands on his hips, warming up his nationally famous team—*on our side of the field*.

We froze.

"Hey, Bo," Mandich said, "he's on our side!"

"Yeah," echoed the other players, "what's he doing on our side? . . . Tell him to move, Bo . . . What's going on?"

So it began. Saturday had finally arrived, and I hadn't even made it to the sidelines before my old coach attacked. Damn that son of a gun. He knew what side of the field was his. It was a mind game. I had seen him use it countless times—but never on *me*.

"Come on," I grumbled to my guys, "let's go."

We marched out there and took our spots, and I stepped up to Woody. "Coach," I said, trying to disguise the trembling in my gut, "you're warming up on the wrong end of the field. You're supposed to be down at that other end."

Woody stared at me. I did not blink.

"Okay, Bo," he said, his jaw set. "Fine." He turned and waved. "Come on, men! Let's go."

Whew. I looked back to my players, and they were whooping it up. They had just seen me send the great Woody Hayes marching downfield. I don't know what Woody had hoped to accomplish, but it had just backfired. We were pumped.

"BEAT THE BUCKS! BEAT THE BUCKS!"

How can I describe the feeling in that stadium that day? From the moment the band played and we came charging out into the cold air, under the maize and blue banner, there was an electricity that I have never felt in any football game since. It was as if all the energy from a season's worth of tackles and body-slams had just been released. We could hardly stand still. The stadium was packed, 103,588 people

—at least 30,000 from Ohio State—the largest crowd in Michigan history. The noise was shocking, deafening; it made you dizzy.

"Are we getting too high?" my coaches kept asking.

"No, let's get higher," I said.

"Bo, they won't remember what they're doing out there!"

"The hell they won't! This is everything!"

The two teams lined up for the opening kickoff, and I glanced across the sidelines at Woody. He paced up and down in that white shirt, the general, the field master. I remembered the time I told him I was leaving him to become the head coach at Miami. *"You can't go. You'll be head coach here at Ohio State as soon as I retire. Why do you want to go?"*

Now I was worse than gone: I was across the sidelines. I had dragged those young men behind me through the most grueling season of their lives—all for this one November afternoon, this one team, this one game. Ohio State. Ohio State. BEAT THE BUCKS.

"AaaaaaaahhhhhhhhhhhHHHHHHHH" screamed the crowd as we kicked off . . .

And here is what happened: on the very first play, Kern, Ohio State's All-American quarterback, scampered twenty-five yards. On the second play, Otis, their All-American fullback, burst ahead for seven more.

"Looks like Ohio State is picking up right where they left off last year," the TV announcers said.

But this wasn't last year. Not even close. We stopped that drive on fourth-and-one at our own ten-yard line. Our defense nearly flew off the field. You could see in their eyes that they were absolutely crazed!

The Buckeyes did manage to score first, a touchdown dive by Otis. But they missed the extra point, and we came right back after them. Glenn Doughty returned the kickoff thirty yards, and Don Moorhead marched us downfield, throwing three times to Mandich to get us to the three-yard line.

"All right," I yelled, over the roaring crowd, "let's go with the off-tackle play. Dark 26."

Any football fan would have seen the irony. It was the play that had made Woody Hayes famous. The play he had practiced a thousand times a year. So had we. Garvie Craw took the ball and blasted through the hole just the way you draw it on the blackboard.

Touchdown.

We went ahead, 7–6.

Ohio State seemed to shrug it off. They drove downfield with their passing game, scored again, but missed the two-point conversion. And *again* we came back. Moorhead led a drive to the Buckeye thirty-three–yard line. No one expected this resiliency from our team. They figured we would roll over and die for the mighty Buckeyes.

"Give it to Taylor," I barked. "Tailback draw." Just another one of our "simple" running plays, the kind we had practiced live all week, all season, until guys were panting and bleeding. Taylor took the ball, and Craw laid a block on the great Jack Tatum that left him flat-out useless. Taylor twisted, turned, and broke tackles for twenty-eight yards, all the way to the five. Pandemonium in the stands! Two plays later, Craw punched through again—"Take *that* for last year!"—and now we were ahead 14–12.

The remainder of that first half was about as much as a Michigan heart could stand. Barry Pierson, our senior defensive back—who would have the game of his life—took a punt and went straight down the middle, busting tackles, gaining speed, and our sideline went wild. *"Go! Go! GO!"* Midfield. Forty. Thirty. Twenty. All the way down to the Ohio State three! A sixty-yard punt return!

"All right, now, let's ram it in!" I hollered. Nothing could stop us. Moorhead took the snap, rolled around and sneaked over the goal line, and we were ahead, 21–12. And we weren't finished yet. We intercepted a Kern pass, drove downfield, and scored another touchdown—and had it called back! Illegal procedure. We kicked a field goal instead.

Ohio State was stunned. With just over a minute left in the half, we were up, 24–12. No other team had scored more than 21 points on the Buckeyes *all year*—and here we had 24 *by halftime!* The crowd was going *crazy.* You absolutely could not hear yourself think! We left the field to an ovation that was still ringing in our ears when we poured into the locker room.

And what a scene *that* was. Players roaring. Coaches screaming. Jim Young, our defensive coordinator, who is normally a fairly reserved guy, stood in front of the blackboard and began pounding it over and over. "They . . . will . . . not . . . score . . . again! Gentlemen, I promise you they . . . WILL (pound!) NOT (pound!) SCORE (pound!) AGAIN!"

What can I say after that?

They did not score again. The second half was a defensive masterpiece, and Pierson was the star. The star? He was on fire out there. He intercepted three passes, made four unassisted tackles, and manhandled the great Jim Otis. He knocked Otis's feet out from under him on one play. He yanked him down by the head on another. Pierson gave one of the greatest performances I have ever seen in a single game. In a single afternoon, he went from a nobody to a fifth-round draft pick by the NFL St. Louis Cardinals. I loved it. Barry was a small guy, maybe a hundred seventy pounds, and all he had going for him was his heart and his toughness. A Michigan man, for sure. And like all the seniors, he was finally getting his revenge against the scarlet and gray.

As the fourth quarter ticked away, it slowly began to dawn on me. Our players were still flying after every tackle. They waved fists after every mean lick. Woody pulled his star quarterback, Kern, and went to the backup, Ron Maciejowski, who fared no better. He threw an interception to Pierson. That was it.

"Jerry! Jerry!" I screamed into my headphones.

"Bo! Bo!" he screamed.

"We're gonna *win* this thing!"

"Whoooo-eee!"

I couldn't believe this was happening. The crowd seemed to stretch as far as the horizon. Suddenly, they began singing: "Good-bye, Woody. Good-bye, Woody . . ." I looked over at my mentor, pacing the sidelines, as he watched his team lose for the first time in more than two years. His national championship was being stolen. His number one ranking was being stolen. The mighty Buckeye offense had committed seven turnovers, six interceptions, and a fumble. And their defense had bent and broken for 24 points.

It was all dying, here in Michigan Stadium, the best team Woody Hayes had ever coached, yet I felt no sense of superiority. He was still the master. A cameraman tried to zero in on him, and Woody grabbed a student manager and placed him in front of the lens. No one would record his face in failure. He would be back.

"Goody-bye Wood-eeeeee, we hate to see you go! . . ."

"FIVE . . . FOUR . . . THREE . . . TWO . . . ONE . . ."

The rest, I must admit, is a blur. The field was mobbed. Tom Curtis, my senior safety, would later tell me that in the final minute, he turned and saw a high school buddy standing next to him on the sidelines. How he got there, I have no idea. I guess even the security guards were celebrating. Fans were everywhere. The goalposts were broken down. The band was blasting "California, Here We Come." I was lost in a sea of arms, legs, and helmets. I was bouncing on players' shoulders. Our locker room was a mass assembly of players, fans, and reporters. They were calling it the "upset of the decade." All that night, people came by my house, strangers, people I had never met, just to say what a great win it had been. We watched the sun rise, too excited to sleep.

Michigan was back as a national football powerhouse. That would be the upshot of the whole thing. No more sleeping on the golf course. No more locker rooms with nails. No more getting lost on the way to work.

Those who stayed were champions.

We had kept our word.

Years later, after Woody Hayes was out of football and I had been with Michigan for more than a decade, we had a banquet. A great banquet. All the players who had ever played for Woody. No press. No wives. Just players.

And I remember Woody, who was pretty old by this point, stood up and addressed his football children.

"You know, everybody always asks me which of you were the greatest team I ever had at Ohio State," he said. "Well, the greatest team I ever had was that 1969 team."

He paused.

"It had great defense . . ."

Another pause.

"It had great leadership . . ."

Another pause.

"It had a great offensive line, great running backs, a wonderful quarterback, a fine kicking game . . ."

He stopped. He sighed. He looked down the dais and glared at me.

"GODDAMN YOU, BO," he yelled, "YOU WILL *NEVER* WIN A BIGGER GAME THAN THAT ONE!"

And so far, he's been right.

The Ten-Year War

CAN you imagine waiting a whole year for one football game? To have your mood for the next 365 days depend on how you did that one cold Saturday afternoon? That's the way I felt about the Michigan–Ohio State game each year from 1969 to 1978. It was everything I lived for, everything we all lived for. Lose, and your world was gray. Win, and you were in heaven. Last game of the season. Buckeyes against Wolverines. Woody against me. Maybe it was a personal thing. Maybe it was just two proud teams. But it was the best of rivalries, with the Big Ten championship on the line every time we teed it up. They called it the Ten-Year War. They were not exaggerating.

I always thought if they made a movie out of those ten games, they'd have just about everything you can find in college football: upsets, bad weather, crunching defense, temper tantrums—Lord, they'd have plenty of those. If there were two men in America who hated to lose more than Woody and me, I wouldn't want to meet them.

So great was our rivalry, that we rarely talked to each other for the entire decade. Before each game we'd meet at midfield and exchange a few pleasantries.

"How you doing, Woody?"

"Not bad, Bo. Yourself?"

"Aw, you know."

"Yeah."

"Umm-hmm."

"Well, OK. Good luck."

"Yeah. Good luck."

Each of us was searching for the slightest advantage. If that meant no conversation, so be it. I don't think Woody ever really forgave me for beating his "Team of the Century" and he relished every chance he got to take revenge.

And I relished every chance to do it again.

For ten years, we went after each other with every ounce of blood and spit, and when the final numbers were tallied Michigan had won five, Ohio State four, and there was one tie. But numbers hardly tell the story of those games. In fact, sometimes the scores were secondary to the performances.

Take the 1971 game. A rainy afternoon in Ann Arbor. Woody had a Buckeye team that, strangely, was going nowhere. They had already lost three games. Their offense was so bad, they couldn't move across the street.

But in the final minute of the game, trailing us, 10–7, they tried a desperation drive. Now when I say desperation, believe me, it was desperation. On a pass play to Buckeye receiver Dick Wakefield, Thom Darden leapt over him and intercepted the ball.

"INTERFERENCE!" Woody screamed.

"No interference," said the refs.

"WHAT?" Woody came charging out. He looked like his face would explode. "THAT WAS INTERFERENCE! THAT

WAS INTERFERENCE!" He went chest to chest with the official. His arms were flailing. His glasses were all steamed up. "WHERE'S THE INTERFERENCE! WHAT'S THE MATTER WITH YOU!"

They threw the flag. Unsportsmanlike conduct on Hayes. Fifteen yards.

"WHAAAAT?"

Good night. Woody began ripping up everything in sight. He tore up the down markers and threw them into the ground, javelin style. He ran to the first down marker, ripped off the orange plastic, and shredded that. The Michigan crowd was roaring.

"Damn you, Woody," I said to myself, "I know exactly what you're doing." It was a smoke screen, that's all. This game was lost. He was setting the stage for next year, giving his team a motive—and at the same time, making people in Columbus forget he was suddenly 6 and 4.

And it worked. To this day, they'll tell you Ohio State only lost because of that play. And to this day, I tell people, as I told Woody, that I would happily have given him the ball at the spot of the so-called infraction. Go ahead, Woody. Take it. He wouldn't have scored in a month!

What an actor.

How about what happened in 1973? Now it was my turn to blow a gasket. We played one of the most bruising, bashing, knock-em-down games you can imagine at Michigan Stadium. The score was 10–10, late in the fourth quarter, and Denny Franklin, our quarterback, was leading us downfield. We reached Ohio State territory, the Buckeyes blitzed, hit Franklin as he released the ball, and he went down. A broken collarbone. We carried him off the field.

We missed two field goals, and the game ended in a tie—the first tie in Michigan–Ohio State since 1949. As a result, we also tied for the conference championship. But

Michigan deserved to go to the Rose Bowl. Even Woody conceded that.

Ohio State had gone the year before. We used to have a no-repeat rule, which would have sent us automatically. But with that rule abolished just two years earlier, the decision was instead left to a Big Ten conference vote. Wayne Duke, the commissioner, was nervous because the Big Ten had lost the last four Rose Bowls. He started calling the athletic directors.

"Look, Denny Franklin broke his collarbone. Michigan doesn't have as good a chance. I think we should send Ohio State."

He got Cecil Coleman from Illinois to change his vote. And he influenced some of the others. He'll tell you it's not true, but it is. And I will never forgive him.

The vote came on Sunday. I was doing my TV show at Channel 4 in Detroit. I parked my car about fifty yards down from the studio. Suddenly there was an avalanche of press and radio and TV guys.

"Did you hear the news?" they yelled.

"What news?"

"They voted Ohio State to go to the Rose Bowl."

I glared at them. "Like hell they did."

"No really. It's true."

I was speechless. I walked away from the crowd, went into the studio, and began kicking everything in sight. Trash cans. Chairs. I have never been so angry in my life. "GOD-DAMN IT! GODDAMN IT! I WANT TO KNOW WHAT HAP-PENED HERE!"

I marched out. I was damn near crying. I mean, you don't do things like this, not to those kids who played all year and didn't lose a game. "You guys don't deserve this . . ." I told them the following morning. And I broke down.

That was the beginning of the end of my relationship

with the Big Ten brass. If they would do something like that, the hell with them. I've called Wayne Duke every name in the book. If the book were bigger, I'd call him a few more.

Of course, that was the beauty of Michigan–Ohio State. We were battling not only for our own rivalry, but for the right to represent our conference to the rest of the country. The whole ten years seemed to be filled with heroes and villains, champions and scapegoats. There was Tom Klaban, a Buckeye kicker who wasn't even listed in their media guide but kicked four field goals to beat us in 1974. And there was our kicker, Mike Lantry, a Viet-Nam vet, a walk-on, a great kid, who missed a last-second field goal that year that would have won it—and is forever haunted, even today, by people saying "Aren't you the guy who missed the kick?"

There was Archie Griffin, the great halfback who won the Heisman twice for the Buckeyes, and Rob Lytle and Gordon Bell, who churned out the yardage for us. There were quarterback wars, like Rick Leach versus Art Schlichter in the 1978 showdown (Leach ate him up). And there were defensive warriors, like Jack Tatum and Mike Taylor, guys who could hit you so hard, you lost your breath.

There were brilliant goal-line stands—Ohio State beat us with two of those in 1972—and muscle-flexing offense— like the 1976 game, which we won 22–0. There was the time Woody got whacked by an overzealous Michigan fan, and the time he threw an ABC camerman off his sideline. There was a time where I tried to play a mind game with Woody by not walking out to shake his hand at midfield.

"Where's Bo?" he demanded to know.

"Gee, we don't know," my assistants said.

A little later on, I realized this was stupid and walked up to him. "Hey, Woody," I said.

He ignored me.

"Hey, Woody."

He turned the other way. "Is that Bo Schembechler who's too good to talk to me? Bo Schembechler who doesn't have time to talk to me?"

I felt like a fool.

Now remember, all this time, Woody and I were not only doing battle on the field, but in recruiting as well. We often went after the same kids. Woody was brilliant; you barely had a chance once he turned on the charm. But he was also shrewd. He always knew when I was coming. Sometimes I think he had policemen at the border. "Bo's in the state! Bo's in the state!"

If I was making headway with an Ohio kid, I would always say, "Listen, son. Tomorrow, Woody Hayes will be in your school to try and recruit you."

And the kid would say, "No way, coach. He's not interested in me."

And I would say, "Son. Listen to me. Woody Hayes will be in your school tomorrow morning, first thing."

And sure enough, he was.

And most of the time, he got him.

More often than not, he beat me to the punch. The most ridiculous example was Schlichter, whom we had tried to recruit as quarterback in 1977. We drove to the house—Jack Harbaugh was with me—and we expected a tough battle. But we were not even there ten minutes when Art's father, who was really running the show, dropped the bomb.

"Bo, let's get down to business here. Woody was in here yesterday, and he promised Art he would start as a freshman in his very first game against Penn State."

"Wait a minute," I said, "Woody's got Rod Gerald at quarterback."

"He's moving him out. What's more, Woody promised Art would get to throw twenty-five times a game."

"He *what?*"

"And oh, yes. He also promised that Art could play basketball if he wanted. Now, are you prepared to match all that?"

I felt a rumbling in my gut. I leaned forward and began to bank on the coffee table. "Now you listen to me! Woody can't promise all that stuff! He knows better than that!"

On the coffee table were these little vases. And as I pounded, they began to hop toward the edge.

"Furthermore," I said, still pounding, "let me tell you this: When the season opens, my quarterback is going to be Rick Leach, who has worked hard and earned the job! If you want your son to compete with him, then send him to Michigan! If not, then *send him to Ohio State!*"

Pound! Pound! The vases were jumping. Poor Jack was watching them, afraid they would fall off. I was seething now.

"YOU LISTEN TO ME, MR. SCHLICHTER! THAT'S THE MOST RIDICULOUS OFFER I EVER HEARD, AND I ADVISE YOU TO TAKE IT BEFORE WOODY COMES TO HIS SENSES!"

"JACK," I screamed. "MY COAT. LET'S GO!"

We marched out the door. Poor Jack was shaking. He figured he had a six-hour ride back to Ann Arbor with one very ticked-off coach. We got in the car, and I reached over and slapped him in the ribs.

"Hey," I said, winking, "pretty good performance in there, huh?"

Woody won that one.

But I got the last word.

The final showdown was 1978, in Columbus. Our defense was awesome. We held Ohio State to a field goal and won 14–3. Leach was terrific. He threw two touchdown passes, no interceptions, did a great job of improvising. The crazy thing was, in the halftime locker room he could hardly walk.

"What is it?" I said.

"Hamstring. Can't move."

"Geez. Can you play?"

"Of course I can play."

That was Leach. The win—our third in a row over the Buckeyes—also marked the third consecutive year that Ohio State had failed to score a touchdown against us. That bothered Woody tremendously.

He was sixty-five years old now, suffering from diabetes. His once-dark hair was now white. His posture was no longer yardstick straight. It had been a cold day, and I noticed when I looked across the field that he was wearing a jacket. He never wore a jacket, remember? The one gray T-shirt? *"If they don't think you're cold, they won't think they're cold."*

The old man was starting to go.

I didn't know it then, but our glorious war was over. Woody would never coach another Ohio State-Michigan game. After that one, he made the press wait an hour before showing up. Then he answered questions softly for ten minutes before a guy from Chicago asked about his team not scoring a touchdown against us.

"What was that?" Woody said, pretending not to hear.

"Are you aware your team hasn't scored a touchdown in three years against Michigan?"

"I'm aware of it," he growled, standing up, "and *you would be the guy to bring it up!*" Woody knew this writer from previous articles. "You're not the kind of person I ever want to spend any time with!"

And he stormed out.

Years later, when he was sick, Woody came to talk to my team. He stayed around to watch practice. I remember him sitting in the stands, watching us go through drills, looking so frail. It didn't seem right, and I looked away.

Michigan–Ohio State was never the same. Not for me,

anyhow. The heart did not pound so quickly, the juices never flowed quite as strong. Woody was the master, I was the challenging student, and for one wonderful decade I got to feel what deep, gut-twisting, all-you-got football was about. Hey, if that was war, sign me up forever.

The Old Man
Is Gone

TEMPER. As most of you know, that's what finally did Woody Hayes in. A few weeks after our game in 1978, Ohio State was playing Clemson in the Gator Bowl. In the fourth quarter, a Clemson player intercepted a pass near the Ohio State sideline. He shouted something, and in a single moment of madness, Woody grabbed him from behind, spun him around, and punched him.

It was captured on national television. Once I saw the tape, I knew his coaching days were over. Still, I was stunned when the news actually arrived. I came into my staff meeting, and I couldn't help it, I began to cry. "The old man's gone," I said. "They fired the old man."

It's been written that the night they fired Woody Hayes was "the last night of his life." That's not really so. Unlike Bear Bryant, Woody lived for a while after football. I will say that the end result of his punching that player was a deterioration in his health; I think that was particularly true of the diabetes and high blood pressure, from which he also suffered. Doctors will tell you his blood sugar count was so far out of whack that day that, in reality, he didn't realize what he was doing.

I know Woody Hayes *did not believe he hit that guy.* I know because we talked about it in one of the hardest discussions I ever had with my ex-coach.

It was several weeks after the incident. One of the team doctors at Ohio State called me and said, "Bo you've got to talk to Woody. He's not going out of the house. He's feeling low."

I called him up. "Look, coach," I said, "I'd like to come down to talk to you."

"Don't give me that stuff!" he barked. "You're just coming down here to recruit."

"I'm not coming down to recruit. Let's just get together and talk."

"I don't want you going out of your way. Tell you what. Doyt Perry called me the other day. How about if I meet you halfway, at Doyt's house in Bowling Green?"

And that's what we did. I drove down from Ann Arbor. Woody drove up from Columbus in his pickup truck. It was the dead of winter. And there we were, the three of us, Woody, Doyt, and I, in Doyt's living room. We started to reminisce, and the old man was loosening up.

Suddenly he said, "You know, I'm continuing to work on my book. You guys wouldn't mind reading the first chapter, would you? I've got it out in the truck. It's called 'Let's Set the Record Straight.'"

"Woody," I said, "what do you mean by 'Let's Set the Record Straight'?"

"Well, I felt that right at the beginning, I better get that thing at the Gator Bowl cleared up."

"What did you write?"

"First of all, I write that I have *never* seen the film of that game. And I have never watched any replays or news accounts on television.

"What I say happened is that we were driving for the winning touchdown, and the Clemson middle guard intercepted the ball and was knocked out of bounds on our sideline and that he got up and he flaunted that ball in front of us, and all I tried to do was to wrestle that ball from his arms."

I looked at him. "Woody," I said, softly, "that's not what it looked like."

He started to get mad. "Well, by God, I know what was going through my mind, and I'm not a liar! I'm telling what went through my mind!"

I said, "Well, that is not the way it appeared on film." I looked over at Doyt. "Furthermore, on the basis of what I saw, Woody, there's a black cloud over your head right now and you've got to take care of it. You must publicly apologize."

"Oh yeah?" he said. "Let me ask you something: should I apologize for all the good things I've done?"

"No, I'm not asking you to do that. And you don't have to apologize to any of us that know you. But the people who don't know you, I think you owe them an apology."

"I don't know about that!" he yelled. "Damn it! Don't you tell me that."

He got up to go to the bathroom. While he was gone, I whispered, "Now, Doyt, support me on this. We've got to get him to apologize."

So when Woody came back, Doyt said, "Woody, I think Bo is right. You ought to apologize."

Woody just stared at us. "Well, by God, I'm not apologizing. I made up my mind. I'm not going to apologize for anything I've done. I'm not saying that everything I've done is good, but I'm not going to apologize!"

And that was that. I never could get him to understand me. But about one week later, he made his first public appearance in Columbus since the incident. It was a banquet speech that he'd committed to a long time before.

The room was packed. TV cameras everywhere. He got up, and he talked about the meeting we had in Bowling Green. And he said, "I'll tell you right now, Bo thinks I ought to apologize for what happened down there in the Gator Bowl . . . but Bo isn't always right!"

That was as close as he would ever come to saying "I'm sorry." It's a shame that one incident blemishes his otherwise incredible coaching career. Those in our business are able to separate the two. I wish I could say that for the general public.

Woody and I talked a lot during his final years, but not enough. He would send me notes at Michigan; they'd arrive out of the blue, just little scribbles that said "Bo—I am proud to have you for a friend," stuff like that. In 1986, I went down to Dayton to speak at a banquet. And there he was, leaning on his cane. He had come to introduce me.

He was in frail health. He couldn't even stand without a cane. I grabbed Bill Gunlock, who had organized the thing. "You bastards," I said. "How can you ask that man to come down here? He is on his deathbed!"

Gunlock said, "We told him not to come, Bo. But he insisted. He wanted to introduce you."

Man, was I angry. He looked so old leaning on his cane. But he got up and introduced me for fifteen or twenty minutes. He went on and on with stories and nostalgic talk. He stayed for the whole banquet, to hear me speak.

And the next day, he died.

I have spent a lot of time defending Woody Hayes. That hasn't always been easy. But I always seem to defend him to people who didn't know him, people who thought they were so damn smart, they knew everything about this man and how terrible he was. But if you could have been there with him all those years, listened to him speak of the great battles in history, heard him sing the praises of the great off-tackle play, watched him eating that meal with Boxcar Bailey in that Nashville airport, or seen his skin turning red under those hot showers, listened to his down-home speeches to mothers and fathers, gazed at him from across the sidelines, seen him direct some of the greatest football teams in the country, watched helplessly as he staggered to the podium to introduce a former player when he was too sick to leave the house—if you had been there for all that, you'd know those people didn't know what the hell they were talking about.

I make no apologies for my affection toward Woody Hayes. He made mistakes. His temper was, at times, inexcusable. But he shaped me and everything I do with a stamp of passion and strength. He was a remarkable coach, a teacher, a winner. I will miss him forever, and I'll never meet another man like him.

Not in this world, anyway.

★ ★ ★

THE BEST
AND
THE TOUGHEST

★ ★ ★

They All Wore
Maize and Blue

knew he was special the first time I saw him. We were working on deep fly routes.

"Are you watching this kid?" I whispered to Gary Moeller.

"Yeah," he said, "he's so fast, *he's coming back for the ball!*"

The kid, of course, was Anthony Carter. And while it's not really fair for a coach to pick his best-ever players, Carter is the one exception I make. He was the best receiver I ever had and the most exciting player I ever coached. There were times when I stood there on the sidelines, watching him dart past two or three defenders, and I tell you, all I could do was smile. That wasn't coaching, folks. That was pure talent.

Anthony played for Michigan from 1979 to 1982, and he would help us win some big games before he left—including my first successful Rose Bowl. But when he first arrived, a shy, skinny kid, my biggest problem was keeping him on the team. Most people don't know this, but Anthony quit Michigan for a few days during his freshman season. He wasn't happy—I think he was a little homesick—and he decided to go back to Florida. As he was leaving his room with a suitcase, his roommate, Nate Davis, saw him.

"Where are you going?" Davis asked.

"Oh, ah, I'm switching rooms," Anthony said.

We had practice that afternoon and, of course, Anthony didn't show.

"Where is he?" I asked my assistants. By this point, word had begun to spread.

"Coach," they said, "we think he's headed home."

"WHAT?"

I grabbed Bob Thornbladh, the receivers coach, and Mike Gittleson, the strength coach. "Now you listen to me! You two get down to that airport and you check every flight that's going to Miami! You find Anthony and you bring him back here immediately, you got it?"

They took off. We went into meetings. Around 7 P.M. I got a phone call. It was Thornbladh. "Bo," he said, "I've checked every flight. He wasn't on any of them. There's one flight left tonight and I'm standing right across from the gate so there's no way he can get on without me—"

He stopped.

"What? What's going on?" I yelled.

"Oh my god, Bo, here he comes!"

"Now you get him! You do not let him get on the plane, you understand me? You tell him I want to talk to him immediately!"

There was a long silence. I heard rustling sounds and distant conversation. Then I heard Anthony, in that high, squeaky voice.

"Hello?"

"Anthony," I said. "What's going on? You weren't going to just go home without talking to me, were you?"

"Oh no, coach. I was gonna talk to you."

"Well, you get back here and we'll sit down and talk."

"I'll talk to you. I promise you that."

"All right. We'll get this all straightened out, whatever's bothering you."

"Yeah, coach. I won't do anything before talking to you."

"OK, then. I'll see you soon."

Two hours passed. Finally, the door opened and in came Thornbladh with his shirt hanging out. No Anthony.

"What the hell happened?" I said.

"Bo," he said, "he hung up that phone and ran right onto that airplane."

Why, that little devil. He said he would talk to me.

He just didn't say when.

Needless to say, we got Anthony back, I talked with his mother every day during his "hiatus"—which only lasted a few days, once he saw his old friends still doing the same old things on the streets—and pretty soon he returned to our lineup and was catching everything in sight. Man, I loved to watch him do that.

I will never forget his freshman year, a game against Indiana, we were tied 21–21, with six seconds left. We had just gotten the ball out of bounds to stop the clock on their forty-five–yard line. We rushed in a play. In the huddle, Anthony looked over at John Wangler, the quarterback, and said, in that squeaky voice, "Throw it to me. I'll be open."

Now, you have to understand. Anthony was a painfully shy kid. For him to say anything in the middle of the huddle—let alone "Throw it to me"—well, you can bet Wangler wasn't looking anywhere else. He hit him cutting over the middle at the twenty-five–yard line, and Anthony's magic just took over. He juked past one defender. Left him in the dust. Cut past another. Lost him, too. Time would run out before he crossed the goal line, but he went in standing up and scored that touchdown, and we won, 27–21 with 0:00 on the clock. He was mobbed by his teammates.

"Unbelievable!" I remember screaming, as I jumped up and down. "Unbelievable!"

And he was just a freshman.

You'd need a wheelbarrow for all of Anthony's amazing moments at Michigan. Heck, he returned a punt seventy-eight yards for a touchdown on the second play of his career. He broke the Michigan career touchdown record for receivers—*as a sophomore.* By the end of his senior season, he was averaging a touchdown almost every fourth time he caught the ball. The amazing thing about Anthony was he didn't really *look* like a supersonic receiver. His stride did not appear fast, his hands were average size, he wasn't very muscular. Let's face it: he was small. Little kids used to love him—partly because he seemed so much like them.

"Isn't he cute?" I used to say to reporters. That was a good word for Anthony. *Cute.* But off the field, he was, as I said, painfully shy. In his early years he was uncomfortable with the press and self-conscious about the way he spoke.

I watched out for Anthony, more than most players, because I was concerned someone might try and take advantage of him—agents, in particular. He came from a pretty poor background in Florida, and I was determined not to let unscrupulous money offers turn his head. When he finally decided to go to the USFL instead of the NFL, I helped find him a trustworthy agent. Maybe I shouldn't have done that —you're really not supposed to—but this was a kid who had been given a chance and I wanted him to keep it.

The things he could do with a football were unreal— catching it at the oddest angles, twisting his body, finding the best position against his defender. My fondest memory of Anthony, however, wasn't during a game. It was after we won the Rose Bowl in 1981. He came wandering into the coaches' locker room and sat down on a stool. Just sat there while we showered.

"Anthony, what are you doing in here?" I asked him. "There's all those reporters out there. They all want to talk to you."

"Coach," he said, "they talk to me enough. If I stay in

here, then they'll have to talk to some of my teammates and give them some credit."

That was neat.

That was Anthony.

I'm not surprised that Anthony has become such a big star in the NFL with the Minnesota Vikings. I had no doubt he would be a great professional player. I felt the same way about Dan Dierdorf back in 1970—long before he went on to star with the St. Louis Cardinals and became famous as analyst on ABC's "Monday Night Football."

Dierdorf was a beauty. Hell of a lineman. I told him even before he was drafted, "Dan, you are the best run blocker in the NFL right now."

"But, coach, I'm still in college."

"I know. Doesn't matter. You're already the best."   And I was right. He was smart, had great technique, and when he got jacked up, look out. The holes would be big enough for a moving van.

Dan had one of those baby faces atop a mammoth body. In his senior season, 1970, I assigned target weights to everyone. I liked smallish, linebacker types. And of course, Dan was built like a truck.

"I want you at 245 pounds," I told him.

He looked at me and swallowed. "Did you say . . . 245?"

You've got to understand, Dan weighed 250 as a sophomore in high school. He had to kill himself to make that weight. Starvation. Exercise. Finally, the weigh-in came. He tipped the scales, nearly dehydrated, at 243.

"Nice going, Dan," I said to him. "Now, would you do me a favor? Would you go down to 239 so I won't have a player who weighs over 240 on my team?"

Well. I might as well have whacked him with a sledgehammer. He looked like he was about to faint. Of course, I knew as soon as that practice was over, Dierdorf would be out eating six hamburgers and drinking a beer.

I was just thinking ahead.

While he was still reeling from that request, I decided to make all my players run the mile. Midway through, Dierdorf started to wobble. He looked like a building about to topple over. Finally, he flat-out stopped in the middle of the track.

"WHAT'S THE MATTER WITH YOU?" I hollered.

He just stood there.

"HOW CAN YOU QUIT?"

He just stood there.

"YOU'RE SUPPOSED TO BE A LEADER OF THIS TEAM!"

He just stood there. Little did I know that he stopped because he thought he was going to pass out.

"FROM NOW ON, DIERDORF, YOU RUN A MILE EVERY MORNING AT 6 A.M.!"

And I left him there, woozy and weak.

Dan ran that mile. Every morning at 6 A.M. Actually, I think he just jogged a few laps, waited for the coaches to leave, then quit. He was always pretty clever. But you know what? As soon as that first practice was over, he went straight downtown and ate enough hamburgers for an entire fraternity—and by the next day, he weighed 257.

Told you.

Dierdorf, Reggie McKenzie, and Tom Coyle developed a system one year of beating the weight check; they stuck electrical tape under the scale. I'm not kidding. One would distract the assistant coach, while the other did the dirty work with a wad of tape. If placed correctly, the tape would keep the needle from going too high. Of course, you had to be careful how much tape you used, or you could wind up as a defensive tackle weighing 177.

Linemen will do that kind of stuff. It's one of the reasons I like them. They are my kind of guys, down there in the dirt, grinding away with little or no recognition. Like Reggie, who later became the man who blocked for O. J. Simpson. Without Reggie, O. J. would have a lot more bruises. And a lot less yards.

Reggie was a gift to me; he was already a sophomore when I arrived at Michigan. The funny thing was, nobody thought Reggie would be a football player back in high school. He was a wrestler, tall and gawky. The story goes that George Mans, who recruited Reggie, was about to give up on him and drive home. He decided to stay for the wrestling match that night. During the match, Reggie was losing when, suddenly, he slammed his head right into his opponent's jaw and knocked out three of the kid's teeth.

George's eyes lit up. "That guy is coming to Michigan," he said.

As a person, Reggie was sort of a big puppy dog. He lived with six other players (including Glenn Doughty, Billy Taylor, Mike Taylor, and Thom Darden) in a house on Geddes Avenue they called "The Den of the Mellow Men." Have you ever heard anything so dumb? The Mellow Men?

Now the lineman who *should* have been in there was Bubba Paris, who played from 1978 to 1981 and later went on to star with the San Francisco Forty-niners (and recently got his second Super Bowl ring). Bubba was sort of mellow. Actually he was just sort of . . . different. He had a mischievous smile and a big, thick body, and he liked to recite poetry. I remember when he first got to Ann Arbor, he came to see me.

"You know, coach," he said, "my real name is William, not Bubba. That's what everyone calls me, William."

"Well, I'm going to call you Bubba," I said. "It suits you, and it will serve you well when you line up against an opponent. You got it?"

I was right, wasn't I? Who's afraid of a William? But Bubba, now *that's* a lineman!

And all Bubba wanted was to play. "Man, I wish I could get some playing time," he said his freshman year. As luck would have it, one of our starters went down before the Northwestern game.

"OK, Bubba," I said. "This is it, baby. We're going to Northwestern and you're starting at tackle."

"Yeah! All right! That's great!"

Game day came, and it was one of those freakish fall afternoons when it's like eighty-five degrees. And we had the ball constantly. We ran over ninety plays. Bubba was in for *every one!*

I walked through the locker room afterwards, and there he was, sitting on his stool, not moving. His arms were hanging down at his side, his head was down. He was wasted.

"Well," I said, slapping him on the back, "what do you think of that, Bubba?"

He barely raised his head. "I want to play," he moaned, "but not that much."

I've had a lot of great running backs at Michigan. Billy Taylor, Butch Woolfolk, Lawrence Ricks, Gordon Bell, Harlan Huckleby, Ed Shuttlesworth, Russell Davis.

Of course the guy who leads them all is Jamie Morris. More yards than anyone in Michigan history.

And you know the funniest part? I never wanted Jamie. I never recruited him. When the coaches showed me his film, I said "What do I need with a five-foot-six tailback?"

"Take him, Bo. He really wants to come here."

"Ahhh, I don't know."

"Really. He's good. Trust us."

Over and over they kept insisting. Over and over I said no. Finally, we took him for kickoff returns.

When he got to Michigan, Jamie came to me. "Coach, can I ask you one thing?"

"What's that?"

"Will you give me a tryout at tailback?"

I had to laugh. He was so small, I didn't even want him,

and here he was asking to be a tailback. "All right, runt," I said. "I'll give you a try."

Let me tell you something. One try was all he needed. I watched him run, and I felt like someone had dropped a treasure chest in my lap. Or on my head.

"Ahem," I said to my staff. "We are going to play this kid at running back . . . and we are going to play him this year. As a freshman."

The rest, as they say, is history.

I'd like to say that was my only mistake. Far from it. How about John Kolesar? I almost lost him without ever knowing it. As a sophomore in high school, John came to a Michigan game with a couple of recruits. Afterwards, he snuck in to our locker room. He was wandering around, wide-eyed, when suddenly, by accident, he stepped on my foot.

I turned and found myself staring at this toothy kid with curly hair. "Son," I said, "I hope you're not planning on coming to Michigan."

"Uh . . . uh . . ."

He ran away.

Lucky for me, he came back. Think of all the Ohio State games we might have lost without him. Kolesar was one of the best clutch players I ever had. In the 1988 Hall of Fame Bowl, he pulled down the winning touchdown with less than a minute to go to beat Alabama. I was watching from my bed, following the open-heart surgery. "Hot damn, he did it again!" I yelled. "Whoo-ee!"

Who was my toughest player ever? God, there were a lot of them. In the backfield, I would have to go with Rob Lytle. This guy was something special.

He did everything. We'd start him at fullback. Then when we'd stick in another fullback, he'd shift to tailback. We'd throw in another tailback, he'd return to fullback. He looked

like a California surfer—blond-haired; All-American face—
yet he played like an ugly outsider trying desperately for the
last spot on the team.

"Lytle practicing today?" I would ask.

"I don't know," the trainer would say, "he's banged up
pretty badly."

"He'll be out there."

He always was. That man took abuse. We used to run
this play called the fullback dive. It was a short yardage play.
When Lytle got the ball, he'd dive between the guard and
tackle and pick up two or three yards. Sometimes we faked
and the quarterback kept it. Now, usually when that happens,
your running back follows through with the fake and dives
in the line, unhurt, he's done for the play. With Lytle, that
wasn't enough. He would take the fake, stay on his feet, track
down the safety—and knock him on his butt. Every time.
Never failed. Boom. Chop. Down went the safety.

Lytle would have been a star in the NFL, I am convinced,
if not for countless injuries that finally ended his career. He
used to call me now and then from the hospitals.

"Hey, coach, how you doing?"

"You hurt again, huh?"

"I'm coming back from this one, coach. I'll play football
again, believe me."

Donny Dufek used to say the same thing. He was in the
NFL for ten years after leaving Michigan—always by the skin
of his teeth.

"Sorry to hear you got cut, man," his teammates would
say to him when his team, the Seattle Seahawks, let him go.

"That's all right," he'd say, "they'll bring me back." And
sure enough, they always did. He was just too tough a guy
not to have on your football team. Donny was the best special
teams guy I ever had. Knock your socks off. He was also one
of the few football players who also played collegiate hockey.
As soon as hockey ended, he'd jump on spring football. The
first few days he was sluggish.

"What the hell's the matter with you, Dufek?" I asked.
"I'm not used to moving without skates, coach."
Now there's an excuse you don't hear often.

There were plenty of other tough guys at Michigan. How about Kurt Becker, who now plays with the Chicago Bears? Or Mark Donahue, who played in the mid-seventies and probably had less natural talent than I do, but, man, what a lineman! Or Henry Hill, the greatest little middle-guard you ever saw. Linebackers? I had some great ones there. Marty Huff. John Anderson. Ron Simpkins. Mike Taylor.

Then, of course, there was Calvin O'Neal, who, on top of being a rough, tough All-American in 1976, also holds the unofficial Michigan record for tossing his helmet.

He was having a bad day at practice. The coaches were yelling at him. And all of a sudden, he took off his helmet, spun around, and heaved it high, way up, over the goal posts! It landed on top of the football building. It went at least thirty or forty yards. And those things are pretty heavy.

"Hey," I said a few minutes later, "what's that guy doing up on the roof?"

"He's getting Calvin's helmet."

"His *helmet*?"

"Yeah, Calvin threw it up there."

"Oh."

I still laugh when I think of that. Guys like Calvin kept the game colorful. So did John Vitale, my center the last few years, who once told President Ford when he came to visit practice that he needed to work on his golf game. Or Jim Mandich, my All-American tight end in 1969, who they used to call "El Diablo." Mandich rode around campus in a psychedelic car. He never wore a shirt under his uniform—even on the coldest days. And he once addressed the pep rally before the Ohio State game by saying "WERE GONNA KICK ASS AND TAKE NAMES!"

Then there was the rather strange case of Brad Cochran,

a great defensive back in the mid-eighties who came into my office in his freshman season, after a loss to Notre Dame, and literally went nuts.

"You never cared about me! You're not coaching me right! This program is all messed up! I don't belong here!"

He was having a fit. I was flabbergasted. He ran down the hall and did the same with the other coaches, insulting them, calling them names, screaming about how he was leaving. Most of us were too stunned to react. He bolted out the door and disappeared. Just left school. He had been a terrific player—in fact he was the only guy who played *well* in that Notre Dame game—but now he was gone.

Over the next few months, we heard stories. *"Cochran has surfaced in Colorado. He's gonna transfer there to be with Bill McCartney."* Or *"Cochran has surfaced in New Orleans. He's gonna transfer to Tulane."*

Eventually, he found his way back to Ann Arbor, and he sought medical help. They discovered that he had a chemical imbalance that was wreaking havoc on his nervous system. He took medicine and began to recover.

One day, in the spring of 1983, he came to see me.

"Bo," he said, "I'd like to come back to the team."

His outburst was still ringing in my ear from six months earlier. "Brad, I don't know where you stand with your eligibility. You've been out of school for a while. If you want to check into it with the Big Ten, go ahead, but I think your time is up."

Well, that kid went out and petitioned the conference to reinstate him. He built a good case, showing medical reasons. And in the end, he was granted his remaining three years of eligibility. He came back to the team. By senior season, they voted him captain.

Cochran was a strange story. Still, the guy who wins the prize for ultimate Michigan character was a running back named Preston Henry. He was a classic. I did not recruit him. He was there when I arrived. A decent player, extremely bright, good-looking, charismatic—and one of the biggest con artists on campus.

He played for me in that 1969 season. The following summer, I got a report saying that Preston was ineligible. Rather than go through the ordeal of trying to explain it to him—because I knew he'd try to con me—I wrote him a letter: "Preston, as you know, you are thirty-two honor points below a 'C' average, and since this is already the summer months, it's impossible for you to make up this work. I want you to know you will not be invited back for football in the fall."

Two days later, guess who's in my office? Preston Henry. Looking sharp. Dressed nicely. He said, "Coach, I know exactly how you feel and I can understand it. But these grades are wrong. Give me until five o'clock today. I promise you, I can get notes from every one of the professors. I can get this done. Please. Just give me until five o'clock."

Well. I figured this is impossible. But he raced around campus all day, and at five o'clock, this man came in and slapped down signed statements from professors that made up thirty-two honor points. If that ain't some kind of collegiate record, I don't know what is.

So Preston was eligible. He played the next year. Had one great game against Washington, where he almost single-handedly beat them, ran for well over a hundred yards. And eventually, he finished up—which was none too soon for me.

But here's the kicker. A year or two later, when he was done with football, he was brought before an Ann Arbor judge for writing bad checks. The judge gave him the proper lecture. Then he said, "Mr. Henry, you must pay a seventy-five dollar fine."

Preston said, "Sir, can I write a check? Believe me, I have the money."

The judge said, "No, they will not accept a check, Mr. Henry. Cash only."

"Well, could I write them a check and have them cash it?"

"No, Mr. Henry. You must have cash or you go to jail."

"Sir," Preston said. "Could I write you a check and you give me the money so that I can get out of here? Believe me, sir, you know I would never do anything bad to a judge."

The judge stared at him. Only Preston would have the gall to try something like that—and the charisma to make it work.

"Well, this is highly unusual," the judge finally said. "I've never done this before as long as I've been on the bench. But, all right. I will consent."

So Preston wrote him a check and he gave him the money, and Preston went free.

And the judge proceeded to cash the check.

And it bounced.

The judge called Don Canham, our athletic director, and he couldn't help but laugh: "Preston Henry," he said, "has done it again!"

Quarterbacks

CRITICS say I won't let my players pass the pota-toes, much less the football, but the truth is, my closest relationships have been with my quarter-backs. They are my alter egos during a game. I want them to think like me, react like me.

No, that doesn't mean hand off to the fullback every play.

Quarterbacks are a special breed. They need to be cocky, and the cockiest I ever had was probably Jim Harbaugh. You know how he got that way? By hanging around my practice field as a kid, waiting for his dad, Jack, to finish work.

Jack was one of my assistants in the seventies. Even then, his son was a devil, running on the field when he shouldn't, playing with his friends. One time he did that, I screamed "GET THAT KID OUT OF HERE . . . *NOW!*" I think he was ten years old. So, for the record, that is the youngest I ever yelled at one of my quarterbacks.

Once I went over to Jack's house and little Jimmy was there, watching TV, wrapped in a blanket. I kidded him. "Hey, don't you have something more productive to do?"

He grabbed a book and started reading.

Even then, he hung on every word I said.

I guess I always knew Jim would come to Michigan. When we finally recruited him out of high school, we waited until the last minute. He came into my office, sat down, and I said, "Jim, I want you here." He nodded. That was that. It was so matter-of-fact, that a few days later, he called on the phone.

"Uh, Bo, one more thing?"

"Yeah?"

"Is that a full scholarship?"

The consensus on Harbaugh was that he was too temperamental to play quarterback. At a freshman practice, after a teammate hit him late, Jim got up and threw the ball in the guy's face. Still, while he was cocky on the outside, deep down he was like the rest of us. I remember his sophomore year, he was having a good season when he broke his arm in the fifth game against Michigan State. I went to see him that night at the hospital.

"Hello, Bo," he said softly. He was lying in bed, with a big cast on his arm. He still had the black under his eyes from the game. God, I hated to see him like that.

"OK, Jim," I said, as unemotionally as I could, "I got the report on the arm. Number one, you're out for the season. No bowl games, either. That's a fact. And you may not be able to participate in spring practice, you got it?"

Silence.

"Now, the other thing is this: I want a damn three-point average out of you this semester. You're not playing, so you'll have plenty of time for class. Understood?"

He didn't say anything, so I got up to leave. He looked at me and the tears started to well in his eyes.

"Hey, Bo," he said, "do me a favor."

"What?"

"Don't forget me, OK?"

I couldn't help it. I started to choke up myself.

"Jim," I said, my voice cracking, "how in the hell am I gonna forget you?"

Of course, he came back to do great things. Led us to the Big Ten title and the Rose Bowl his senior season. And he never lost a game he started against Ohio State. In fact, he "guaranteed" the win in 1986. Remember that? I said to him, "Jim, are you crazy? Did you really *guarantee* a win to the press?"

He said, "Yeah. I believe it."

I said, "Well, damn it, you better be right."

And he was.

The best play I ever saw him make came against the Buckeyes, too, the year before. Just prior to kickoff, he had come up to me on the sidelines.

"Bo," he said, "whenever you need a play today, whenever this game gets critical, just make sure the ball is in my hands, OK?"

Sure enough, late in the game, we were leading, but Ohio State had scored and was coming after us. On a corner stunt, their strong safety came blitzing in, untouched, and headed straight for Harbaugh. I mean, he was just barreling in! And Harbaugh saw him coming—and he *ignored* him. He let go a bomb to John Kolesar a split second before that safety crunched him, head-on, an awful collision, and they both went down. Jim never saw where that ball went, which is too bad, because it landed in Kolesar's hands for a seventy-seven–yard touchdown that clinched the game for us, 27–17. A lot of people talk about Kolesar's catch, but Jim Harbaugh made that play. If you only saw that pass alone, you would know this kid was something special.

Of course, Jim wasn't the only quarterback to help us win big over Ohio State. I guess Donny Moorhead takes the cake on that one. He quarterbacked the game of our lives in 1969, my first win over Woody, and the game that really reestablished the Michigan football program.

"Moorhead, are you prepared to outplay Rex Kern, the great All-American?" I had asked him before that game. Afterwards I told him that he had.

We used to call Moorhead "The Warbler" because he talked like he had a mouth full of marbles.

"Here comes The Warbler!" the players used to say.

"Aw, come on, guys."

He was an excellent leader, the first guy to practice, the last to leave. And he and Jim Mandich must have had some sort of telepathy going. He hit him fifty times that season.

"Sky pass, coming to you."

"Right," Mandich would say.

It was that quick zip over the middle, where you just split the linebackers. Mandich had such great hands, it worked all the time.

"Sky pass."

"Gotcha."

I owe Moorhead a lot. Even though I didn't recruit him, he accepted me right away. And that made it a lot easier to coach the team. I still hear from Donny now and again, and that makes me happiest of all.

My most unappreciated quarterback had to be Tom Slade, the guy who followed Moorhead. He only played one season, and he was probably the weakest passer of all the quarterbacks we had. But Slade was willing to do something few quarterbacks would do: block.

I remember that season we were going to East Lansing to play Michigan State. They had a safety by the name of Brad Van Pelt.

"Tom, you see that big guy there," I said to him during the films.

"Yeah," he said.

"You've got to block him. All day."

"No problem."

A quarterback? Yep. He did a great job, too. We won that game, and all the others that year. That was the best rushing team you have ever seen. We lost only the Rose Bowl, 13–12 to Stanford, the sole defeat we ever suffered with Tom Slade at quarterback. You won't find him in the record books under passing, and I'm not sure I ever really showed my appreciation for the role he played. I'll say it now.

Tom, you did a hell of a job.

The hardest luck quarterback I ever had was Denny Franklin. Now here was a kid who could do it all, a good passer, a great option quarterback, fast, slippery. He slogged through dozens of regular season games, playing excellent football, leading us to victory—and he never got to play in a post-season game. Something always happened.

Denny came from Madison, Ohio, what they used to call "the mecca of Ohio football." Woody was after him to go to Ohio State, and he was one of the rare guys I pried away. The thing you had to like about Denny, from a coaching standpoint, was that, for all his natural talent, he was willing to listen to whatever you said. I remember the Michigan State game in 1973, which was played in the heaviest rainstorm I have ever seen. I mean, we were *underwater*.

"Listen," I told Denny, along the sidelines, yelling to be heard over the whipping rain, "I want you to know this is exactly what I expect out of you today! Number one, get the ball from center! Number two, hand it to the running back! I am not going to grade you on passing! I am not going to grade you on technique! I am going to grade you on *not dropping the football! You got it?"*

"Whatever you say, Bo," he said.

We had one turnover all game. Michigan State was losing it left and right. We won, 31–0.

Still, tough luck would shadow Denny. In the final game of that season against Ohio State, we were trailing 10–0. Denny brought us back. Scored a touchdown to tie it. And as you know, we were driving in the closing minutes when he got hit hard, went down, and broke his collarbone. Without him, we were unable to move. We missed a long field-goal, the game ended, 10–10, and then the Big Ten voted to send Ohio State to the Rose Bowl instead of us, which was only maybe the dumbest football decision of all time.

So Denny never got a Rose Bowl that year, when he deserved one. He never got one in 1972 or 1974, when we tied for the championship but lost to the Buckeyes. In his career at Michigan, Denny Franklin won thirty games, lost two, and tied one. It seems to me he should have played in about a dozen bowl games, not zero.

Rick Leach, on the other hand, went to a bowl game four years in a row—three of them Rose Bowls. So what if we never won any? Hey. This guy was a beauty. He was probably the most naturally athletic quarterback I ever had. And the most competitive. He plays baseball now for the Texas Rangers, and he was certainly the only passer I ever had to play a college football and baseball game on the same afternoon.

It was his junior year. We had our annual spring game. Michigan baseball had a doubleheader against Minnesota.

"What should I do, Bo?" Rick said as the day approached. "I don't want to miss either one."

"Well, I don't know, Rick."

"Hey. How about if I play the first half of the football game, then leave and run over to the baseball field. I'll make the second game of the doubleheader. Can I do it that way, Bo?"

Why not?

And that's what he did. He quarterbacked the first half, performed well, then ran off the field, peeling away his uniform as he went. Quick change in the locker room. Ta da! He was out there on the baseball field. Played the second game.

The next day I picked up the newspaper. Guess who drove in the game-winning run?

That was Leach.

You could say Rick was born to play at Michigan. In fact, he was born at the University of Michigan hospital. His father played baseball for the Wolverines. So did his uncle. Let's face it. This kid was maize and blue before he could walk. He turned down a big bonus from the Philadelphia Phillies in order to go to school.

We started him as a freshman, which is not something we usually do with a quarterback. Heck, we *never* do it with a quarterback! The day before his first game, I took him aside and walked him around the field. "Listen, Rick, we're going to start you tomorrow. There's going to be pressure, but I want you to forget about it. You just go out there and do what we taught you, and you'll be fine."

"OK, coach," he said.

He went out the next day and threw three interceptions. So much for my speeches.

Still, even in that game—which we won anyhow, 23–6 over Wisconsin—you could see he ran the option like a veteran. And before long, he was one. God, what a competitor! Tough. Ornery. You want to take Rick Leach out of the game, you better bring a forklift. Once, just before the Notre Dame game, he stepped in a hole and badly sprained his ankle. All the newspapers said no way Leach could play. He not only played, he starred, outshining Joe Montana in that game and leading us to a 28–14 win.

Some people say the reason Rick and I got along so well was that he's a lot like me: competitive, stubborn, consumed with sports. Maybe that's true. I do know I never had any problems with him. Only when he left.

"My god, what are we gonna do now that Leach is gone?" we asked. We had grown so used to having him at quarterback, we almost forgot about recruiting a new one.

For pure speed at quarterback, you couldn't stop Steve Smith. Let me give you an example. We were playing Illinois, and Smith had been instructed by Gary Moeller to run the quarterback draw-play whenever they were in the bump defense, where the linebackers and corners play man-to-man.

Of course, the quarterback draw is not designed for big yardage. On the last play of the first half, we were on the fifty-yard line. People figured "OK, go for a long bomb. Take a chance." That's what we figured, too. But when Smith stepped to the line, the defenders came up in the bump defense. Smith looked it over, said to himself, "Nah, not this time" and began calling signals for a pass play.

"GODDAMN IT, STEVE," Moeller screamed from the sidelines, "IT'S THE BUMP! THE BUMP!"

"Check, check," Smith said, changing the play.

He took the snap, went back, let the defense spread, then took off down the center of the field—so fast that nobody touched him. Fifty yards and a touchdown with no time left on the clock! On a quarterback draw?

Now that was speed.

Steve was a sensitive kid. His dad was killed in an automobile accident, and we talked about that a lot when I recruited him. A lot of schools were after him, and I think he may have chosen Michigan, to be honest, because he sort of needed a father figure.

That's why I stuck by him, even when the fans began to boo him. It wasn't fair. He took over a veteran team in 1981 and we were ranked number one in the nation in pre-season. In the opener against Wisconsin we flat-out blew the game, 21–14, and Steve had a lousy day. He was three for eighteen, with three interceptions. We never came close to the national championship after that. And by the time the 1982 season started, he was being booed every time he made a mistake.

"Why are they on me, coach?" he asked. "I'm not the first quarterback to make a mistake."

"Listen," I said. "There's only one person on this team you have to please and that's me. You don't worry about the people in the stands."

In the end, my faith was justified. He came back from the boos. He came back from having his shoulder separated in the 1983 Rose Bowl. And he played well his senior season. Set new passing records for competions and yardage. In the final game of his senior season, he beat Ohio State on a dark, wet day at Michigan stadium. Threw for over two hundred yards and two touchdowns.

"I think today was a personal triumph for Steve Smith," I told the press. "He is one tough kid."

And pretty damn fast, too.

And finally, there was John Wangler. If each of my quarterbacks has had one special characteristic, then he must go down as the most beloved passer I ever coached. You won't find a soul who didn't like "Johnny Wangs." Some of those linemen would die for him. He was clearly Anthony Carter's favorite quarterback. Wangs knew the secret: if you ever see Anthony anywhere close to open, throw it to him.

Johnny's life changed in the 1979 Gator Bowl against North Carolina. He came out smoking. Threw for over two hundred yards in the first half.

And then came disaster. He was sprinting out when he got hit by linebacker Lawrence Taylor (now of New York Giants fame). Wangler was left in a heap on the field. His knee was severely injured; the cruciate ligaments were ripped. He would not touch a football for nearly ten months.

"Wangs, it kills me to tell you this," I said to him after that game. "But the doctors say they have to operate on this knee and do reconstructive surgery. You won't take part in any spring football and you won't be able to play next season, either. I'm sorry, son."

He didn't say anything. He underwent the operation. And as soon as he was able to move, he began to rehabilitate that knee on his own. Every day he was in the weight room. Every night he was the last to leave. I would close up the building at seven o'clock and he'd still be in there, another set of repetitions, his face squeezed in pain, over and over.

"You still hanging around, Wangs?" I would tease him.

"I'm gonna be ready for next season," he would grunt.

"Well, OK." I nodded. But inside I was saying no way. I felt awful for that kid. He was never coming back from that injury.

The other guys on the team saw Wangs punishing himself in that weight room. They said so long to him on Friday nights when they were headed out for parties. They said hello to him Saturday mornings, when they came in for a workout. He lived in that building. He never gave up.

John Wangler never saw a minute of work in spring practice. He did not touch a football all summer. When the 1980 season arrived, we had to go with Rich Hewlett at quarterback.

"We'll have to run the option a lot," I said.

"Seems a shame with a receiver like Anthony," my coaches said, shaking their heads.

"I know. But what are we gonna do? Hewlett's an option guy."

Wangler was on the team. There wasn't a soul on that squad who would deny him a spot. He was not very mobile. But his courage had brought him back into uniform. And— although he hadn't taken a snap since the Gator Bowl—I snuck him into the opening game against Northwestern, just for a few plays at the end of the first half.

We won that game 17–10, then, the following week, went down to South Bend to take on Notre Dame. This was a big game. We wanted to avenge a loss the previous season in Ann Arbor. It was a sunny day, and the Notre Dame crowd was wild, as usual. Just a few minutes into the first quarter, I could see our option was going nowhere. We fell behind 14–0. The game was slipping away. Damn, this was frustrating! Here we were with Anthony Carter, the most feared receiver in the Big Ten, and we're running an offense that can't utilize him. I looked down the sidelines at Johnny Wangs. He knew what I was thinking.

"Can you go, Wangs?"

"I can go, coach."

"All right . . . I'm putting you in there," I said, almost choking on the words. "I need you to throw, you got it? Throw. Just throw!"

"I'll do it."

I then gathered the offensive line. "Now you listen to me! Wangs is going in this game and damn it, I don't want anybody to *touch* him! Nobody! You don't let those Notre Dame guys get a finger on him, because he can barely move, and when he goes back to pass *that's where he's staying!* There will be no scrambling here! If any Notre Dame defender touches Wangs, I'm blaming *you!* Understood?"

I didn't have to say any more. You could see the look in their eyes. They *loved* Johnny Wangs, I mean, absolutely *adored* him. They would have blocked a tank if necessary. Wangs went into that game and led one of the gutsiest comebacks I have ever witnessed. He threw a touchdown pass to Lawrence Ricks. He threw another one to Norm Betts. He threw another one to Craig Dunaway. With four seconds left, we were leading by a point, but Notre Dame kicked a fifty-one–yard field goal to beat us, 29–27. It was like being stabbed in the heart, that's how much emotion we had in that afternoon.

"Son," I said to Wangs afterwards, "that was one hell of a performance. I don't care if we did lose."

Johnny Wangler started the rest of the season. He did not run. He could barely move in that pocket. But he directed us to eight straight wins and a trip to Pasadena. And, perhaps fittingly, he gave me my first Rose Bowl win. We clobbered Washington. It was his last game as a Wolverine and more than anything, I wanted him to score a touchdown. In the fourth quarter, comfortably ahead, 17–6, we drove to the one-yard line.

"What's the play?" the coaches asked.

"I want an option for Wangler."

"An option?"

"Yeah. I want him to score."

We tried, we really tried. But it was hopeless. Washington stuffed him, he just couldn't run. It killed me to be one damn yard away and not be able to give Wangs a piece of the glory. Finally he handed off to Stan Edwards for the touchdown. That was it.

"Hey, I did everything I could to try and get you in that end zone, Wangler," I said, teasing him afterwards, "but you just *couldn't cut it*."

"Thanks anyway, Bo," he said, laughing.

No, John. Thank you.

The Bear

AS long as we're talking about great ones, I should tell you a story about Paul "Bear" Bryant, whom many consider the best college coach ever. It's hard to argue. Bear was one of a kind. A man's man. An old-fashioned, knock-em-down, drag-em-out football coach. Everyone knows how he won more games than any coach in Division I college football. And everyone knows about those great Alabama teams he had. And everyone knows about the national championships he won, and players like George Blanda, Joe Namath, and Ken Stabler, who grew up under his wing.

But I got to know Bear in a different way. They say you never forget your first kiss or your first car? Well, you surely never forget the first time you coach alongside Bear Bryant. It was a hell of a thing.

The year was 1972, The Coaches All-America Game, an all-star game which doesn't exist anymore. We played it in Lubbock, Texas, in July. Have you ever been to Lubbock, Texas, in July? You play at night just to avoid heat stroke.

Anyhow, Bear was head coach of the East, and I was his assistant, along with Tubby Raymond, from Delaware. We flew in about a week early. Now, as you can imagine, it's tough to get players in July. Who wants to risk injury *and* sunburn? But somehow the West team—coached by Chuck Fairbanks, then of Oklahoma—was loaded. They had all these great players from Southern Cal and Nebraska, including Jerry Tagge, the Huskers quarterback.

And we were at least ten men short.

"What are we going to do?" I asked Bear, who by this time was in his late fifties, a little wrinkled, but still the toughest looking son of a gun you'd ever see.

"Well, Bo," he said, in that deep, gravelly voice, "we got to get us some players. How many you got up there at Michigan that can play?"

"Plenty. But we're only supposed to have three guys from any one team."

"The heck with that," he said. "Get all you can."

We ended up with five Michigan guys. Bear brought Johnny Musso, his great running back, and a few others from Alabama.

It was all last minute, none of which seemed to faze Bear. He told me, "Bo, coach the offense." He told Tubby, "You coach the defense."

"And me," he said, "I'm gonna play golf."

And that's exactly what he did. Every day. Tubby and I would start practice and sooner or later, Bear would roll in, wearing some fancy plaid golf shirt and golf shoes. But there was never a question who was head man. One afternoon, I called a meeting for the offense, and right in the middle, Joe Gilliam, the quarterback from Tennessee State (and later the Pittsburgh Steelers) lit up a cigarette. Now, if one of my Michigan players did that, he'd be kicked out the door. But these weren't my guys. So I went out in the hall where Bear was just wandering around.

"Hey," I said, "I want to tell you something. I'm not teaching football to any son of a gun smoking a cigarette."

He looked at me and waved his hand. Without saying a word, he walked into that meeting.

"Hello, men," he said. They all straightened up. "I want to tell you something: we're here to play football. I don't care what you do when we're not playing football, but when you're in a meeting, or practicing, we'll do things the way they're suposed to be."

He paused for effect.

"And there ain't going to be no . . . smoking . . . in . . . here. Now, Gilliam, you get that cigarette out!"

That was the end of the smoking problem.

As the game drew closer, everyone figured we'd get killed. We still didn't have enough players. We were trying to get Lionel Antoine, the outstanding tackle from Southern Illinois. He was supposed to play, but he was married, and his baby was in the hospital at the time.

I called him every day in Chicago, hoping maybe he could make it down. Finally, on the morning of the game, I tried one last time.

"How's it going, Lionel?" I asked.

"Everything is fine, now," he said. "The baby's all right. But it's too late to play in the game, right?"

"Not really. We need you. We don't even have a tackle."

He was flattered. "Well, I don't see how I coul—"

"Look, hold on there a minute." And I went to Bear. I told him the kid could play, but he was up north.

"Tell him to get ready," Bear said. "I'll send a jet for him."

"What jet?"

"The university jet."

"Well, gee, can you get the jet at this late notice?"

"For God's sake, Bo. I bought the goddamn thing for them! I guess I can get it if I want it!"

Believe me when I tell you, Lionel was down there in a matter of hours. I scribbled a few plays on a piece of paper—"You block here, then you block here"—and we stuck him on the bus.

The weather was hot and sticky. Riding to the game, we saw one of those temperature signs at a bank: it read 101 degrees. Bear was wearing his traditional button-down shirt and checkered hat. We got to the field, and the first thing he said was, "Well, God damn! Look at that! Their bench is over there in the shade and we're in the sun!"

He looked at me. "Bo, I want you to get some guys and carry all our benches to the other side. In the shade."

"OK, Bear," I said.

And we moved our whole team. Carried the benches across the playing field, to the same sideline as the West. Set up right next to them.

And you know what? Nobody asked us a single question.

That was the power of Bear Bryant.

The game started. Early on, the West had to punt, and Ron Curl—remember him? from Michigan State?—broke through and blocked it. We got the ball and quickly scored a touchdown. It was 7–0.

We kicked off. They didn't move. We got the ball. Went eighty yards and scored again. Now it was 14–0. Less than seven minutes had passed.

O. J. Simpson was on the sideline for ABC. He found Bear, who was just standing there, watching all this, not calling any plays. And O. J. said, "Coach, that was a great drive! You sure are moving that ball."

Bear said: "Uh, yeah, absolutely. We figure we can, uh, run on these guys. We are well prepared."

"Thanks, coach."

"Sure."

O. J. walked away. I glanced over at Bear and we both laughed and shook our heads.

At halftime, Tubby and I went over some plays. This was

Bear's only suggestion: "Bo. The sun is down. You tell them to bring those benches over to the other side now."

"OK, Bear."

And we moved back across the field.

And nobody said a word.

By the fourth quarter, we had rolled up a big score, 35–20, and time was running out. All of a sudden, Bear was standing next to me. I looked up.

"Well, come on, Bo," he said, "what are you waiting for? Ain't you gonna run my play?"

"His" play—the only one he suggested all week—was a trick play in which you toss the ball to the running back out of the I formation, and he runs left, then throws it back across field to the quarterback, who takes off down the sideline. If it works, it makes the defense look bad.

"Gee, coach," I said, "You run that play, you're really going to rub it in."

He glared at me with those thin, steel eyes. "So what?" he snarled. "It's only the goddamn All-Star game. What the hell. I want my play run!"

"OK, Bear," I said.

I called the play. Sure enough, it worked to perfection. Our quarterback, Paul Miller, from North Carolina, was wide open and scampered all the way to the two-yard line. And Fairbanks was over there, across the field, screaming at me: "You son of a bitch, Bo! You no-account son of a bitch!"

So I opened my arms and said, "Wait a minute! I'm not the head coach! I didn't call that play."

He couldn't hear me. I hope by now he's forgiven me.

We punched it in for a touchdown and that was it. 42–20. After the game, Bear gave all the credit to Tubby and me. "These guys did all the coaching," he told the press. "And they did great. Bo, I'd like to take you back to Alabama with that offense. You did a job, man."

That night they had a buffet dinner for everyone. Tubby and I were standing in line, and all of a sudden, over in the corner, we heard that voice, as thick as mud: "Hey, Bo! Tubby! Come on over here! We're not gonna eat that crap! We won the game!"

Bear.

"Men, I had a few steaks flown in. Sit down. We're gonna eat like champions." And they brought out these porter-houses that were the biggest things I ever saw. We sat there and ate until way after midnight with the old coach, just talking and laughing about the game. What a week. I wish every young coach could get a chance like that.

There are two other stories about Bear that I think sum up his legend pretty well. One happened when we were coaching the East-West Shrine game together up in Palo Alto, California. Jackie Sherrill was with us that time. We were getting killed. The worst part was, Bear had to be in Houston that night. And the game was running long.

At halftime he said to us, "Now, look, fellas. If this game runs a little late I'm going to have to go. I got a guy with a car waiting on that little road outside the stadium. You guys can handle it, right?"

Sure.

So right after the start of the second half, Bear left. We wound up losing the game, At the press conference after-wards, we sat down, and all of a sudden, someone came rushing up to me. "Emergency! Emergency!" he yelled. "You've got to come to the phone, Bo! Hurry!"

I went to the phone, and I was trying to think what the problem could be.

"Hello?"

"Bo?"

It was the assistant athletic director from Alabama.

"For God's sake, Bo, what happened to Bear? The phones are lighting up down here! They saw on television he wasn't there the second half. Is he all right? The whole state of Alabama is up in arms!"

"Hey, relax. He had to catch a flight. He's on his way to Houston."

"Oh. Thank God. You're sure?"

"Yeah. He's on an airplane."

"Thank you. Thank you."

And he hung up.

That should tell you how big Bear Bryant was in Alabama.

The other story came late in Bear's life. He was in his sixties and had already coached the Crimson Tide for twenty years. Now, remember, Bear had grown up dirt poor in Arkansas, had run the most brutal football program ever at Texas A & M, had molded young men from dusty Southern towns into hard-hitting, tightly disciplined football players. He made them heroes, stars, champions. He had won all those SEC titles and bowl games and national championships. At the time of this story, he had just broken Amos Alonzo Stagg's record for most victories by a college coach. Let's face it. He was a living legend.

And at the time, I was being pursued for the head coaching job at Texas A & M. Bear knew about it, and we were at the East-West Shrine game again, and he came up to me in the morning and said, "What's goin' on?"

And I said, "Coach, they seem pretty interested."

And he said, "Well, I think we oughta talk."

That afternoon, we were back at the hotel. He called my room. "I'm comin' down," he said.

He came down and sat at the table. I sat down, too. He stared at me. "Well," he said, "aren't you going to offer me a drink?"

"Oh. Sorry. Wait a minute."

So I ran to the bar and got a fifth of bourbon and set it on the table.

"I'll need some Coke, too," he said.

I ran and got him some Coke. He mixed the drink, and

he started to talk about Texas A & M. He remembered how small it was when he was there. He said he should have bought land back then; it would be worth a fortune now. He just kept talking and talking, reminiscing, maybe an hour. Finally, he banged the bottle down and said, "All right, Bo. We've talked enough about *your* goddamn problems. Now it's time to talk about *my* problems."

I was stunned. Bear had just become the winningest coach in college football history. He was famous, wealthy, they worshipped him in Alabama. What problems could he have?

"Bo," he croaked, "I don't wanna go back to the office. I don't wanna recruit one more kid. I don't wanna coach any more."

He looked sad and, suddenly, very old.

"Well," I said, thinking it over, "I can understand that. You've done everything you can possibly do in the game. If you want out, you should call your president right now and say the time has come for you to retire."

I grabbed the phone and put it down in front of him.

He glared at me. His words were thick as paste. "Aw . . . no . . . you . . . don't," he said. "You're gonna find this out someday. I hired forty-seven people at the University of Alabama athletic department. If I quit, what happens to them? What happens to those assistant coaches, and office people, and all them that I brought in there?"

I never thought about that.

"What happens to them?" he repeated. "Here's what. They're out in the cold. The new guy will replace them. Now, how can I do that to them?"

I didn't know what to say.

"You'll face that someday, Bo," he warned, standing up to leave. "You will. And, damn it, I hope you're smart about it."

Bear Bryant went back to Alabama and coached another

year. He leaned against the goal posts, doing something he was too sick to do, because of the people he had hired. He was not happy. He did not enjoy his work. He quit after that season. He died a few months later.

That was loyalty. You won't find that much anymore. And you certainly won't find anyone like the Bear. I'm just glad I got a chance to know him. I can still hear him saying "Bo, ain't you gonna run my play?"

Anytime, Bear. Anytime.

It's Not Temper, It's Coaching

I F you believed all the stories about me, you'd think I was the toughest, meanest bastard that ever lived.

Not true.

You'd think I had a temper made of lighter fluid.

Not true.

You'd think I kicked trash cans, Coke trays, and defensive linemen. Fired coaches, ruined locker rooms, hurled headsets. Made referees cringe, sportswriters shake, and had players so frightened they wouldn't breathe for fear of doing it the wrong way.

That part is true.

But I can explain.

There is a method to my madness. It's not temper, it's coaching. Like the time I made one of my Miami players run around the entire campus in his football uniform. Or the time I told Jim Brandstatter he was "the worst lineman in the history of intercollegiate football!" Or the time I chased this stupid official up and down the sidelines in Minnesota while he ignored me, until I finally yelled "AND YOU KNOW SOMETHING ELSE? YOU RUN LIKE A FAT BROAD!"—and he hit me with a fifteen-yard penalty.

In each case, I knew exactly what I was doing. Let's be honest. There's something about a temper that affects people. Particularly in football. You can charge up a team, make the referees think, inspire your assistants—or just plain scare the hell out of somebody.

Take the sidelines, where some of my more embarrassing tirades have been captured on television. Have I smashed my share of headphones? Yes. Sometimes I rip them off and throw them so hard that when we find them they don't work anymore.

Have I hollered at the referees? Yes. Now and then. Particularly if they do stupid things like call a phantom touchdown for USC at the Rose Bowl.

You know what I tell my players before the game? "Listen up, men. I don't want anybody arguing with the officials out there, you got it? We only need one ass on this team—and I have designated myself."

I live up to that role—but only when necessary.

The fact is, temper is a part of my act. I use it when it accomplishes a purpose. It could be in game situations. It could be—and more often is—in practice situations.

Back at Miami of Ohio, one of my quarterbacks, Kent Thompson, had a bad habit of fumbling the football. Whenever he did, I exploded. "DO NOT DROP THE DAMN FOOTBALL! UNDERSTAND? DO NOT DROP THE DAMN FOOTBALL! DO NOT DROP THE DAMN FOOTBALL!" I didn't whisper. I screamed. You call that temper; I call it motivation. But eventually, Kent improved. And you know what he told me after the season was over? Every time he called the play in the huddle, he ended it with "Do not drop the damn football . . . *break!*"

See? It worked.

* * *

Now, if we're going to talk about my temper, we'd better distinguish between the different types. There is sideline temper (heat-of-the-battle), practice temper (motivational), office temper (between myself and a player), and staff-meeting temper (you're fired, you're fired, you're fired). Those are real.

And then there is my "legendary" temper.

We might as well clear that up right now.

I have had a temper since I was a kid. I used to fight with my sisters over who got to use the bicycle, or who got to ride in the front seat. And I was always very competitive in sports, which led to a temper when I lost. So much so, in fact, that once, in a high school basketball game, one of my teammates cursed at an official, and the official spun around and threw *me* out of the game. He just figured "It must be Schembechler."

My good friends know this. Usually, they ignore it. Joe Hayden, my buddy for thirty years, once sat with me while I got so mad that I picked up a glass and threw it across the room. He didn't even turn his head.

"You dropped your glass, Bo," he said.

"You're right, Joe, I guess I did."

That much temper, I admit. But as I get older, I hear more and more stories about myself, almost all of them having to do with me exploding, losing my cool, ripping somebody to shreds. People imitate me. The imitations get wilder and wilder. The stories become incredible. Sure, my memory is sketchy. And I don't always realize when I am raising my voice. But I still shake my head when someone says that:

• Before a game in the early seventies, I was going through our last-minute huddle drills with the team. Just as I was calling a play, an ABC-TV guy broke in to tell me that we had to clear the field because the band was ready to come on. "DON'T INTERRUPT MY HUDDLE!" I screamed, then I grabbed him and threw him to the sidelines.

• After a loss at Miami of Ohio, I was so upset I went into a room and began kicking everything in sight, smashing chairs, knocking stuff off of shelves. My assistant coaches were outside the door, afraid to enter. Two reporters came looking for me, but my coaches stopped them. "You don't want to go in there," they said.

• During our first team-meeting of the season, Mike Husar, our offensive lineman, showed up wearing a tank top, in clear violation of our dress policy. I made him stand up, in front of everybody, and yelled about how "THIS IS NOT THE WAY A MICHIGAN MAN DRESSES!" I then tried to rip the shirt right off his body. It didn't work. I tried again. No luck. Finally I screamed at the equipment man to get him a different shirt and told him to sit down.

Are they true stories? God, I hope not. But I suppose I could spend this whole book rebutting stories about my temper. It's not nearly what it's cracked up to be, especially as I get older. I learned a lot of great things from Woody Hayes, but one of the not-so-great things was that if you don't control your temper, it will control you.

So I pick my spots. Guys on my team will tell you I'll let them get away with one or two things, but if they keep it up, I'll come down hard. And when I do, I won't sit around thinking about it. I can't. If a kid is messing up or breaking the rules, I don't sleep until I talk to him. I get antsy. Despite my passion about football, I'm worried about those kids under the helmets. These are lives we're dealing with here.

That's why I always take action immediately when I hear something. "Get me such-and-such in this office in the next five minutes!" You may call it temper; I call it taking care of business. I did that with Leroy Hoard, when I found he'd cut several classes. I did that with Jim Harbaugh when I got a report that he'd been involved in a disorderly conduct incident.

"YOU ARE OFF THIS TEAM!" I told him as soon as he walked in.

"What?" he gulped.

"IS YOUR NAME JAMES JOSEPH HARBAUGH?" I said, holding the police report that had him listed along with several other students.

"Yes."

"THEN YOU ARE OFF THIS TEAM!"

"Bo," he said, rising, holding back the tears, "it wasn't me. It wasn't me!"

"WELL YOU BETTER GET THIS STRAIGHTENED OUT, BECAUSE UNTIL YOU DO, YOU DO NOT PLAY FOOTBALL HERE ANYMORE!"

Eventually, we learned that it wasn't him, that he had been around the scene but hadn't done anything wrong. Fine. Jim was back with the team. But if he was ever *contemplating* making trouble, I think we nipped it in the bud right there.

That's office temper, by the way. Behind closed doors.

Practice temper is something else. Understand that practice is the time when you motivate your players to concentrate, to execute, and not to make mistakes. I will not yell at a player if he fouls up *during* a game. What's the point? He already feels bad enough. It's like Mike Lantry, our place kicker in the seventies who missed the field goal that would have won the Ohio State game. That poor guy has had to drag that kick around for years. Why? What does it accomplish? You still don't get to win.

Now, there are some coaches who never raise their voice in practice. I can't do it. I coach from the heart and from the throat. The kids in my program know that when they come to practice they better be 100 percent ready or they're going to hear about it. Literally.

"NO MISTAKES! WHAT THE HELL IS THE MATTER WITH YOU?"

"IF YOU BLOW COVERAGE ONE MORE TIME YOU CAN JUST KEEP RUNNING OUT THAT TUNNEL!"

"YOU ARE THE LOUSIEST BLEEPING PLAYER TO EVER PLAY YOUR POSITION!"

We call that the language of practice. It goes back to Woody Hayes and Bear Bryant and back even beyond them. It is not used all the time, but it is used during drills—hard, sweaty, undesirable drills. It motivates. And it isn't always fire and brimstone, either.

Humor works just as well. I might say, "Men, today is Labor Day. And we are here to *labor!*" Or "Hey! I don't want a whole lot of smart son of a bitches who ask me questions! I want a lot of dumb son of a bitches who *just do it!*"

Back in the 1969 season, I told the team we would not tolerate any racial unrest. "I don't care if you're black, white, or purple," I hollered, "you will all get along. The only group we have to worry about . . . is the *Italians*. Hey, Calderazzo, Zuccarelli, isn't that right?"

And Brandstatter—who probably took more abuse from me than any single player—once heard me tell him "Damn you, Brandstatter! I'd kick you in the butt, but I'm afraid I'd lose my foot!"

Let's talk about sideline temper. What an image I have! The TV broadcasters like to say, "Well, if the officiating is bad today, old Bo will surely let us know about it." And then they keep a camera ready, just in case. I must look pretty bad, because whenever people meet me, they always say, "Oh, you look much younger than on TV. On TV you look like Attila the Hun."

Hey. Sorry, folks. When you're on the sidelines, you don't have time to worry about being polite.

Picture this: you are wearing a headset, and in your ears you can hear all the coaches in the press box, plus all the people on the sidelines who have that same headset. The crowd around you is roaring, so you have to scream to be heard. Your heart is pounding. Your pulse is racing. You are so locked into the strategy of the game that a bomb could go off in your underwear and you wouldn't notice. You can feel when things are going your way. You can see the mistakes you made and wish to hell you hadn't. You're thinking about tendencies and formations and personnel and play-calling and what down it is, and what yard line it is, and which way the wind is blowing, and who's your hot running back, and all the time you're doing this, there's a 25-second clock going tick, tick, tick.

Now, this is not the place to take aside one of your players and calmly say, "Tommy, tell me how you are feeling. Is everything OK? Do you think you'll be able to catch this screen pass if we throw it to you?" We are not in a negotiating position here. We are not here to discuss theory. Damn it, man. We're at war out there.

So I make no apologies for being abrupt. Purpose. Everything is for a purpose. Usually sideline temper will get a referee's attention. It'll let him know I'm there. It'll show my players that I am 100 percent into that game and they had better be the same.

And then sometimes, I'm just mad as hell.

Last season, down in Iowa, we were trying to run a play and the crowd was just brutal. You couldn't hear a thing. Our quarterback, Michael Taylor, came to the line, called the team back, returned to the line, and it was worse. The linemen set, the backs set, but Taylor stood there.

"HE CAN'T HEAR, REF!" we yelled.

And all of a sudden—can you believe it?—the ref called us for delay of game, five-yard penalty! He said that Taylor had failed to put his hands under center before stepping back from the line and, therefore, the clock had continued running.

I went nuts! The situation was so obvious! Why were *we* getting the penalty? "COME ON, REF, THAT WAS A HORSEBLEEP CALL! COME ON REF!"

And he threw a fifteen-yard unsportsmanlike conduct penalty *on me*.

"WHY YOU GODDAMN SON OF A —"

So we ended up losing twenty yards in that fiasco. I was furious. I threw the headphones. I stomped up and down the sideline. "YOU'RE BLIND! YOU'RE INCOMPETENT! YOU STINK!"

I don't call that calculated temper.

I call that rage.

Referees will do that to you. And most people think I hate them. After all, I have a file full of reprimands from the Big Ten telling me to cool my stack. But the fact is, the officials that are good and that I've had confrontations with are still friends of mine because if they make a mistake, I tell them about it and often they admit it. Hey. I make mistakes, too.

I only carry one grudge, and that's against Gil Marchman, the guy who in the 1979 Rose Bowl called Charles White in for a touchdown when he clearly fumbled three yards from the end zone. And the reason I carry the grudge is not because he made a mistake, but because he never admitted it. That was a critical call. We ended up losing by a touchdown.

All he needed to do was come up afterwards and say, "Bo, I blew it."

He never did.

Sometimes you can use a bad ref to your advantage. Back in 1977, we were playing Texas A & M in our stadium. It was a split crew of officials, and one of them was from Texas. The Big Ten guys told him, "Don't mind Bo. He gets upset every once in a while, but he's OK. You don't have to take it too seriously."

And this Texas official jumped up and said, "He better not say a word to me. I'm not taking any crap from him."

So the first time the least little thing happened, I think it was a holding call, he didn't tell me what the penalty was. I yelled at him. And he threw a flag for unsportsmanlike conduct! Just threw it and marched off fifteen yards! And I looked at him and said, "Why, you son of a bleep." And he marched off fifteen more!

I was boiling mad. My players saw the whole thing. And you know what?

They were so jacked up, they went out and pounded the Aggies, 41–3.

I never did get a chance to thank that old Texas boy.

Finally, let's talk about staff-meeting temper. This is something altogether different. For one thing, nobody throws a flag. So the sky is the limit. I always joke that if someone walked by one of our staff meetings, not knowing anything about how football coaches talked, they would think there was a riot going on. They'd think this ship was in deep and dire trouble.

"Only an idiot would block that play that way!"

"You're crazy! If we do it your way, we won't gain two feet!"

"SHUT UP!"

"What the hell do you know about anything?"

"Both of you guys are wrong!"

"Who asked you?"

"SHUT UP!"

It is true, I get so mad during some of these meetings, I have nothing left to yell but "You're fired!" Not that I ever mean it. What I really mean is damn it, I'm tired of talking about this and we're not going to debate it anymore. But what I say is "You're fired!" And sometimes the guy walks out and goes down the hall and gets a drink of water and then he comes back. Deep down, he loves it. We all love it. Football coaches screaming in smoke-filled rooms are like little kids playing in the mud. The joy is in getting dirty.

So you really can't make anything out of staff-meeting temper. Woody and I used to have some beautiful arguments, as you know. Many is a room that was not the same once we were finished with it. And he threatened to fire me (and once did, of course) the same way I do with the guys on my staff. Over and over.

After a while, guys just develop a defense. Jerry Hanlon has been with me since the Miami of Ohio days. There's not much I can fool him with anymore. When we get into an argument, he'll pull out a crossword puzzle and start doing it.

"DAMN IT, JERRY. PUT DOWN THAT CROSSWORD PUZZLE OR YOU'RE FIRED."

"Bo," he'll say, glancing up over his glasses, "you fired me last week."

Now that's the best way to handle temper I've ever seen.

★ ★ ★

WE'RE NOT
HERE TO
DEBATE THIS

★ ★ ★

Three Yards and
a Cloud of Dust

"HEY, Bo," a reporter asked me in the press conference following our victory in the 1989 Rose Bowl, "did you use a new offensive game plan this time?"

"Of course not," I said. "We approached this game in typical Michigan fashion."

Pause.

"We decided to throw the bomb on first-down."

The room exploded in laughter. If it's one thing the press has loved to attack me for over the years, it's my conservative offense. No pass, they say. Rush, rush, rush. Three yards and a cloud of dust. Well. First of all, as usual, they don't know what they're talking about. We have thrown the ball plenty at Michigan. Secondly, as long as that cloud of dust keeps resulting in first-downs, I don't see why we should knock it.

Of course, I know exactly where I got my reputation as a rush-loving coach. It was the 1971 season, when my quarterback was Tom Slade. Now, Tom was a good athlete, he had good mobility. But he had a very average arm. I chose him, over better pure passers, because I knew I could put a tremendous cast around him. We had a running attack that you just couldn't stop. Billy Taylor and Glenn Doughty were in the backfield. Our offensive line featured Reggie McKenzie and Paul Seymour, both of whom would make All-American. I mean, we were brutal. So I decided to emphasize the run —along with an ironclad defense—and literally rush our opponents into submission.

"Now, Tom," I said. "You understand you're going to have to do some blocking here."

"No problem," he said. "I can block."

He was great. One of our best plays in that running-attack back was a power sweep, where the quarterback reverses a pivot, tosses the ball to the tailback—then leads the way with a block. Now, you would never do this with a quarterback who was going to throw the ball often. He'd get the crap knocked out of him. Can you imagine Troy Aikman throwing the lead block eight times a game?

Of course the press saw this quarterback out there, playing guard, throwing his body around. And then it saw our total passes attempted all year: 114. *For the entire year!* I think Brigham Young may have thrown that many in one game. Anyhow the media dubbed me "Mr. Off-Tackle" and it has stuck ever since.

Hey. I don't care. I had made up my mind I could win with that offense. And you know what?

We finished the regular season 11–0.

Would you argue with my judgment?

I like the run. What can I say? My favorite thing in football is probably an eighty-yard drive in which I've shown some dominance up front, opened some big holes, made some beautiful blocks. And on the final play, from inside the five, we knock it home. That's football to me.

But that doesn't mean I don't like or appreciate the other

parts of the game. The publishers of this book, at one point, suggested we call it *Bo: How I Learned to Relax and Love the Forward Pass*. Ha, ha, ha.

What a stupid idea.

Here are my thoughts on the key elements of football:

DEFENSE: As much as I like the run, defense is the most important element in football. Plain and simple. You will not win big without a great defense. Last year, people talked about Notre Dame and USC, but the team I would have dreaded playing the most was Auburn. They had an unbelievable defense, so gifted up front, quick and strong. You could not score on that group.

Defense wins games. Defense sets the tone. Even in the pros, it's usually the best defensive team that wins the Super Bowl. And in order to have a great defense you must first stop the run. The run will beat you quicker than anything I know, because it not only beats you physically, it beats you mentally. It saps your spirit. "Geez," the players seem to say, "we're getting the hell kicked out of us. We have to get down there and bang *again?*"

Before the Rose Bowl last year, all the talk was about USC's fine quarterback, Rodney Peete. I told our defense, "Forget Rodney Peete. Just forget him. If you don't stop the USC rushing attack, we don't have a chance. Stop the rush, and you'll take care of Peete."

We stopped the rush.

We won the game.

Above all, your defense must be nasty. If you talk to my defensive players, one thing they will always complain about is how I side with the offensive players whenever there's a conflict. "Don't you dare touch that quarterback again!" I will scream. Or "Who do you think you are starting a fight with that offensive lineman? You're not tough enough to try that!"

Doesn't matter who the defensive player is: Calvin O'Neal, Mike Hammerstein, Mark Messner. They all get treated the same: lousy. And I do it for a reason. I want to make them tougher and nastier than anybody they play against, because nobody is going to side with them.

One time, back in the early seventies, we were running a skeleton drill and David Brown, our free safety, made an aggressive play on the receiver. The ball was thrown high and David tagged the guy and he went flying. Jack Harbaugh, who was coaching the secondary, began clapping.

"All right, David," he yelled. "Way to go."

"HEY!" I screamed at Jack. "I don't want any hitting in that secondary."

"But, Bo," Jack said, "he made a great play . . ."

"I SAID I DON'T WANT ANY HITTING AND I MEANT I DON'T WANT ANY HITTING!"

Poor Jack. His knees were shaking. He slinked away. Later that night, the defense had a meeting. And when Jack walked in, the players stood up and applauded.

That's fine. That's what I want. Those defensive guys should stick together and feel the whole world is against them. It makes them nastier. And they need that on Saturday.

OFFENSE: If you have a great defense, you are likely to have a good offense. You can take more risks, because even if you turn it over on your forty-yard line, their chances of scoring are not real good.

Hey, the best teams I've had were defensive, not offensive, and yet if you go back through the history of the twenty years, there are probably few teams out there which rolled up more yardage or scored more points than Michigan. That goes all the way back to the great Fielding Yost and his teams in the early 1900s. Yost was a defensive coach; he played defense. That's how he stopped everybody. He got the ball, went and scored, so they thought he was a great offensive genius. Actually, he emphasized defense. And anybody in their right mind would do that.

So why do I coach the offense? Most head coaches coach offense. The offense will set the tempo of the game, and the offense is still the most complicated phase of the game. Head coaches want that kind of control.

And yes, that means the passing game. And we might as well dispel this myth right now. I like the pass. There, I said it. I LIKE THE PASS! And Michigan has had some great passing teams. Don't tell me Jim Harbaugh wasn't a great passing quarterback. Don't tell me Rick Leach or Steve Smith couldn't throw the ball. And don't tell me Anthony Carter didn't get a chance to catch any passes.

The point is, you construct your offense around the talent that you have. When we had Anthony, we were going to find a way to pass and pass-block, so that we could take advantage of him. The same way we emphasized the run back in 1971 when we were loaded with rushers.

No, I am not the kind of coach who goes bombs away on first-, second-, and third-down. Why should I? It's not smart. Any good coach will tell you that turnovers are killers, and there's a much higher chance of turning over the ball when you're constantly throwing downfield. But there is a safe way to throw the football. We proved that last season. How in the world can you pass for 153 yards a game and have just two interceptions all season? Now, come on! There's something good going on here.

And we won. That's the most important thing, isn't it? It's like I tell the quarterbacks I recruit. I go into their homes, and coaches have been there before me warning the kid "Don't listen to Bo. If you go to Michigan, you'll never pass more than 10 times a game." Hey. Baloney. First of all, they're still working off that 1971 reputation, and this is a long way from 1971. Secondly, even if that quarterback does pass a little less, odds are he's going to win a lot more. Now, what's more important: throwing for 350 yards in a nothing game against Kansas State, or throwing a touchdown pass to win the Rose Bowl? You tell me. And if you said the Kansas State game, see ya later. You're not the kind of guy I want for a quarterback.

FIELD GOALS: Field goals frustrate me, to be honest. You get tired of the damn things unless you're the guy kicking them. When you get beat by some kid kicking four field goals, you say, "Come on. What the heck kind of way is that to lose a game?"

It's particularly bad in college football. We have the wide goalposts, and until last year, we let them tee it up as much as they wanted. I see some of these little guys who can't really play the game, not from a blocking and tackling standpoint, and yet they are instrumental in deciding the outcome. It bugs me.

(That's why I always liked our kicker, Mike Gillette. He was a stone-cold athlete. He liked to hit, and his teammates respected that. He was a football player who happened to kick—not a kicker who happened to play football.)

The problem with the field goal is that it rewards penetration by allowing you three points when you are not in the position to score six. That's not inherently bad. But when you only have to cross the 50-yard line to do it, then it doesn't make sense. And that's where we are headed.

As a kid in Ohio, I used to play this game called Kick Goal. Two players kick the ball back and forth, catch it where it lands, and kick it again. Eventually one kid moves in close enough to kick it over a tree—and he wins. Is that what we want? Well, that's what football is becoming with these long field goals. Kick Goal. Come on!

I don't say take the field goal out of college football. But I'm glad they took the tee away. Make it a little harder. It's so damn frustrating to bang bodies with the opponent, down after down, knocking open holes, slamming holes shut, then, on fourth down, have the game decided by everyone watching a ball sail over their heads.

Doyt Perry took over as Head Coach at Bowling Green in 1955 and hired the serious, clean-cut young coach you see here. My style hadn't changed much when I arrived on the free-spirited campus of Ann Arbor fourteen years later.

(*Above*) Ara Parseghian gave me the chance to move up to Big Ten football as one of his assistants at Northwestern. He had one of the greatest minds in college football, and yet in 1957 we went 0–9.

(*Below*) Although I loved working under Woody Hayes at Ohio State, in 1965 I felt ready to become Head Coach at my alma mater, Miami of Ohio. My staff, surrounding me *left to right*: Jerry Hanlon, Jerry Stoltz, Jack Hecker, Jim Young, Dave McClain, and Joe Galat.

Nobody could fill a lineman's shoes quite like Dan Dierdorf. God knows he weighed enough! All kidding aside, I knew Dan would be an NFL star before he ever left college. He was maybe the most talented offensive lineman I ever had.

After our stunning 24–12 upset of #1 Ohio State in 1969, my first season as Head Coach, I met with reporters in the locker room. Woody Hayes once told me, "You'll never win a bigger game." He was right. (*AP/Wide World Photos*)

Here I am making a few subtle suggestions to the referees. Actually, my sideline temper is usually a controlled outburst with a definite purpose in mind. Then again, sometimes I'm just mad as hell. (*Photos by Bob Kalmbach*)

Anthony Carter was the best receiver I ever had, and the most exciting player I ever coached. He also helped get me my first Rose Bowl victory in 1981, bless him. (*Bettmann News Photos*)

Rich Leach was a student of the game—and one tough quarterback! He also was the only passer I ever had who played college football and baseball on the same afternoon. (*Bettmann News Photos*)

I didn't even want to recruit five-foot-six tailback Jamie Morris. He had to beg me for a tryout at running back. After just a few plays, however, I decided he would start as a freshman. Shows you what coaches know.

Michigan football has had a winning tradition ever since Fielding Yost posted a remarkable 165–29–10 lifetime mark. Here I am with his successors, *from the left*: Fritz Crisler, Bennie Oosterbaan, Harry Kipke, and Bump Elliot.

Though in frail health, my mentor and dear friend Woody Hayes insisted on coming to introduce me at a banquet in Dayton in 1986. He regaled the crowd with nostalgic stories and stayed until the end, when this picture was taken. The next day he died.

I met Millie Cunningham over the phone in the summer of 1968. Within three months we were married. With her three sons, Matt, Geoff, and Chip, I had a ready-made family.

Millie gave birth to Glen Edward Schembechler III the second week of the 1969 season. We called him Shemy because that's what my father was called. Sometimes the best way to unwind after a game was to hold him in my arms until we both fell asleep. (*Photo by Ted Walls*)

In 1983, my oldest son, Chip, took me on a surprise visit to meet my namesake, Bo Derek, and her husband, John. Three years later they came to dinner in Ann Arbor during Ohio State week, and I introduced her to my team after practice, where she gave me a big kiss. Some of my players are still in shock.

I've learned a lot about being a father watching Shemy grow up, and about the importance of listening to my children. That's one reason I treasure moments like this father-son walk along the Pacific Ocean. (*Photo by Michael S. Green, The Detroit News*)

I'm all smiles watching my players whiz by during their laps on the first day of spring practice, the promise of a new season ahead. I hope we never lose sight of the fact that this is a game young men play for enjoyment and lifelong memories of accomplishment. (*Photo by Pauline Lubens*)

They Call It
Motivation

A LOT of people ask how I motivate players. I'll answer that with three stories:

1. It's the mid eighties. Mike Mallory, one of our better linebackers, is falling behind in his studies. Upon receiving this information, I instruct one of my coaches to get him in my office immediately.

"Okay, Mike," I say as he walks in the door, "this is it."

"What, coach?"

I yell to my secretary, "Get Bill Mallory on the phone for me, will you?" Bill Mallory is Mike's dad, a friend of mine, and the coach at Indiana.

"I told you, Mike, I'm not putting up with any crap. I'm not playing around with you. I know you're not studying. You're screwing around!"

He's speechless. He can't believe I'm doing this.

Too late. I pick up the phone. "Bill, I've got your kid here, and I want you to know this kid has not done what I've asked him to do. I'm tired of telling him. I want you to talk to him right now."

I hand over the phone.

Mike looks like he's five years old. "Uh-huh," he mumbles into the receiver, "uh-uh, uh-uh, uh-huh . . ."

He hangs up.

"Now," I say, "are we going to have any more problems with you?"

"No way, coach. It's over."

"Get out of here."

No more problem.

That's motivation.

2. It's the early seventies. Middle of a practice. The receivers are working a drill where they run down the sideline and catch passes over their shoulder. Without realizing it, I stand directly in the path of a kid named Thom Darden, who is coming at me full speed. My back is turned. He's looking over his shoulder. I spin around just at the last moment, and he crashes into me headfirst in the hardest collision I have ever suffered as a coach.

I am knocked flat. My body is yelping in pain. Suddenly, I am surrounded by my players, looking down at me, waiting for my next move. I muster every ounce of strength that I can and hop to my feet as if nothing has happened.

"Hot damn!" I say. "That would have killed an ordinary man."

They walk away shaking their heads.

That's motivation.

3. It's 1970. Third game of the season. We're playing Texas A & M, and we are not moving the ball. All of a sudden, Dan Dierdorf, our offensive lineman—who is probably the best in the country at that point—comes rushing over to the sidelines, fed up with our performance. He yells at me, in

front of everybody: "DAMN IT! RUN EVERY PLAY OVER ME! OVER ME! EVERY PLAY!"

And I do. I run off-tackle five or six times in a row.

And we march right down the field.

And we win the game.

That's motivation, too.

Here's my point: there are a lot of ways to motivate football players. Sometimes you have to scare the crap out of them. Sometimes you have to lead by example. Sometimes, you just have to get out of the way.

And always, you have to keep up your act.

As a coach, I am the consummate actor. I am acting every minute of the day. Everything I say, every comment I make, is designed with an effect in mind.

I may walk by a player and bark at him: "I hope you're on your way to class." That's my subtle way of letting him know I've seen his midterm grades.

I may yank a player aside during practice and holler "Son, with your body and my brains, I would have been unstoppable!" He knows that he better concentrate a little harder.

I may snarl. I may whisper. I may slap a guy on the back or yank him down by the face mask. It is all calculated. It is all designed for maximum effect. Acting. Always acting. I've taken a lot of ribbing over the years for all the great players I've told would "never play a down at Michigan." But that's been acting, too. And it's been motivational. Take Jamie Morris. In his freshman year, he made the same mistake two or three times during a practice. I exploded. "Will somebody shoot me the next time I recruit a *five-foot-six tailback!* I must have been *out of my mind!* YOU WILL NEVER PLAY A DOWN AT MICHIGAN!"

Jamie, of course, went on to become our all-time leading rusher and now plays for the Washington Redskins.

Jim Harbaugh was no different. He was late to his first meeting as a freshman. I'd known Jim since he was a kid. And here, in his very first practice, he's coming in late? "I can't *believe* you!" I said. "Don't even *bother* to come into this meeting! YOU WILL NEVER PLAY A DOWN AT MICHIGAN!"

Of course Harbaugh became one of the best quarterbacks we've ever had. He now plays for the Chicago Bears.

The point is, I knew exactly what I was doing in both cases. In front of the whole team, I was setting a tone. With Jamie, I was saying, "Don't ever make the same mistake twice." With Harbaugh, I was saying, "I don't care who you are, you follow the rules." And you can bet those players watching took good mental notes; they didn't want to be the next guys yelled at.

Motivation. It is, quite simply, the spark that makes someone do that which he might not otherwise do. You need a ton of it in football. Let's be honest: it's unnatural for people to want to hit each other. You can't just tell a player, "Go out there and cream that guy because I told you to."

Football is a tough, bloody sport, with contact so fierce it can make you wince. If you expect your players to excel, you better have a pretty good reason, and that reason must be the pursuit of excellence. Not for the individual; for the team. You will never get the same level of effort from one man seeking glory as from a group of men pulling for a shared goal. You just won't.

I have seen the power of a team. I saw it that halftime locker room in Ann Arbor, 1969, when Michigan was supposed to be chicken feed for Ohio State. Remember Jim Young, pounding on the blackboard?

"THEY ... WILL ... NOT ... SCORE ... AGAIN!"

Motivation. It inspires every comment I make to a player. Of course, as coach, it is my job to know where and when to say something.

Some players, for example, are great practice players. They show motivation every day of the week. Greg McMurty, our excellent wide receiver, is like that. You will never see him inattentive in a meeting. If I were to rip Greg when he messed up, I'd be a fool. All I need to say is: "What a disappointing play for you."

He'll be thinking about that all week.

John Kolesar was a different case. He was also an excellent receiver and a great clutch performer. But during practice meetings, you could see him staring at walls, looking out the window, drifting away. Sometimes you'd need an alarm clock to get his attention.

Now, if John screwed up, I'd yell. I'd explode. "Get your head into practice!" But it *worked* with him. And that, as they say, is the bottom line.

Here are some keys to football motivation:

1. You must know your players like a book. Know their personalities. Know what works.

2. You must be true to your own personality. There are some guys who can be very soft and say, "I wish you had done better," and it hurts a player's feelings. I'd probably say, "DAMN IT! I'M GOING TO KILL YOU!"

But that's just me.

3. Deep down, your players must know you care about them. This is the most important thing. I could never get away with what I do if the players felt I didn't care. They know, in the long run, I'm in their corner. They are, after all, still young men, aged seventeen to twenty-two. They have to feel if they have a problem, they can come to you. They have to believe you are watching out for their best interests. Why else would they trust you? Somewhere beneath that crusty exterior, you must be human. I will not hesitate to cry in

front of my team. I cried when I told them they wouldn't be going to the 1973 Rose Bowl. I cried when I had to tell Al Sincich, my middle guard in the early eighties, that his mother had been killed. Tears are not—as some might accuse me of thinking—a sign of weakness. I *want* that kind of emotion.

Of course, for every tear there's a yell. I'll get on them for missing class or for not scoring well on a test. Last season I suspended Leroy Hoard, our fullback, because he cut a class. No class, no football. He came back and wound up MVP of the Rose Bowl.

Bear Bryant used to tell of how he presented himself for the first time to his Texas A & M team:

"I took off my coat and stomped on it.

"Then I took off my tie and stomped on it.

"Then, as I was walking up to the microphone, I rolled up my sleeves."

That'll motivate you. Or at least get your attention. Most coaches have done things like that. I've walked out of meetings, cursed, slammed the door, left them sitting there. I've kicked things. I've thrown an eraser or two. During punting drills I carry a yardstick, to measure the distance between each player on the line. I'll drop that yardstick between the players' legs, and if it doesn't measure up, I give them a whack.

There are countless little things you do to motivate your team. Mostly, however, you talk. That is a coach's greatest motivational tool. That is what I work at the most.

When I talk, I am passionate about the game. I may speak about Michigan, the school, the tradition. I may speak about the opponent and how little regard they have for us. I may speak about courage or pride. It depends. I never prepare a speech; whatever comes out, comes out. For a big game, like Ohio State or Michigan State, I might begin: "Men, many others have played in this game before us. Tradition demands that you play like *Michigan!* That is why you're *here!* You did not come to play in a mediocre program, and if you did, you are at the *wrong place . . .*"

The words come from the heart. The delivery comes from practice. Acting, always acting, remember? Sometimes being a college football coach is like playing a lead in a movie.

My dramatic style is simple.

I steamroll.

I am not passive. I don't want some guy looking up into the sky, and I don't want him looking down at his desk. I want those eyes on me, and if I'm good, that's where they'll be. I will raise my voice, then lower it to a whisper, I will pause to let it sink in.

I will be honest. I will be direct. After we beat Ohio State last year, I could have been happy. I could have said, "Hey, we won the Big Ten championship. We're going to the Rose Bowl." But the fact is, our second half that day was awful. We gave up thirty-one points. So I chewed them out. "THIS GAME WAS NOT GOOD ENOUGH FOR CHAMPIONS!" I said.

On the other hand, during the Rose Bowl, at halftime, we were losing to USC, 14–3. In the locker room, I did not speak of mistakes. I did not scream about a lousy first half. I simply said, "We can beat this team." I knew we could. They knew we could. We made the adjustments. And we won.

That's another key to motivation. When your team is winning, be ready to be tough, because winning can make you soft. On the other hand, when your team is losing, and the fans and press are getting on your players, stick by them. Keep believing. Last season, after we lost to Miami, 31–30 —in the craziest final seven minutes of football I have ever seen—I told my team, "You men will *win the Big Ten championship.*" I told the press as well. We were 0–2.

We did not lose again.

By November, we were the champions.

Motivation. It is the transference of your heart and soul

into your players' minds and bodies. When you do it well, you feel in sync with your team, you can sense its mood. Of course, you can still overact. I remember one year, we were about to play Northwestern. I had been looking at film, and on this particular reel, they looked good. I began to worry. We were at the hotel, it was 9 P.M., the players were about to go to sleep. I ran from room to room, telling every one of them, "We are not ready for this game! We are not mentally prepared! *We are going to lose this game!*"

We won, 69–0.

Uh, never mind, guys.

OK. Let's talk about fear. A lot of my younger players may say they're afraid of me. But contrary to what you may believe, fear is not all that important in motivation: *fear of making a mistake* is what works. That's what we had with Woody. You were so damn afraid of messing up in practice, that you concentrated like a heart surgeon.

I suppose my players feel the same way about me. They probably fear me as freshmen and sophomores. By junior year, they know all they have to be afraid of is playing below their potential or messing up as students.

Then I explode.

No mistakes. We can't afford them. One guy's mistake can deflate the effort of an entire team. If you work on eliminating mistakes in practice, you'll have a lot less to worry about in a game.

I remember in 1968, my last year at Miami of Ohio, there was a walk-on defensive back named Kent Thompson. He was a skinny, wiry kid and a good athlete.

We were out at spring practice one day, a full scrimmage, and it was a mess. My quarterbacks were awful. So I said, "Come here, Thompson. I'm going to try you at quarterback."

We tried a pass play. He drops back, sets up, boom! Bangs it in.

"Okay," I say, "that was a good one. Now we're going to roll out to the right . . ."

He rolls out, looks, boom! He bangs it in.

As you can imagine, the guys on defense are getting ticked off. This brand new quarterback is making them look bad. Third play, he goes back in the pocket—and they put the blitz on. This big defensive tackle, Errol Kahoun, comes through and hits Thompson head-on, knocks his helmet off, the ball goes flying. He gets up, blood dripping down his face, and I say, "Kent, I'm going to tell you something; that's going to happen to you every once in a while. But, damn you . . . *DON'T YOU EVER DROP THAT FOOTBALL AGAIN!*"

Motivation.

Woody Hayes used to say, "No back is worth two fumbles." I often say, "No player is worth fifteen yards." If it's mistakes we're talking about, I want my players to be afraid. If it's a violation of team rules, I want them to be *petrified*. Every player makes mistakes on the field, and I'll blow up, and we'll both get over it; violating team rules is something else. Serious violators are gone. I don't care who they are. You want to motivate a group of players, let them know what happens if they break the rules.

Ask Calvin O'Neal, our All-American linebacker in the mid seventies. Once, at the team dinner before the first game of the season, Calvin and another guy came sneaking in late. As an excuse, they concocted this ridiculous story about riding down an eleavtor with this fat woman who suddenly passed out and they had to help her to an ambulance.

"Do you really expect me to believe that?" I asked.

"Oh, yeah," they said. "It's the truth."

I let this violation go until after the game was played. Then at the next team meeting, I walked over, in front of everybody, and said, "Calvin, stand up and tell the team what you told me about why you were late."

He stood. He told the story. The guys were cracking up.

"There was this fat woman . . ." he said.

"Hee-hee-hee . . ."

"And she passed out . . ."

"Ha, ha . . . HAHAHAHA! . . ."

What the team did was substantiate exactly how I felt about that excuse, namely, that it was a crock. Then I said, "OK. You guys are going to run every day for the rest of the season." And that's what they did. I stood there after every practice, every day, my arms folded, making sure they finished.

So motivation is using what works at the moment. At that moment it was group embarrassment. Sometimes it can be a joke. Sometimes it can be a scolding. As long as your players know, deep down, that you are trying to make them as good as they can be, then you can use just about anything. Even a disappearing act. Once, in 1978, we were losing to Notre Dame at halftime. Here was my halftime speech: "Gentlemen, it's one thing to be beaten. It's another to be embarrassed." And I walked out.

We won, 28–14.

By the way, the notion of fiery halftime speeches is vastly overrated. Oh, I've made a few. And that Ohio State game in 1969 had one of the most electric halftimes I've ever experienced. But by and large, halftime is for adjustments, questions, and quick answers. Rarely will I launch into any motivational lectures at halftime. And I never asked Michigan to win one for the Gipper.

I came close, however. Back in 1979, I had a strong safety named Jeff Cohen, who was Jewish. Our game against Notre Dame that year was an afternoon game, and it fell on Yom Kippur, the Jewish high holy day. Cohen, it turns out, had always spent that holiday in synagogue.

He decided to play anyhow. That morning, just before we went out for the kickoff, I walked by him, patted him on the back and said, "Hey, Jeff, let's win one for the Kippur."

That's motivation, too.

＊　＊　＊

So verbal, physical, emotional, or comical motivation is a beautiful thing when it works. You must keep up your act and remember that you are coaching attitude as much as skill. I work on a guy's attitude from the minute he gets here. Encouragement. Criticism. Screaming. Winking. Kicking. Yelling. Nodding. Ignoring. It's all part of coaching attitude, because attitude equals motivation. Michigan may not have the biggest or fastest players in the country, but if I coach the right attitude, we can win, we can beat anybody.

I learned that lesson the hard way. And this is probably the best story about motivation that I know.

The year was 1980. Andy Cannavino was the captain of our defense. We opened with a meek win over Northwestern, 17–10. We then lost to Note Dame on a "Hail Mary" field goal, 29–27. Then we came back to Ann Arbor and lost to South Carolina, 17–14. I couldn't believe it. It was the worst game I've ever coached. I did a terrible job. At home, no less.

The following night, we were in a staff meeting, and Bob Thornbladh, one of my assistants, said, "Bo, we've got a problem with this team."

"I know," I said, "it's obvious from the way we're playing."

"It's more than that, Bo. These guys are complaining. They say your practices are too hard, that we're hitting too much in practice, that the coaches are way too critical, and that football isn't fun anymore."

I stared at him. "Well, who the hell is saying this?"

"Cannavino, for one."

I swallowed hard. "My captain?"

"Yeah."

I didn't think it over. I didn't take a night to sleep on it. I said to Thornbladh: "I give you five minutes to get that son of a bleep in my office."

Within five minutes, Cannavino walked through my

door. He was a big, six-foot-two, 225-pound, dark-haired, good-looking guy. I told him to sit down.

"Andy," I said, "I've been hearing about morale problems on this team."

"Yeah, coach," he said, "I think we have some."

"Well, what are the players saying?"

"They're saying we practice too long and that the coaches are pretty critical and we spend a lot of time looking at film."

I paused.

"Did you ever say that, Andy?"

"Yeah, coach . . . I did."

I leaned forward. My words were slow and deliberate. "Now let me tell you something. When you were back there in Cleveland, at St. Joseph's High School, Ohio State, where your daddy went to school, didn't even offer you a scholarship. We brought you to the University of Michigan. The coaching staff here made you an All–Big Ten player. Your teammates elected you captain of the team. And you have the *audacity* to criticize Michigan football? How *dare* you?

"I'd like to stand you up before all those guys who played here in the past, all those guys who won championships, went to bowl games, did all the things you want to do in college football, and I want you to tell them that your practices are too hard, that they're hitting too much, that you spend too much time watching film! And you know what they're going to tell you? Grow up! Grow up and be a man! And if you won't, then get the hell out of *Michigan football!*"

He was stunned. He began to cry. But I wasn't finished.

"Cannavino," I growled, "we have one problem on this team, and only one problem, and that is *you!* And until *you* change, we will never win. You are the captain of this team. What you say, the other players and especially the young ones will listen to. How can you possibly ruin this team by criticizing the leadership here? You are the problem. Understand me? *You are the problem!*"

He got to his feet, tears coming down his cheeks. And he walked out the door without saying a word.

Folks, as I sit here writing this book, I promise you, Andy Cannavino became the greatest captain I ever had. We did not lose a single game the rest of the season. His defense kept opponents from crossing our goal line for twenty-four *consecutive quarters*. We went to the Rose Bowl and beat Washington, 23–6. That 1980 football team, by the end of the season, was as good as any team in the United States of America. And the only reason it didn't win a national championship was that I did a bad job of coaching attitude. I assumed that because a guy played for Michigan he automatically had a great attitude. I was wrong. It needs help. It always does.

That may have been the single greatest motivational speech I ever gave, but only because it was born out of frustration with myself. Nothing motivates like your own failure. Nothing.

The Accidental
Celebrity

WHEN they first offered me the head coaching job at Michigan, I was not the number one choice. I was not the number two choice. I was so far down the list, that the day after I accepted, one of the Detroit newspapers ran the headline: "BO WHO?"

They don't say "Bo Who?" anymore. My teams have won too many championships, played in too many Rose Bowls, and my picture has been in too many dumb TV close-ups— usually when I'm ticked off on the sidelines—for me to claim anonymity anymore. Heck, I've even been in a movie. *The Big Chill.* Got nominated for an Academy Award. The movie. Not me. I was in it for two seconds—and nobody told me until the film was already released.

The actors, who were supposed to be Michigan graduates, are watching a Michigan game on TV. We get a clipping penalty to nullify a long gain. I appear on the screen, and the character played by Jeff Goldblum says "Come on, Bo, you're not supposed to fold until the *fourth* quarter."

And he throws popcorn at me.

Some movie career, huh? That's OK. The truth is, I have never been comfortable with celebrity. Because of my job, and Michigan's success, I've been thrown into a lot of celebrity situations and I think I've learned to handle them. But I am not, by nature, an out-front guy. I'd rather sneak to the back of a cocktail party with a couple of old buddies and a couple of old cigars. Dinners, roasts, TV interviews—even after all these years, I've never really felt at ease with them. I'm a football guy. I always will be. I think I realized that most strongly, believe it or not, the night I met Elvis Presley.

It was back in 1973, and I was in Las Vegas for a clinic along with Frank Broyles and Darrell Royal. One night we went to see Elvis at one of the big casinos. We had a table right in front. He came out and did his show. I'm sure, by that time, he was heavily into drugs. He was puffy and pale. Afterwards, we were told that he wanted to see us in his dressing room.

I was surprised. We went back there, and it was a big fancy room with a bar at one end. I figured to see all these beautiful women there, but I was wrong. There were just half-a-dozen men. His bodyguards. Finally, Elvis came in. He was very cordial, but he looked, to me, like a troubled guy. I really didn't know what to say. Finally I made some remark about his sequinned jumpsuit. "Hey, those are neat. How many of those suits do you have?"

His eyes lit up. "Come here," he said, and he took me into the back room, his real dressing room. He started to show me his suits. There were dozens of them. Every color.

"Okay, Elvis," I said, "you wore this suit tonight. How many times will you wear it again?"

"That's it," he said.

"One time?"

"Yeah. I've got a guy that makes 'em for me. A thousand bucks a suit. As soon as I wear one, it's over. I ship it to the Elvis Presley Museum or someplace."

"Really?" I said.

"Yeah."

He went on and on about these suits. "Look at this one. How about this one? . . ." Now, shoot, I'm a football coach. I don't give a hoot about jumpsuits, but he's showing me every one. He's taking me around, just me and Elvis Presley, in a closet. This was a lonely guy.

I tried to be polite. But it got a little embarrassing. Finally, we ran out of things to say, so we went back out front. We sat around and talked a little more, then we left.

Now, when some people hear that story, they get all excited. Wow! You talked to Elvis Presley! But you know what I was thinking that whole time? "I'm glad I'm not him. I don't ever want to be like this poor soul."

If that's fame and fortune, you can have it. I am a football coach. I find it strange enough to be writing a book. Jumpsuits are a little out of my league.

Woody Hayes used to tell me, "I've seen these coaches running all over the country playing golf, going to banquets, getting on TV, traveling with Hollywood people. I just want you to know one thing, Bo: every time you do that, you're taking time away from what you're supposed to do—which is coach your team."

And I agree with him. Football comes first. That's the problem with these "face men" coaches, who are more interested in getting TV time and magazine stories than they are in coaching their teams. You can always spot a "face man." His mug will be all over the place during the week, local TV, network TV, ESPN. Then, during the game, he'll be standing on the sidelines like someone dropped him in from outer space. How the hell can you coach like that?

Last October, George Bush called me on the phone. He wanted me to join him in Grand Rapids and help him campaign. Now let me tell you, I was flattered. I like Bush and I planned on voting for him. And here he was, on the phone asking me to help.

"Mr. Vice President," I said. "I'd be happy to do it, but this is football season. I have practice. And if I went with you to Grand Rapids, all the time I was up there, I'd be thinking: 'I'm cheating my players.'"

And I didn't go.

And he understood.

(Millie didn't exactly understand. In fact, when I came home and told her, I believe her reaction was: "YOU DID WHAT?")

Sorry. That's the way I work. Now, I don't mind if the President comes to *us*. We'll make room. We did it for Gerald Ford, an ex–Michigan Wolverine, who stopped by while he was in office.

Of course, if you want to screw up a football practice, have the President of the United States drop in. The day before, they come in with dogs, and they've got secret service men checking everything out, police everywhere; it's a mess. Finally, the next day, Ford arrived, amidst a sea of human protection. He stood out on the field as we ran our plays. After a while, he wanted to hear the huddle.

Here's where things got tricky. They had this one secret service guy, I remember he was bald, and his job was to always look back over the President's head to protect him from behind. You got it? Well, as I said, Ford wanted to stand near the huddle, which meant this secret service guy had to stand near the line.

"Okay, twenty-eight, twenty-nine, check with me." A toss sweep. And the quarterback looked up and saw this secret service guy, right where the ball was going to go. He looked at me as if to say, "What do you want me to do?"

So I yelled to the guy, "Excuse me, sir. Would you please move?"

He wouldn't look at me. His job was to keep his eyes locked behind the President.

"Excuse me, sir, would you please *move?* We've got a play coming your direction."

He wouldn't budge. And Ford was standing there as if nothing's happening, and my quarterback was throwing his hands in the air, so finally I yelled, "Aw, go ahead with the play. Run the guy over if you have to."

And we ran the toss sweep. And let me tell you, that guy just barely got out of the way.

Like I said, nothing interferes with practice.

As you can tell, I am not overwhelmed by politicians, and I don't think I'd be much of one, either. Football is my world. I'm most comfortable on the sidelines, calling plays, or in the weight room, slapping players on the back.

Besides, what do I know from celebrities? I don't exactly spend every free minute at the movies. I don't own a lot of record albums. I remember once we were in Hawaii, my mother was with us, and she wanted to see this singer. His name was Don Ho. After the show they took us backstage to meet him. My mother was very excited.

"Bo, meet Don Ho," some there said.

"Say, you're pretty good," I said. "You ever get over to the mainland?"

My mother just about killed me.

What do you want? I had no idea who he was. Like I say, this whole celebrity thing is a little baffling. What's truly strange is when *you* become the celebrity. Sure, autographs are flattering, as are people taking your picture, but it gets out of hand—especially as college football has gotten bigger and bigger. Gifts come in from unexpected places all the time. I have to refuse most of them. Once a truck pulled up to my house, and they unloaded a beautiful player piano. Said it was "a gift from a Michigan supporter," a man named Jim Betchek. A piano? I hadn't even met the man before.

Another time, a parent named Mike Baldouras offered to take Millie and me to Greece, his homeland. I coached Mike's kids, Art and John, from 1981 to 1986; the man has never stopped thanking me. "Mike, listen to me," I finally

said. "There will be no trips and no favors while I am coach
here. We can't do that. You got it?"

He still offers.

Millie and I have lived in the same house in Ann Arbor
since 1969, and just about everybody knows where it is. Kids
will ring the bell and ask for autographs. That's OK. It's when
they take my license plates that I get a little annoyed. One
morning I came out and both the plates were taken off my
car. They're on some frat house wall, I bet.

Sometimes, in the middle of the night, a car will roll by
and a student will scream "HEY, BO, WAKE UP!" And if we
leave a Michigan flag outside, like we used to on game day,
forget it. Someone takes off with it. We've been given maize-
and-blue Christmas ornaments, maize-and-blue toilet paper.
Now and then, if people know Millie is out of town, I'll come
home to find a couple frozen steaks on the front step with a
note: "Bo—figured you could use some dinner . . ."

It sounds pretty crazy. But, believe it or not, Ann Arbor
is relatively calm compared to the way some communities
hail their coaches. Woody Hayes was once the most popular
man in Columbus. He could have been elected Mayor by a
show of hands. And Bear Bryant in Alabama? Talk about
revered! There's a joke they tell down there about a man who
goes to heaven and sees a figure walking around with a whistle and a cap with an "A" on it.

"Who's that?" the newcomer asks. "That's God," he is
told, "but he thinks he's Bear Bryant."

If a football coach succeeds in a football-crazy town, he
can have carte blanche. That's crazy, but that's the way it is.
Take some of these speaking engagements, for example. This
is the truth: if I wanted to make money, speaking at the
highest priced functions, going anywhere they asked, I could
increase my income by probably three hundred thousand
dollars a year. Just for speaking! Can you believe it? What
do I have to say that's worth that kind of money?

Which is the reason I won't do them. I'll speak at banquets for friends, fellow coaches, former players. And if something fits into my off-season schedule, and they're willing to pay me money and I want to do it, that's fine. But I rarely bother. I get embarrassed when I'm with people who make a fuss and talk about things that I've done. The truth is, I might have done them, but they weren't that earth-shaking. And I promise you, I didn't do them alone.

Sometimes I feel like I have to live up to other people's expectations. I find myself flying all over the country to give talks and speeches and accept awards, and all I'm really thinking about is how nice it would be to be stuck on some island alone for a month, nothing but sun and water and peace and quiet. That part of the job has gotten harder and harder for me as I get older. So many speeches. The funny thing is, when I was a freshman in college, I got D's in my public speaking. The whole idea left me petrified.

Besides, fame can have a way of backfiring on you. Last fall I was sitting in the house of perhaps the most highly recruited high school quarterback in the country. It happened to be the Monday night that the Chicago Bears were playing the Los Angeles Rams. And Jim Harbaugh was starting at quarterback.

"Do you mind if we watch the game, coach?" the kid asked.

"Nah, sure, why not?" I said.

After all, I coached Harbaugh. And here he is on national TV. A good recruiting aid. So we turn on the game. And not one minute later, the announcers—*including my own Dan Dierdorf!*—begin to laugh about how long it's been since a Michigan quarterback started in the NFL. "Of the fifteen thousand passes thrown on 'Monday Night Football,' how many have been thrown by a Michigan quarterback?" they joked. I mean, they were cutting on us something awful. And here I am, in the living room of the nation's top *quarterback* prospect.

He looked at me. I looked at him. What could I do? I

grabbed his arm, stared him straight in the eye, and said, "Son, you're gonna change all that."

He didn't come to Michigan.

So much for fame.

I'm gonna kill Dierdorf the next time I see him.

All right. Now, before you get the idea that I am some hermit that prefers to crawl into the film room every night, let me tell you a story about one of my good friends.

Her name is Bo Derek.

By now, a lot of people around Michigan kid me about Bo. She has been to several of our games. At the 1988 Rose Bowl, they brought her to the pep rally as a surprise guest, and she ran onstage in the middle of my speech and gave me a kiss. How does a guy like me get to be kissed by a woman like that? It began with a practical joke.

Back in 1980, Keith Jackson and Bill Flemming from ABC sports were driving through Universal City, California. They stopped in a store and there was this picture book of Bo Derek—who was very popular then with the success of the movie *10*—and somehow they decided to send it to me as a gag. They signed the inside cover with a note: "To my namesake, Bo. I admire your work at Michigan. I hope I get to meet you at the Rose Bowl. (Signed) Bo Derek." And they mailed it from Universal City so the postmark would seem real.

Well, I got this thing and, to be honest, I wasn't sure what to make of it. I showed it to my staff and said, "Men. There it is. We go to the Rose Bowl this year, we get to meet Bo Derek."

I showed it to everybody. It was a neat thing to have. Then, a few weeks later, Flemming called on the phone. He was laughing. He said, "Did you get anything strange in the mail lately, Bo?"

And I knew it was him.

Now, that might have crushed some guys. But in 1983,

after we lost the Rose Bowl, my oldest son, Chip, took me on a surprise trip. We boarded a small, single-engine plane and flew north along the California coast. Chip said we were going to a lodge that he knew of, where we would watch the NFL play-off games and relax. I was so tired from the Rose Bowl, I didn't ask any questions.

We landed in the middle of nowhere, at this airport that looked more like a garage.

"Chip, where are we going?"

"Oh, we'll just go to this lodge up here and have some lunch and watch the play-offs," he said.

"Where are we going to go to get a car? We've got to drive somewhere."

I looked around. I didn't see a thing but landscape. All of a sudden coming down over a hill a hundred yards away I saw this blond-haired woman. As dumb as I am, I could tell this was a pretty good-looking woman, and she was coming my way. She got closer and closer, and I looked at Chip, and I said, "Hey! That's Bo Derek!"

She said, "Hi, Bo."

I said, "Bo! . . . uh . . . This is a pleasant surprise. I never expected this."

"Well, welcome," she said. "Let's go up to the ranch for lunch."

And we did. She introduced me to John, her husband, who at the time looked really wild with a beard and long hair. Bo cooked stew. We ate.

Now, I tell you this: the woman didn't know a damn thing about football. Why she agreed to meet me, I have no idea. I later found out that Chip had arranged the whole thing. Anyhow, we hit it off, despite our lack of common interests. She and John showed me around their house, including the bedroom, which had a steam bath and a rubbing table and even a grill for barbecuing. John took some pictures, including one of Bo and me by the pool, which I keep in my office, for people who don't believe this ever happened.

Three years later, I got to prove it. It was the Thursday before the 1986 Ohio State game. We were at the peak of our preparation. This, you might remember, was the game for which Jim Harbaugh, our quarterback, had "guaranteed" a victory to the press—which made me want to slug him.

Anyhow, Thursday morning, the phone rang. It was Bo Derek. "Hi, Bo," she said. "I'm in town. We're picking up a new car. How about coming out tonight for a hamburger?"

I said, "Whew! . . . Um, Bo, it's Ohio State week."

She didn't understand that.

"Maybe you can come by the game Saturday?" I suggested.

"Gee, I don't think we'll still be here."

Now, I wasn't about to miss practice. But you hate to let an opportunity like this slip away. I had an idea. "Look," I said. "How about if we send a helicopter out to pick you up, and you come out and meet the team after practice?"

She said, "I'd be happy to."

And so we did. That afternoon a helicopter—provided by Tom Monaghan—took Bo Derek from Dearborn to Ann Arbor. Landed right on schedule. Of course, the team knew nothing about this. At 5:30, practice ended, and I called them together for a little talk. It was speech time for Ohio State. We all knew how much this game meant. I said a few words about our goals and the tradition of the game.

"Now, men," I added. "Before we break up, a friend of mine is here and I want to introduce her to all of you."

Out came Bo Derek.

"Hello, dear," I said.

"Hi, Bo," she said, and planted a big kiss.

I don't know which the team had a harder time believing—that their old coach was getting smooched by Bo Derek or that he was allowing it to happen during Ohio State week. They were in shock. I wish I had a camera to catch all the mouths that were dropping open. Anyhow, the whole thing seemed to have a positive effect. The players all had souvenir pictures taken with Bo. I looked like a hero. Bo and John came to our house for dinner.

And we won the game.

Just another week at the ranch.

Why My Bowl Record Stinks, and Other Thoughts

OUTSIDE the door, my players were going wild in celebration, singing, laughing, slapping high fives. In the stands beyond the tunnel, the Michigan band was playing "Hail to the Victors."

I was alone in a small room where the coaches dress. I reached into the pocket of my sports coat and pulled out a cigar. I hadn't smoked one of those in years. Bad for the heart. But the hell with it. I was going to smoke one now.

We had won the Rose Bowl. Final score: Michigan 22, USC 14. That might be an average celebration for some coaches. But if your last name is Schembechler, you'd better savor every second. Jonah had his whale. Captain Hook had his crocodile. And I have January 1.

Let's be honest here: my bowl record stinks. As of this book, I've got five bowl wins, eleven bowl losses, and seven of those losses were in the Rose Bowl. In twenty years at Michigan, I have brought more Wolverine teams to Pasadena than any other coach—and have only won twice.

Does it bother me? Sure it does. Losing tears the heart out of you. And I don't have a very good heart to begin with. Going all the way to California to lose is even worse. Which explains my joy at finally getting a win last January 2. It also explains why, with less than two minutes left in the game, fourth-down, the ball on the USC one-yard line, I called a time-out and signalled my team over to the sidelines for a huddle.

"Listen to me!" I screamed, trying to be heard over the sold-out crowd. "We're going for it! I don't want any damn field goal. I want a touchdown!"

The players nodded. We were already ahead, 15–14. A field goal would have been the safe choice. But there are moments in football when you simply *will* the ball into the end zone. And I swear to you, one hundred Michigan men were willing that ball in there at that moment.

"All right, Leroy," I said to Leroy Hoard, our hot back, "we're giving you the ball. You gotta get it in there, you understand me!"

"I will, I will" he said, panting. "I'll get it."

And he did. Took that ball and charged for the end zone as if I were right on his butt. The refs cleared the bodies. Touchdown!

Finally, it was Michigan fans cheering in California. Finally, it was the Michigan band playing our music—after getting pelted with seat cushions at halftime. We won? We actually won? As time ran out, the players hoisted me on their shoulders, the officials handed me a huge trophy, and I screamed something into the TV cameras. God, that was sweet. About the only negative was that while I was in the air, some dirty rat stole my play sheets. I had them in my back pocket and, just like that, they were gone. I like to keep those sheets—sort of a personal souvenir. Instead someone is out there showing them around, saying "Look, here are the plays Bo used in the Rose Bowl."

Jerk.

* * *

Why is my bowl record so bad? Who knows? If I were 11–5 in bowl games, I'd probably be too cocky, so maybe this is God's idea. "Hey, Bo, we're gonna kick you in the butt with this bowl thing. OK? It's for your own good."

Some people have suggested I play too conservatively in bowl games. They say I worry about not losing instead of winning. Maybe we did keep the wraps on too tight in earlier years. I remember in 1969 we really overworked our guys. Glenn Doughty wrecked his knee in practice and needed surgery. Several other players went down with injuries. It wasn't fun at all. And then I had the heart attack.

Last season, as we got ready for Pasadena, I told my coaches, "We're going to do things differently. Let's be more relaxed than ever. Let everybody have fun, enjoy the sights. And let's open it up a little bit."

"Open it up?" they said.

"You know . . . pass?"

They looked at me and saw I wasn't kidding. What made me loosen up? Who knows? Maybe I'm like the old man who retires and buys a red Corvette, trying to make up for his lost youth.

Whatever. It worked. We won. That explains *that* Rose Bowl. As for the others, well, I should say right here that with a record like mine, there are no excuses.

But let me make a few . . .

First of all, I think it's tough to establish a strong bowl record coming out of the Midwest and going west or south to play. Your opponents, at the very least, are playing in familiar weather and field conditions, while you have to adapt. And in some cases—such as UCLA at the Rose bowl —-you're playing on their *home field*.

Secondly, opposing teams have become a lot better since the old days, when the Big Ten used to dominate the Rose Bowl. The Pac-10 has enormous talent. At this point, I'd say the Big Ten can only win about half the time. Hey, there were times we went out there and were simply outmanned.

Thirdly, in the seventies, the Michigan–Ohio State game was so big that, to be honest, the Rose Bowl semed anticlimactic. We were never able to reach the same peak twice. Sure, I wanted to win those early Rose Bowls, but not as much as I wanted to beat Ohio State and Woody. And I think he felt the same way. Woody's record in the Rose Bowl during the Ten-Year War was 1–4. His overall bowl record during that time was 2–6. So he wasn't faring much better than me.

We peaked for each other. Some years, we were so emotionally wrung out after that game, I'm surprised we had enough energy to board the plane.

And then there were the games themselves. I can't say we've had the best of luck out in sunny Pasadena. In 1970, my first Rose Bowl as head coach of Michigan, I had a heart attack a few hours before kickoff. That didn't help. We lost to USC 10–3, and I didn't find out until the next day.

In 1972 we were a better team than Stanford—in fact, we were undefeated—but we fell for a fake punt and got beat by a last-second field goal, 13–12.

We came back to face USC in 1977 leading the nation in total offense. It was a great, heavy-hitting game, and we were threatening to tie at the end. We reached their seventeen-yard line but ran out of downs. We lost, 14–6.

Same thing next year. We buried ourselves against Washington, crawled back from 17–0 deficit, and had the ball on their eight-yard line in the closing moments, trailing, 27–20. Rick Leach rifled a pass to our fullback, right into his hands, but he missed it and the ball rolled off his shoulders and into the hands of a Washington defender. Interception. That finished us.

And then there was the 1979 game. This one still ticks me off. If only the referees had *eyes*. If only they had seen that Charles White, the great USC tailback, fumbled the ball on the three-yard line while going in for a touchdown, and that Michigan linebacker Jerry Meter recovered at the one. Instead, the line judge ruled that White crossed the plan of the goal line before the fumble. Bull! USC was given the score. We lost, 17–10. An invisible touchdown? Come on!

What else could happen? We finally won a Rose Bowl in 1981, beating Washington, 32–6. Thank goodness. I must have sighed for a half hour. Butch Woolfolk had an unbelievable day, 182 yards, and we rolled.

But two years later we were back to our old problems. Against UCLA we lost our starting quarterback, Steve Smith, when Don Rogers smashed him in the second quarter and separated his shoulder. We had to go with junior Dave Hall, who did an admirable job but wasn't able to overcome those odds. We lost, 24–14.

And in 1987, we couldn't run the ball against Arizona State. I think we had fifty-three yards net rushing, and for a guy who lives by the run, that was death. We lost 22–15.

So that's my Rose Bowl saga. A whopping two wins and seven losses. Sure, it bugs me. But I don't mind the teasing about it. It's been with me my whole career, and I don't think I have enough years left to overcome it. Besides, I'm not sure anybody wants me to anymore.

I think they all kind of like it.

The national championship is a different story. We've never won one of those. We have been ranked number 1, but something always happened before the end of the season. For years I told my team, "We are not concerned with winning a national championship! At Michigan, we aim to win the Big Ten and the Rose Bowl! *Those* are our championships!"

Yet, as I get older, I have to admit, I'd like to win one of those national suckers. Just once. Oh, it wouldn't kill me if we didn't. In fourteen of my twenty years at Michigan we've finished the season ranked in the top ten. That's not too shabby. But before I quit, it would be fun to see what a national championship is like. Especially after seeing our basketball team capture the national crown last spring at the Final Four in Seattle. That was neat.

There are problems, however, with a national championship for Michigan—or any conference school. The big thing is, we can't set our schedule. We are locked into eight conference games and choose three nonconference opponents. If I focused on winning a national championship, I might load up those first three games with pushover teams. I won't do that. I can't.

Can you see me telling my administration: "OK. I've got our schedule all set. We open at home against Bowling Green. Then we travel to Slippery Rock. Then we come back to host Grand Valley State."

"Uh, Bo?" they would say. "Have you lost your mind?"

That's why many of the national champions the last few years have been major independents—like Miami, Notre Dame, and Penn State. A school like Miami can pick and choose its opponents. They'll take one or two tough teams like Notre Dame or USC or Michigan, but they can fill out the rest with nobodies, keep their record pure, and hover near the top of the rankings.

No knock against independents, but let's face it: Big Ten schools can't do that. I'm playing Ohio State and Michigan State every year. I've got Iowa, Illinois, Minnesota, Purdue, Indiana. *Every year.* And of those three nonconference games, two are almost always against big-name teams. In the last few years, they've included Notre Dame, Miami, Florida State, Washington, UCLA.

Fine. That's the way it should be. Big boys should play big boys. But chances are we're going to drop one here or there, and that will probably take us out of the national championship picture. It has in the past. Last season our only two losses were to Notre Dame (the eventual national champion) and Miami (the eventual runner-up), both last-second defeats by a total of *three points*.

Does that mean we're not as good as a team that is undefeated but plays a lightweight schedule? Not necessarily. I still remember when we played Brigham Young in the Holiday Bowl in 1984. We had lost Jim Harbaugh at quarterback. We were 6–5. Folks, we were not good. Yet we almost beat BYU, which, thanks to its undefeated record against mostly weak teams, was ultimately voted national champion.

"They're number one?" I remember asking people after that game.

Now don't misunderstand. I'm not saying most major independents aren't great teams. Miami and Notre Dame are damn tough. And I am in awe of what Joe Paterno has done at Penn State, winning several national championships while running as clean and tough a program as he does.

But in most cases, major independents do have an easier route to the national title than many conference schools, Michigan included. And it wouldn't surprise me if the Wolverines continue to have wonderful, winning teams—and never get there.

Let me tell you something about the Heisman Trophy. Who needs it? A few years ago, in Jim Harbaugh's senior season, there was a lot of talk about his being a front-running candidate. During one of our meetings I walked over to him and put my hand on his shoulder.

"Look at this guy," I said to the rest of the players. "They're talking about him for the Heisman Trophy. The best football player in the country. Yes, sir. It might mean a lot to old Harbaugh here to have that trophy. Right, Jim?"

I didn't give him time to answer.

"Well, I'll tell you something," I said, my voice rising. "Harbaugh isn't interested in any damn Heisman Trophy, because he knows at Michigan, *we do not promote one player over another*. Isn't that right, Jim?"

I didn't give him time to answer.

"We do not promote one player over the other because football is a *team game!* And Harbaugh will not be setting any passing records if the line in front of him doesn't *block like crazy!* And he will not be throwing touchdowns if the receivers *do not run perfect pass routes!* And he will not be scrambling for yardage unless everybody else on the team *knows their assignments on that football field!* Isn't that right, Jim?"

I didn't give him time to answer.

"So you can forget all that Heisman talk, because I can tell you this about old Jim Harbaugh. He is a Michigan man. And he knows what counts at Michigan is the team! *If the team is successful, he is successful!*"

I stared at him. *"ISN'T THAT RIGHT, JIM?"*

"Right!" he finally said.

Good kid.

I have nothing against the original concept of the Heisman Trophy, which was to recognize the most outstanding football player in the country. But today, the award is largely hype. It's based on how well you promote as much as it is on how well you perform. It's such a big media event, that they start the "Heisman Watch" before the first game of the season is played.

I never understood that. They base Heisman hopefuls on what they did the previous year. But isn't it an award for what you do *this* year? You mean to tell me if I have a great season, I can't win it unless I had enough momentum coming in from last year?

Schools send out posters, press kits—even records and buttons—as early as July. I can't see that. It puts tremendous pressure on the kid. I remember when Harlan Huckleby was in his senior year, a local TV broadcaster started a campaign "Huckleby for the Heisman!" Soon everyone around town was saying it. They printed up bumper stickers. "Huckleby for the Heisman!" Harlan didn't have as great a senior season as expected, and I think some of the pressure from that affected him.

The Heisman has been diluted. That doesn't mean deserving players don't win it. I was happy to see Barry Sanders from Oklahoma State get it last year. But even with Sanders, it was a statistical thing. People counted all his yards. How else can you really judge? The award is voted by sportswriters who, if they're lucky, only see a few games per week. They have to rely on "Heisman Watch" like the rest of us. Crazy.

Call me old-fashioned, but I prefer what happened with Mike Hammerstein. Mike was a defensive lineman who played with us from 1981–1985. Coming out of his junior season, he was an unknown. A great player, but he wasn't even voted All–Big Ten.

The following season, our defense played like mad. We led the nation. We shut out three teams and held four others to seven points or less. People began to read about us around the country. They said, "Hey, that defense has got to have some star players, right?" And the next thing you know, Mike was voted consensus All-American. No promotion. No hype. The team put Mike in there, and when he won that honor, the team celebrated. They felt like it was for all of them.

I like that. But to start a Heisman promotion campaign for one player goes against our concept. We've had some players at Michigan that have deserved Heisman consideration, and one, Anthony Carter, who probably deserved to win it. I hope my attitude hasn't hurt them. I think they understand where I'm coming from.

Right, Jim?

Dad, You Never Listen to Me

WHEN Alex Agase quit my staff a few years ago, he said, "Bo, I love spending time around here. But I neglected my kids my whole life. The only way I can make up for it is not to neglect my grandchildren."

I know exactly what he means. I think every football coach does. I haven't exactly been a great father over the years and am probably not a great husband. There are times I wonder how Millie puts up with me. And I'm sure she wonders the same thing.

We met over the phone, in the summer of 1968. Within three months we were married. I don't know if it was the right timing or the right chemistry or maybe just love at first sight. She had been married before, to a sportscaster in St. Louis. I also had been married before, briefly, to a woman who worked as Woody Hayes's secretary. I was young, in my twenties, and really only did it because I thought it was the thing to do. It was probably doomed from the start. My hours and lifestyle did not lend themselves to marriage. She couldn't understand that. We were too young. And it ended.

Few people even know about that marriage. But it kept me cautious about women—or at least about *me* and women—until late in my thirties.

"What did you say your name was?" Millie asked me that first night over the phone.

"Bo Schembechler."

"How do you pronounce it?"

"Schem-bech-ler."

"How do you spell it?"

"S-c-h . . ."

The call had been set up by friends of ours, Merl Pollin (wife of Marv Pollin, my trainer at Ohio) and Cheryl Smith (Larry's wife). It was summertime, and they had bribed me to come by their place one night and take out the garbage in exchange for a beer. Afterward, they showed me pictures of their friend, Millie Cunningham.

"Why don't you call her up?" they said.

"Nah."

"Well, we're gonna call her, and you talk to her."

"OK."

Anyhow, we liked each other enough over the phone to arrange to meet when I came to St. Louis. Millie picked me up at the airport, we went back to her house, and the first thing I knew, I was surrounded by her three kids, Matt, Geoff, and Chip. That was fine by me. I took them out back and played a little football. "OK," I said, directing traffic, "you be the receiver, and you be the defender, and you be . . ."

As it turns out, that was probably the best thing I could have done to win Millie's affection. Raising three kids by herself was not easy, and she certainly wasn't going to get involved with some man who wasn't interested in family. We went out to dinner that night at a floating restaurant on a Mississippi riverboat, and we stayed up until sunrise, talking, laughing, and comparing stories about our first marriages.

The next day, we took the kids to the zoo and the St. Louis Arch. I played cards with them and let them win all the change in my pocket. By the time I left (I was only supposed to stay one day; I stayed three) I felt like I already had a new family.

"I'll call you, OK?" I said to Millie at the airport.

"Good," she said.

We spoke every night. Within two weeks we were talking about getting married. I made up some reason to go to St. Louis again and stayed at the airport hotel. I invited Millie and the kids to come by, because it had a pool. Those kids wouldn't leave us alone.

"Let's lock the door to the room," Millie said, trying to get a few minutes' privacy.

"Good idea," I said.

We weren't in there five minutes when we heard a clicking, and then the door swung open. The kids had picked the lock.

Anyhow, it became pretty apparent this was the right woman for me. She was smart, independent, loved children, and even liked sports. Our jobs were not all that dissimilar. I was a football coach. She was a nurse. I got them banged up. She healed them.

I'd like to tell you a wonderful story about how I asked Millie to marry me. I'd like to, but I can't. The fact is, neither one of us can remember exactly when we decided. I think I said something like, "Aw, hell, let's get married."

Mr. Romance.

Millie always jokes that I courted her according to my schedule for 1968:
1. Finish recruiting
2. Finish spring practice
3. Find wife
4. Get married
5. Return to football

I laugh, but it kind of worked out that way. I met her in June, and we were married in August—a few weeks before we returned to football. We had a terrific wedding. It was in St. Louis, at the Ladue Presbyterian Church. The three boys stood on the altar with us, which was neat. As soon as we exchanged vows, the kids shook my hand and called me "Dad." I was crazy about them, still am, and with Millie on my arm I felt as rich as I could be.

I remember the reception at a nearby hotel. There were a lot of ex-Cardinal baseball players there, because Millie's first husband had broadcast the St. Louis games. Stan Musial, Marty Marion. And then, of course, there was my coaching staff, Smith, Moeller, Hanlon, and the rest. At one point, when things were pretty quiet, my guys went up to the band.

"Hey, don't you know anything fast?"

"Pardon me?"

"Something fast, buddy. Play some rock and roll."

They did, and all of a sudden the dance floor was filled with these football coaches, shaking around with their wives, acting crazy. I don't know what Millie's family thought of it. But I was cracking up.

We went on our honeymoon to San Francisco. Stayed in a tiny room at the St. Francis Hotel. Had a great time. And when the honeymoon was over, for Millie, anyhow, the honeymoon was probably over. I went back to work in football. And although that first season I actually came home for lunch—something which ended when I got to Michigan—I still was gone most of the time. One day I got a call from Millie at the office.

"Bo, it's so hot here. Can't we get an air conditioner in this house?"

"Well, gosh, Mil, it's kind of expensive, you know?" I was only making eighteen thousand dollars at the time. "I'll think about it, OK?"

A few days passed. She asked again. A few more days passed. Then one morning I was sitting in a staff meeting. My secretary came in. Millie was on the phone.

"Yeah, Mil?"

"Now you listen, Bo," she said. There was no mistaking the tone in her voice. "If you don't get an air conditioner in this house, I'm leaving."

"Stay right there," I said. I had two delivered that afternoon.

You have to know when not to mess with Millie.

Still, it was hard for her to get used to my work habits. Or my obsession with football. Remember, we met during the off-season and were married before any serious practicing had begun. After the first game of the 1968 season, which she attended, I came home and could tell she was upset.

"What's the matter?"

"I waved to you today and you didn't wave back."

"When?"

"Just before the game. Didn't you see me?"

"No," I said sheepishly.

"Didn't you hear me?"

"No."

That's the way I get. Totally absorbed. And of course, I was my usual charming self after losses. Back then it was far worse than it is now. I would sulk, I would pout, I couldn't be talked to. When we lost the season finale to Cincinnati, everybody gathered for a good-bye party. I was supposed to meet Millie there. Instead I stayed in my hotel room. She called and called, but I didn't answer the phone. Finally around midnight, I picked it up.

"Bo, where are you?" she said, exasperated.

"Aw, you know . . ."

I was ashamed after losing. It was stupid, but that was my personality. And it was probably not the only hard part of having a football coach as a husband.

*   *   *

I have four great kids, and I have learned something from each one of them. Shemy has probably taught me the most—only because I got to watch him grow up from day one. He was born in September, the second week of the 1969 season at Michigan. We were preparing for Washington. Millie woke me that morning and said, "I think we better go to the hospital." I started running around in my underwear. Hurry up, hurry up. It was like something out of *I Love Lucy*.

Millie was in labor for several hours, and finally, they took the baby by cesarean section. In one of my first visits to see him, the nurses had put him right next to the little baby daughter of Garvie Craw, my fullback. It was kind of strange. I was forty, he was probably twenty-one. Yet we both stood together by the glass, waving.

"Hey, Garvie," I said, "you've got a daughter and I've got a son. Wouldn't that be something if one day . . ."

"Yeah, coach," he said, "that *would* be something."

We named him Glenn Edward Schembechler III, but I was determined that he not be called Bo. Little Bo, or anything like that. Millie suggested we call him Shemy, because that's what my father was called. My mother loved the idea, and that's how he got his name.

Now, I'm wild about having kids around, and had Millie and I met when we were younger, I would have wanted ten. Maybe eleven. A whole offense. It's probably a good thing that didn't happen, because as much as I love them, I don't pay enough attention. I realize that about all my boys. Think about the changes that Geoff, Chip, and Matt had to go through! In less than two years, they moved from St. Louis to Oxford to Ann Arbor, switched schools three times, gained a baby brother, and barely saw their father half the year. And then I had a heart attack!

They probably never understood why I had to be away so much, and I probably never did a good enough job explaining. I wanted to be a good father. I love those kids desperately. But I didn't anticipate my life going so fast in those years. It just happened. I thought about my own father, how I never really got to know him until the last year of his life. We took a fishing trip together in Northern Michigan, went out on the lake every morning and fished, talked, laughed. He smoked his pipe and shared with me things I never knew he had inside him. How wonderful this was, I thought, to suddenly discover my father after all these years. And how sad that it had taken me this long to do so. I vowed to be closer with him from that point on.

But the following year, he died.

Was I doomed to repeat his mistake? Would I miss the best years of my sons' lives, too wrapped up in blocking schemes and defenses?

Once, when Shemy was four years old, we were walking downstairs. I said something to him and he didn't respond.

"Shem, I asked you a question."

Nothing.

"Shem, I'm talking to you."

Nothing.

"Shem, why don't you answer me?"

"Because," he said matter-of-factly, "you don't answer me when I talk to you."

My heart fell to my feet. Had I been that neglectful? Had I been that terrible a father? Had I really shut out my own child because of football? Shemy taught me a hell of a lesson on those steps. And it wasn't the last.

Six or seven years later, we had a road game scheduled against Minnesota. "I'm going to take you on this trip," I told Shemy.

"Great!" he said. We played the game outdoors, in the old Minnesota stadium. Shemy sat on a bench in front of the stands. Eventually, we gained control of the game and we were winning. There were two minutes left to play, and

I looked over, and I saw him slumped over with his head in his chest. He looked so sad.

I called to him. "Hey, Shemy, come here! Come here!"

He walked over, and I saw his eyes were red. "Hey, man," I said, "be happy. We're going to win this game. We're going to win!"

And he started crying, just sobbing.

"What's the matter, son?" I said. "What's the matter?"

"Those names they called you—those names they yell at you!"

"What names?"

"Those people in the stands."

My god. I hadn't even thought about that. All those Minnesota fans were right behind him, screaming at me—like most opposing fans do—calling me a son of a bitch and a bastard and worse. To be honest, I don't even hear that stuff. But Shemy couldn't take it. This was his father they were insulting!

On the bus ride home, I put my arm around him. "Now, son, you've got to understand that those people don't really mean that I'm that kind of a guy. That's just the way sports is. When people get involved they yell at the other coach like people yell at the umpire. They were probably drunk and just yelling those things."

I looked at him, so young, so trusting. "Do you understand that?"

"Yeah, I understand."

When I came home, I told Millie what had happened. "I wonder what he gets in school," I said. "I mean, every day around here, he could probably hear something."

Once again, I had been oblivious to it all. My other sons endured the same thing, maybe worse, because they changed their names from Cunningham to Schembechler. If I were smarter, when we got to Ann Arbor, maybe I would have suggested they keep their old names. It might have made life easier for them.

*   *   *

About the only typical mistake I didn't make with my sons was pushing them into sports. I can honestly say I never wanted them to follow in my footsteps or to be the best players on their teams or anything like that. Sometimes, I was of no use at all. We went to watch Matt pitch a little league game once, and we were sitting on blankets along the first-base side. He walked the first batter, the second batter, the third batter, and the fourth. All of a sudden, in the middle of the inning, he ran off the mound to where we were sitting. He was almost in tears.

"Dad! Dad! What am I doing *wrong*?"

"Um, I don't think you're getting it over the plate, Matt."

"*Daaad!*"

All my kids wound up playing a little football, nothing special, nothing spectacular. Matt was probably the best. He played defensive back and was a walk-on at Western Michigan. What happened to him there taught me a lesson as well.

The trainers had him doing weight-lifting, heavy squats. And apparently they didn't have the proper belts, or the belts weren't tight enough. Matt suffered an injury.

"The pain's down the side of my leg," he told the people there.

"It's a hamstring," they told him.

He waited a few days. It didn't go away. He told them again, and again they said it was a hamstring. He couldn't play. The pain was too great. They started teasing him, calling him a goldbricker. How can a little hamstring keep you out?

Finally, Matt went to see an orthopedic specialist. He took X rays and tested him, and he sat him down. "Matt," he said, "we can do it here if you want, but I suppose your dad will want someone back in Ann Arbor. You'd better get home right now. You've got a crushed vertebrae."

By the time Matt got back to Ann Arbor, we had to put him in an ambulance. He could not even get out of bed. Dr. Farhaupt operated on him for a bad back. He was through in football.

And those people at Western didn't even know.

My kids are grown now. Shemy is in college at Miami. I've made more than my share of mistakes with them, mostly mistakes of neglect, and I'm a lucky man to have a wife and family that manages to see past what I do and tries hard to see what I am.

A few years ago, we had the annual football bust. In a break with tradition, they asked Millie if she would be the master of ceremonies. She was a little nervous about addressing a crowd, but when the night came, she was in rare form.

"Bo and I lead a normal life," she told them. "When he comes home at night, I kneel down and kiss his Big Ten championship ring."

The audience broke into laughter.

"And before dinner, we sit under Woody Hayes's picture."

More laughter.

"And after dinner, if we get a few private moments, we go downstairs and look at film."

The room cracked up. And so did I. She was wonderful, she always has been, and believe me, you need someone like that to have a successful marriage as a football coach.

That, and an air conditioner.

☆　☆　☆

AND NOW, FOR OUR NEXT CONTROVERSY...

☆　☆　☆

Texas A & M, Canham,
and a Courtroom

THERE comes a time in every coach's career when he wonders if he's done all he can do, if maybe it's time to move. I was feeling that way in 1981. We'd had a team that was ranked number one going into the season and we blew our opening game against Wisconsin. We lost again to Iowa and lost again to Ohio State. It was the worst job of coaching I've done since coming to Michigan. I didn't get the kids motivated the way I should have. I had coached over a decade's worth of Wolverines and I was in my early fifties.

"Hell," I said to myself, "maybe I'm slipping."

And then the phone rang.

It was Gil Brandt, the player personnel director of the Dallas Cowboys. "Bo," he said, "there's a job open down here at Texas A & M and I think you ought to consider it."

Thus began one of the more controversial episodes of my career. You stick around long enough, you'll have plenty of those, and I'll tell you about a few in this chapter. First let me explain what really happened down in the Lone Star state, because, for all the accounts, I don't think the whole story has ever really been told.

At that time, if you remember, the Midwest was kind of depressed, the economy was bad, and everyone seemed to be moving to the Sun Belt. Oil was big. And the money was flowing in Texas.

"What's the deal, Gil?" I asked.

"Well, the man you want to talk to is named Bum Bright. He's chairman of the Board of Regents at Texas A & M. I'll tell him to give you a call, OK?"

"Well, all right. We're just talking, though."

"Yes, of course."

I was in Chicago for a meeting when I got the call from Bright. He was an Aggie, all right. Texas through and through. Tremendously wealthy—and very interested, it seemed, in having me work for his school.

"Bo," he said, "I sure could see you in this position. We're talking about football coach *and* athletic director. We're talking some serious money."

That was intriguing, I admit. But I still wasn't sold on the idea. "Listen, Bum," I said, "I'm not really looking for a job or anything like that. Thanks for your interest, but it's probably not the right time."

We left it at that. Our team went down to Houston to play in the BlueBonnet Bowl. While I was there I got another call from Brandt.

"Hey, Bo. The Cowboys have a play-off game the day after your bowl. Why don't you fly up to Dallas and come see the game as our guests?"

I said sure. We played the BlueBonnet Bowl, beat UCLA 33–14, and the next morning there was a tremendous fog in Houston. All the flights were delayed. Millie was with me— we were headed to San Francisco the following day for the East-West Shrine game—so I called Gil and said, "Hey, I don't know if I can get out of here."

He said, "Keep trying. No matter what happens, no matter how late, I'll have somebody there to pick you up."

"You sure?"

"No problem."

Eventually the fog lifted and we flew to Dallas. When we landed, a short, stocky guy with a crew cut came up and introduced himself.

"Bo," he said, "I'm Bum Bright."

To say I was surprised would be an understatement. I looked at Millie. What could we do? He took us straight to a hotel, because the Cowboys game was already half over.

"Bo, why don't you and me ride out to the house before dinner and talk a little?" he said.

In the car, I laid my cards on the table. "Look, Bum, I'm a little concerned here. You pick me up at the airport. We're going out to your house. I don't want people to know I'm talking to you about a job. I don't want my name in the papers."

"Hey," he said, "don't worry about that. This is strictly you and me."

We drove to his house and, my God, this was some house. His next-door neighbor was Bunker Hunt, the billionaire. I noticed *six* cars in Bright's driveway.

"I thought you said there wasn't anyone else," I said.

"Those are all *my* cars, Bo."

Oh.

We went into his library, and he began to talk about Texas A & M. He had a small statue of himself dressed as an A & M soldier on the mantel.

"Bo," he said, "before you leave here tonight, we're gonna have ourselves a deal."

"No, we're not," I said, politely but firmly. "I don't work like that, Bum."

Later that night we went to dinner at his country club, then returned to the house.

He began laying it on thick. "This is a fine opportunity, Bo. You could really do things here. You be football coach and athletic director and after two or three years, if you want out of coaching, you just slip into the AD job full-time, same money, same everything."

He began talking dollars. A ten-year deal worth somewhere around $2.25 million. Now if that doesn't make your eyes spring out of your head, you must be dead. I was making $60,000 a year at Michigan with no contract.

"Where will all that money come from?" I asked. I knew the university didn't have that kind of funding.

"Don't you worry about that," Bright said—which immediately made me worry. I knew where it would come from: alumni. People like Bright. People who felt they could buy anything. You have those kind of people paying your salary and you are indebted to them every minute you're on the job.

We talked past midnight. Finally I said, "Let me ask you a question: what does your president think of all this?"

"The president knows what's going on."

"Don't you think I should talk to him?"

"Wait a minute."

He grabbed the phone and dialed the president, Frank Vandiver. "President Vandiver? Bum Bright here. I told you I'd call you anytime night or day when I had Coach Schembechler available. He is here at my home now. I would like to have you here at 9:00 tomorrow morning. Okay, sir. I'll see you at 9 A.M."

I went back to the hotel.

"Millie," I said, sitting on the bed, "this is a weird deal."

"It's so much money," she said.

"I know. But there's something fishy here."

At 9 A.M. the next morning, I was back at the house. The president was there. I asked to speak to him alone.

"Mr. President," I said, "do you know what's going on here?"

"Well, vaguely," he said. "I know they're making a strong pitch for you. Actually, I should thank you."

"Thank me? For what?"

"For getting me a raise. Because of the money they're going to offer you, they had to raise my salary as well."

Great, I figured. Now I'm really starting to wonder. "Listen, Mr. President, I want you to understand what kind of guy I am. I'm a straight-arrow. I just follow the rules and do the best I can. I won't tolerate any cheating or violations."

"Good. That's exactly what we want."

"I hear all these rumors about the Southwest Conference. I'd be a thorn in their side because I won't operate that way."

"That's fine."

"And if I'm your athletic director, I'll fire anyone in your department who violates the rules."

"Fine."

I said I'd get back to them, Millie and I went to San Francisco, and on our way home, we flew to Houston without telling anyone, rented a car, and drove down to Texas A & M. We just wanted to take a quick look around. College Station was not exactly Ann Arbor. I mean, it was a nice campus, but it was really in the middle of nowhere.

"Can you image recruiting down here?" I said, sighing. "You'd be doing a lot of driving."

"How about the school system?" Millie wondered.

We never got out of the car for fear of somebody recognizing us. We ate in a McDonald's along the way. It got dark before we could see everything, so we drove back to Houston and flew home.

When I returned to Michigan, I laid everything out to Don Canham, my AD. It was a lot of money, that was for sure. And I began to wonder whether I should take it. My family would be set for life. We would never have to worry —no matter what happened to me or my heart. At the beginning, Canham and Michigan didn't seem too concerned. They didn't jump to raise my salary or anything like that. That bothered me.

"I don't know, Mil," I said to my wife one night, "maybe I'm more appreciated elsewhere than I am here."

I wavered back and forth. I still hated the idea of leaving Ann Arbor, and I detested the idea of my paycheck coming from alumni. That meant any time there's some stupid dinner at the country club, they could call you at home and expect you to attend. You'd be a puppet on their very expensive strings. Did I need that? Was it worth it?

And then the story leaked to the press.

What a nightmare. I couldn't go anywhere without people asking me what was going on. The mail started to pour in. *"Don't leave us, Bo." "Don't let that Texas money turn your head."* One letter even arrived simply addressed: "Bo, Ann Arbor, Michigan." I guess the post office got pretty used to our delivery.

I talked with my staff. Under the deal, I could have taken all of them. Hell, I could have taken a circus if I wanted! Canham finally came to the house, and after some heated discussion, made me an offer of a twenty-five thousand dollars a year increase, which would bring my salary to eighty-five thousand dollars a year—versus the two hundred twenty-five thousand dollars annually that the A & M worked out to. And all this time, Bright kept calling me at home. "The airplane's on the runway, Bo. It's just waiting for you. We'll come pick you up and fly you down on a minute's notice. Remember, we're talking money, two cars, membership at the country club, an expense account for entertaining . . ."

After a while, it got ridiculous. Reporters were camping outside our house. The phone wouldn't stop ringing. On the day I promised to make a decision, Joe Falls from the *Detroit News* kept knocking on the door, demanding to be let in, demanding to know something. I was down in the basement, trying to make this decision, talking on the phone to a lot of people. My son Matt answered the door a few times and had to say "Sorry, Dad's not ready to talk now."

"Millie," I said, downstairs, "what do you think?"

"What's in your heart, Bo?" she said.

"God, Mil, that's a lot of money. We'd be set for life."

She was crying. I started crying. I thought about the kids I had just recruited, how I promised them if they worked hard, by senior year, they could be starters. I looked around my basement, at the projectors and the clipboards and the football memorabilia.

"Millie," I said, shaking my head, "I just can't leave Michigan."

"Then don't. We can get by on any amount of money."

She was right. The whole attraction was money, and that's no reason to take a job. I called the Texas A & M people and told them thanks but no thanks. That would be the last time I would seriously consider leaving the Wolverines.

I came upstairs, and the first person I saw was Tom Monaghan, owner of Domino's Pizza and a huge UM supporter. I don't know how long he had been there.

"Bo," he said, before I even had time to speak, "I've got to talk to you. I've been thinking there's no way we can lose you to Texas. You can't go. I want to make it right for you here. I want to give you a pizza franchise."

I laughed. "Tom," I said, "forget it. I made my decision. I just told them no. I'm on my way right now to a press conference on campus. I'm late."

"Bo, I'm giving you this pizza franchise."

"Tom, I just told you it's not necessary. It's over. I turned them down." I looked out the window. It was snowing like mad. "Hey, I've got to go to this press conference. Come on. You want to ride along?"

"OK."

We got in the car and I drove down to the press conference, and as we got out of the car, Tom grabbed me and said, "Bo, I want you to take the franchise anyhow. I know you're staying. But I just want you to have it. Please."

I looked at him and shrugged. "OK, Tom," I said. "Thank you."

We walked up the steps. He opened the door.

"Oh, there's one thing I forgot to tell you," he said.

"What's that?"

"This franchise?"

"Yeah?"

"It's in Columbus, Ohio. On the Ohio State campus."

I cracked up, and went in to face the media. In one night I'd turned down millions in Texas and gained a pizza store in Woody Hayes's backyard.

I might as well deal here with my relationship with Don Canham, my former boss and athletic director. I don't know how controversial it is, but there has been some speculation and some rumors and, as usual, most of them are wrong.

First of all, Canham and I were two different people. He was more reserved than me, but there was no doubt he was in charge while he was at Michigan. It was a one-man operation. I admired the fact that when he hired me, I did not have to go through a committee of seventy-two people. I interviewed with him and the faculty rep and that was it. I got the job.

And for the first twelve years I was here, Don and I got along fine. We might have disagreed over some minor things, but fundamentally, we felt about the same on scheduling, TV, recruiting, and things like that.

Our relationship changed after the Texas A & M incident, and I guess I can understand that. The things offered me to stay at Michigan were largely offered by the president, and maybe Don felt a little ramrodded on the whole deal.

Whatever the reason, we drifted further apart after that.

I went my way, he went his. We didn't fight, but we didn't spend much time together either. We never socialized.

I don't feel Don ever cheated football, but there were times he dragged his feet. Toward the end of his term, I felt we should have reacted a little quicker to the aging football facilities—especially when we were building a multimillion-dollar swimming pool. But maybe every coach feels that way about his own sport.

Anyhow, he's retired now, and there's no point in re-hashing our differences. Don did a lot for Michigan while he was AD. Let's leave it at that.

Of course, I can't have any disagreements with our current athletic director. That's because I *am* our current athletic director—along with Jack Weidenbach, who handles most of the day-to-day responsibilities. Taking on that additional position created a lot of questions. After all, I was just coming back from my second open-heart surgery.

Why did I do it? I don't know. Half the time I still think I'm crazy. But back then—April 1988—I felt it was the right move for several reasons, all of which could be summed up in one sentence: it beat the alternative.

"Bo," they had said to me several months earlier, "we'd like you to be the athletic director, but it would mean giving up football after the 1988 season. You couldn't do both jobs."

"No thank you," I said. "I'll stick to what I'm doing."

They then began to consider outside possibilities. I wasn't crazy about any of their candidates. I suggested several people who were interviewed but never considered. I don't know why. For some foolish reason, there was nobody from the athletic department on the selection committee. Doesn't that seem a little strange? At least have Canham, or myself, or somebody.

After a while, I heard from Robben Fleming, the interim president, and Jim Duderstadt, who was the provost.

"Bo," they both said, "we'd like you to reconsider the job."

"Aw, we've been through this before," I said. "I already turned it down. I don't want somebody else telling me when I have to give up coaching football."

"Well, what if you didn't have to give up coaching football? . . ."

The rest, you know. I took the position, and on the days when it really gets to be too much, I console myself by remembering that I probably won't be fired, since I'm the guy who would have to do it.

The Kenney Gear incident is a little more serious. It brings up the whole issue of danger in football, who is responsible for injuries, and just how violent what we're doing out there is.

Kenney Gear was a wide receiver for us in the early eighties, a wonderful kid, a good player, a real hard worker who backed up Anthony Carter. One day, during practice, we were on the twenty-yard line and we called a pass. The quarterback was under duress, so he rolled out to the right. In a play like that, he is instructed to throw the ball away if no one is open and that's what he did.

Kenney Gear followed that ball, which was thrown very high and headed for the seats, and instead of letting it go, he ran through the end zone, lifted off past the end line, leaped through the air and smacked into the wall that surrounds the field. Hit it right in the midsection. It was awful when you saw it, and you knew he was hurt.

I had two team physicians out there and they rushed to his aid. We carried him out and took him to the hospital.

He had lacerated his liver, a terribly serious injury, the kind you suffer sometimes in automobile accidents, and he was fortunate that perhaps the greatest liver-trauma surgeon in the world was there at the hospital, and they got him in and saved his life.

We visited Kenney in the hospital and he was in good spirits. I told him the doctors said he would be all right, not to worry about anything. We would take care of him. But after he was released, he stopped coming around. I kept calling.

"Hey, Kenney, I want to see you. I want you here with this program."

"Yeah, OK, coach."

When he still didn't come around, I knew something was up. And sure enough, not long after, I got a letter saying Kenney Gear was suing the university. The lawyers had hopped on him real quick.

The case was in litigation for years, and in March of 1988, I went to testify in the Lansing court. Kenney and his lawyers were seeking $1,025,000 in damages from the university, claiming the wall was too close to the playing field. They claimed Gear had been deprived of future earnings as a professional football player, and deserved reimbursement for trauma already suffered as well as for future pain.

It was a very difficult thing for me to do—testify against someone I coached—and to top it off, I had never testified in a courtroom before. I felt sure our team and the school were in the right. The wall was not too close. Kenney just went beyond what he should have done. That ball was headed for the seats.

As for his deprived career in professional football, I had to be realistic. I don't know if he would have had such a career. But he was a good kid, and I always liked him, and testifying there made me very uncomfortable, even though I wasn't the one named in the suit.

The case was eventually thrown out of court, after the judge declared that Kenney "had clearly tried to do something . . . that it was not intended for him to do." He pointed out that a football stadium is not a public playground, and people who play the sport know there are risks involved.

Kenney Gear is perfectly healthy today, he has a degree

from Michigan and a masters from a school in New York, but his whole case made me think about our sport and its inherent dangers.

When Kenney hit that wall, my stomach turned to knots. I could not sleep until I found out the extent of his injuries. You've got to understand, I've seen guys get hit that I felt were going to get killed. And they get up and walk away. But this was different. He was in surgery, and of course, I wasn't allowed in the operating area, so I went back to my house and sat in my basement, nervous as hell, until they called and said he was out of danger.

That's the most frightened I've been over a player that I've coached. I went out to that stadium a week later, and as crazy as it was, I called over the construction guys and said, "I want padding put around the entire wall."

"For real?"

"Yeah. Do it."

It probably wasn't necessary. No one else had ever injured themselves like that. And it's not like the wall was in the field of play. But I had the whole damn thing padded and it cost a hundred thousand dollars. It was worth it for the peace of mind.

You see, a football coach is always frightened about how much time he should spend scrimmaging. You can't prepare a team unless you simulate what's going to happen on Saturday, but if you hit too much, anything can happen. Every time you hit, every time you scrimmage, there is that fear that somebody is going to get seriously hurt, and you must weigh that against getting them ready to play on Saturday.

I've seen some terrible injuries in football. Knees twisted and gnarled. Broken bones. Limbs hanging loosely. Shoulders that pop out of their sockets. Sometimes it's just the timing. Kirk Lewis was our team captain in 1975, and in the final scrimmage before the first game, he broke his arm and was out for the season. You torture yourself when that happens. "Why didn't we hold him out of that scrimmage? Why couldn't he have just skipped it? Why did we have to tackle him so hard?"

I know injury from personal experience. I was always a pretty good baseball player. But one day in football, during a game, I got my arm caught in a pass protection and hyperextended my elbow. I could never pitch after that.

There are no easy answers. Football is a violent game, and people who watch it and play it are aware of that. In many ways, football is our nation's substitute for war, combat without weapons. But there are casualties, there are injuries, and as a coach, you never really get over them. The bigger and faster they get, the tougher their collisions, and it seems the smack of bodies today is louder than it ever was.

I may love the hard hitting and the great tackles, but as a coach who thinks about his kids, I am never completely at ease until I get my injury report and it says "nothing serious."

Adventures in
Basketball Land

W*HAT AM I DOING HERE?*
That's what I was thinking as I ducked away from reporters at the Seattle Kingdome Monday night, April 3, 1989. The bands were blaring. The teams were taking lay-ups. Basketball? What was I doing on a basketball court—not just any court, but the NCAA championship game between Michigan and Seton Hall?

I tried to make my way to my seat.

"Bo! Bo!"

I looked up. It was Brent Musberger from CBS.

"How you doing, Brent?"

"Bo, I'm glad I found you." He pulled out some sort of ticket. "Here. Take this floor pass. After the game, if Michigan wins, how about coming up while we're interviewing Steve Fisher, maybe put your arm around him, and announce to the world that you've hired him as head coach?"

I stared at him. "Are you serious?"

"You're the athletic director, right?"

"Yes."

"You make the decision, right?"

"Yes."

"Well, this will be a great way to make the announcement, don't you think?"

"Brent, you little rat," I said. "I have to live with this guy for the next five or ten years, I'm not gonna make a decision just so you can get good ratings on television!"

I looked around at the wildly cheering crowd. So this is what it meant to be athletic director: I had an interim coach that had won five tournament games; I had an ex–head coach who was somewhere out in Arizona; I had TV people wanting me to make a major decision on camera. And I had a basketball team that was playing out of its mind.

What am I doing here?

It all began, for me, with a late night phone call nearly four weeks earlier. A local sportswriter rang me at home.

"Did you hear about Frieder?" he said.

"What about him?"

"I think he's taken a job at Arizona State. Our sources tell us he's on a plane out there right now."

"Come on. I haven't heard anything like that."

"Bo, I think it's true. Do you have a comment?"

"No. I don't have any damn comment. That's just rumors, and I don't comment on rumors."

An hour later, he called again.

"Bo," he said, "it's for sure. He's on that plane, and someone in the Arizona State office has confirmed that he's taken the job. Can you make a comment now?"

I said something very noncommittal and hung up. I know this writer. He's pretty reputable, and if he bothered to call twice, the story was probably true. I called Jack Wiedenbach, my co–athletic director. "Jack," I said, "I think we've got a problem . . ."

Bill Frieder, who had coached our basketball team for nine years, had indeed accepted a job with Arizona State the day before the Wolverines were to leave for the first round of the NCAA tournament. He never bothered to inform me until *after* he'd been hired.

"I didn't have Bo's home phone number," he told reporters. But that's a bunch of garbage. You mean to tell me reporters can get me at home and he can't? Frieder told Steve Fisher, his assistant, that he'd accepted the job hours before he left Ann Arbor Tuesday afternoon. I was in my office. He could have called me then!

Instead, he called my secretary, Lynn Koch, at her home at 3:30 A.M. the following morning. He told her he had taken the job and again said he didn't have my phone number. At 7 A.M. he reached Jack Wiedenbach and told him.

And around 11 A.M. Wednesday morning—after the whole world knew about his departure—he finally called my office.

"Bo," Lynn said, "Bill's on the phone."

I picked up the receiver, never even bothering to close the door.

"Yeah, Bill?"

"Bo, I tried to get hold of you. I didn't make my mind up until three in the morning so, you know—"

"You should have called before you went out there, Bill."

"Well, look, don't worry about a thing. They've provided me with a jet so I can fly directly to Atlanta, and I'll coach the team in the tournament."

"No, you won't," I said. "Your coaching is through here at Michigan. I've put Fisher in charge of things."

Now, folks, that decision took less than thirty seconds to make. No way would I let someone who had made a parallel move to another school coach one of our teams. Hey. No coach takes off to even *look* at a job—let alone to accept one—without first consulting the athletic director. I mean, that's just common courtesy. Had Frieder come to me after the last game of the regular season and said, "Look, I'm interested in this Arizona State job," here is what I would have said:

"Bill, if those people want you, they'll wait until after the NCAA tournament. This is not a proper time for you to be looking at jobs. Finish your season here and then, of course, you have my permission to look at any opportunities you want."

He didn't do that. He didn't come close. Even if he were moving, let's say, into professional basketball or the corporate world, it might have been different. But to simply go to another school, and they couldn't wait three weeks until the tournament was over? I say forget them. And if you don't want to, we'll finish the season with the assistant coach.

And that's what we did.

And we won the national championship.

Why didn't Frieder call me earlier? I don't know. Was he afraid of me? No. Was he intimidated by me? Maybe. I have read a lot of stories about how "poorly" we got along, but the truth of the matter is, I had no major problems with the guy. He is different from me, and he just does things differently.

Remember, I did not hire Frieder, I inherited him when I took over as athletic director. Five years ago, I talked to him about gambling and playing cards at the Washtenaw Country Club, which he had done now and then. I didn't think it was a good thing.

Outside of that, we had very few direct confrontations. But as soon as I became athletic director, Frieder apparently told people, "Bo's out to get me."

That is not true. Yes, there were rumors about his recruiting methods, but they were only rumors. Part of the problem was the way Bill looked—always frazzled, always on the go, talking fast. People don't trust that. And he brought in a lot of big-name recruits, which made people suspicious.

It is also true that two years ago, someone at the *Michigan Daily* prompted a university investigation of recruiting in Frieder's program. The university lawyers checked it out and found sloppiness, but not proof of wrongdoing.

Not long before Frieder left, there were questions about the recruiting of Michael Talley, a star player from Detroit. Jud Heathcote of Michigan State had complained that Frieder had called Talley during the season, in violation of an agreement they all had with the high school coach. But again, nothing was proven.

Now, as athletic director, it is my job to make sure all our programs—baseball, swimming, tennis, and the rest—are run cleanly and correctly. And there were things in the basketball program I was going to change. We were going to get some quality competition in the first half of the season, for one thing. There were too many games against the likes of Tampa University and South Dakota State.

Also, I wanted our players to project a better image when they traveled; they had been wearing whatever they wanted—jeans, sweatshirts. I thought it would better represent Michigan if they wore Michigan sweaters. Shoot me. I'm old-fashioned.

I would not call that being "out to get" Bill Frieder.

Would you?

Just the same, he began to act extra careful with me. He would leave me notes about all sorts of things. *"Bo—the car that such and such is driving is completely legit and paid for by his family."* Or *"Bo—this kid missed several classes and I kept him out of practice and now he is back to good habits. Just wanted you to know."*

And finally, he left—badly, if you ask me—and I know he is not making as much money in Arizona as he was at Michigan. Why did he go? I really can't tell you. There wasn't much to discuss on that telephone once I said Fisher was coaching the team.

"Well, Bo, I respect your opinion," he said.

"OK, then, we understand each other?"

"Yeah."

"OK."

"See ya."

"Bye."

That was it. A few hours later, I was standing before the basketball team, explaining to them why I had done what I had done.

"Look, men," I said, "I think you have an excellent chance of winning the national championship if you put your minds to it, and I think with Steve Fisher as your coach you'll be able to do that."

I looked at their faces—Glen Rice, Rumeal Robinson, Terry Mills, Sean Higgins. They did not ask a single question. They did not raise any objections. I felt bad for them. No athletes deserve that sort of treatment from a coach they trusted.

"Hey, you've had an unlucky blow here," I said. "But I think you can rise above it and play like Michigan. You can be champions. See you in Atlanta."

The team went to Atlanta, beat Xavier and South Alabama, although they did not play particularly well, and came home to await the next round. I had flown down for the games and come back in between for football practice. I was living on that airplane. But it was important to be there. I went into the locker room after each win but didn't say much, just "Good job, way to go, men."

Along the way, I was getting to know Steve Fisher a little better. You have to understand, we did not know each other before that shake-up. It is not uncommon for a head football coach and an assistant basketball coach to be little more than "Hi, how are you?" acquaintances. And I had only been athletic director for a year.

Just before they left for Lexington and the second round, Steve asked me to talk to the team again. I was surprised. I really didn't want to get in his way.

"They like when you talk to them," he said. "It gets them pumped up."

"You sure?" I asked.

"Oh yeah," he said.

"Well," I said, leaning forward, "if I talk to them, I'm going to speak my mind. And if I do that, you may have one less player when we're finished."

"That's OK," said Fisher, smiling, "I think it will be good for him."

He knew who I was talking about: Sean Higgins, a six-foot-nine sophomore guard with so much talent it could make you cry, but whose head was not in the game. He was sauntering up and down the court, making mistakes, losing balls and not diving after them. He was also quoted in the newspaper that week saying he was thinking about transferring—or going pro!—now that Frieder was gone.

When I got to the practice, the kids were all sitting on the edge of the court. Steve introduced me, and I began by addressing each player, same way I do sometimes in football.

"Every one of you guys is important to win this damn thing," I said. "I keep hearing about this North Carolina team, how they've beaten us the last two tournaments. Let me ask you something: If Glen Rice goes down there and scores 30, *do you think they're going to beat us?*"

I whirled toward Terry Mills. "If Mills over there plays like he's capable of playing, he gets down in there and throws those elbows around, do you think they're going to beat us, J. R. Reid or no J. R. Reid?"

I spun and pointed to Rumeal Robinson. "We've got the best guard here in the United States of America—I mean, this kid's the best in the business—if he plays ball, we'll *win.*"

One by one I went through that team. Mark Hughes. Loy Vaught. Demetrius Calip. Finally I came to Higgins. And I lowered the boom. "Now, Higgins, I'm going to tell you something. There isn't a soul here that gives a *damn* what you do three weeks from now, a month from now, a year from now *or five years from now!* As a matter of fact, we don't give a damn whether you get on the bus to go to Lexington! I'm gonna tell you something: if you want it, your damn release is *on my desk right now!* It's written up! We can go get the son of a bleep and you can pack your bags . . ."

I paused. "Or you can go down to Lexington and *dive* for loose balls! And when you're taken out for a substitute, you *run* back to your coach, not walk! And you keep your head in the game, like your *teammates!* You bust your ass and see if you can be a basketball player. Otherwise, STAY HOME!"

His eyes bugged out of his head. I don't think anyone had ever talked to that kid like that before. I don't know what effect—if any—it had. I do know Higgins was diving for balls the next game. I do know he played well the rest of the way. He shot out the lights against Virginia. And he made the winning basket against Illinois to send us to the finals.

"Tell Higgins I said he played a helluva game," I whispered to Fisher after the North Carolina game.

And after the Virginia game, Higgins found me in the locker room and gave me a hug. Put the clampers on me, as we say in football. I was a little embarrassed, but I was happy, too.

OK. All the time this was going on, the mail was pouring into my office. "When are you going to hire Fisher as permanent coach?" "What are you waiting for with Steve Fisher?" "How come you won't give Steve Fisher a vote of confidence?" It was amazing. With each win, the response grew. We were getting fifty letters a day, easy.

I was also hearing from other coaches interested in the job. In most cases, however, those who expressed interest were not coaches we would hire. Did I ever interview anyone for the job? No. Did I consider other people for the job? Yes, of course. As soon as Frieder left, I made some calls to people I knew, asking who might be a good candidate.

One of those calls was to Bobby Knight. A Detroit sportswriter wrote that I was considering Knight as new coach, but that was crap. I only wanted Bobby's opinion.

"You know I put Fisher in charge of the program," I said.

"Hey, Bo. I would have done the same thing," Knight said. "Under those circumstances, you have no choice."

"So, do you have anybody in mind?"

"Yeah, I got a few names."

I checked them out. I also got some recommendations from Digger Phelps of Notre Dame and, without any prompting, from Dick Vitale. He called me up.

"Bo, I got some guys. They'd be great."

"Yeah. Who?"

"Rollie Massimino, from Villanova?"

"Um-hmm."

"Great guy. Perfect choice. Here. Lemme give you a few others . . ."

You know Vitale. You'll get them whether you want them or not.

The point is, I wasn't violating any trust by considering other coaches. Steve Fisher was originally an interim selection, and he knew that. My thought when Frieder left was that I would like to see an entirely new program. I wanted to hire the people, to be sure they had a lot of character, to be sure they knew discipline, and to be sure things were done, always, in the best interest of the players.

Frieder's program was run too loosely for my liking. There were too many hangers-on, for one thing, and that always worries me. Basketball junkies. Booster types. Sometimes they rode the bus or sat near the bench. No good.

So before I made any hirings, I checked out everything I could about Frieder's operation. As a football coach, that might be called "none of your business." As an athletic director, it's called "your job." I asked a lot of questions of a lot of people.

Meanwhile, I began to hear good things about Fisher. Knight had told me his assistant coaches "think real highly of the guy." And I was already observing a change in the team. They had more cohesiveness. They had more self-control. I watched him in the locker room and I was impressed with his preparation. The players rallied around him. So did the fans. I mean, few people have captured the imagination of the sports world the way he did.

And then, that championship game! Wow. Michigan came from behind, forced it into overtime, and won by a point, 80–79, on two Rumeal Robinson free throws. It was a great performance, and it required some great coaching. I was sitting just a few rows in front of Rumeal's mom and dad, and when he hit those free throws, we all went crazy.

I headed down towards the locker room, trying to escape unnoticed. The CBS people found me and shoved a microphone in my face.

"Well," the reporter asked, "does Steve Fisher have the job now?"

"I, uh, think he'll be the first person we interview," I said.

What the hell? I wasn't going to give them an announcement just because they wanted one. Hey. My job is athletic director, not public relations director. I was thrilled with what Steve did, absolutely *thrilled*—and anyone who thinks that I am somehow jealous of the basketball team for winning a national championship has obviously never sat next to me at a basketball game. I am into Michigan, I don't care what sport. I want us to win *everything!* You don't get jealous of your own school, for Pete's sake.

"You did a hell of a job," I said, hugging Fisher in the locker room. "I don't know how you pulled it off, but you did!"

* * *

And, of course, a week later, I gave Steve the job for real—after we had spoken at length about the program. We really didn't have a chance to do that during the tournament, which is why I waited. Steve answered every tough question, smartly and candidly.

"Fisher, you got the job," I told him that Monday morning. "I'm happy for you."

"Hey, Bo. I'm gonna run the kind of program we both want."

"Great."

That was that. Could I have hired someone else—even after Fisher led us to the title? Absolutely. National championship or not, hiring a man who has won six games is not the same as hiring Dean Smith or Bobby Knight. There is still a gamble. Fisher did not recruit those kids. He was in an ideal situation—no one expected him to win. Had I taken someone else, it would have had to be a top echelon guy. And I would have been buried in hate mail, but so what?

The point is, by the end, Steve had convinced me he would do a great job. He certainly earned the chance. He is our coach now, I am proud of him, I support him, and I hope he goes all the way with the basketball team again this year.

And Higgins? I'm watching you.

This Old Heart
of Mine

WILL die one day from a bad heart. I've pretty much accepted that. Already I have suffered two heart attacks, two open-heart surgeries, and I'll probably go through another episode before I'm finished here on earth.

In some ways, that's a terrible thing to live under. On the other hand, each time I come through one of those scares, it makes me appreciate the life I have that much more. When that doctor told me a few years ago, as I lay on that hospital bed with tubes coming out of my body, that, yes, I could coach again, I swear it was one of the happiest moments of my life.

Of course, by that point, I was a veteran of heart surgery. That wasn't the case in 1969. I still remember the moment that first heart attack struck. I was walking up a hill the night before the Rose Bowl, all alone, in total darkness, and suddenly I felt like someone had stabbed me between the shoulder blades. I grabbed onto a tree, and tried to hold myself up. What the hell was going on? I was forty years old and I could barely stand!

It was one of the weirdest incidents of my career. Who would have thought I would miss my first Rose Bowl because of a heart attack suffered hours before kickoff? That whole week, I had been having problems getting up for the game, and you know that's not like me—especially in 1969. We were coming off a miracle season, my first at Michigan, the big win over Ohio State, and here we were in Southern California, preparing for the granddaddy of them all. Yet every day I felt more and more queasy. I had stomach pains, odd little aches, and I just couldn't shake this feeling of blah.

Three days before the game, we had sneaked down to a small clinic and had an electrocardiogram taken. No one knew—except the team doctors and Millie. It came back negative. So I figured great, whatever the problem is, it's not my heart. In fact, I celebrated the good news by ordering a nice, big, juicy hamburger back at the hotel.

Brilliant, huh?

The next day we practiced at Brookside Park, right outside the Rose Bowl itself, and I felt terrible. I could not focus. I made myself take the ball and run it from hash mark to hash mark, trying to wake up, trying to get going. "Come on," I said to myself, "what's wrong with you? You're playing USC in two days!"

Like a lot of men that age, I figured I was sort of invincible. After all, I never really had any major illness. And the only injuries I ever suffered were sports related—broken nose, lost teeth, things like that. I ignored the pain, as I had always done, and went on.

On New Year's Eve, we took the team up to the Catholic monastery, where we were to stay the night. It was on the side of a big hill, with guest quarters and a dining hall and a long circular drive that went winding through it. The priests had a little party going and they invited us down. I drank a 7-Up there, hoping it would help my stomach. I still felt lousy. Then word came that President Fleming was at the guest house and wanted to talk to the team.

"Okay," I said, "I'll be right up."

I went out into the dark, and I started to walk up the path. The pain hit me like a sledgehammer. I could barely move. I staggered to that tree and held on for dear life. I was dizzy and weak. I was sweating. I saw the lights from the guest house, and the president's car parked out in front. I knew I had to get up there, but it seemed as if it were a hundred miles away.

Looking back, I'm sure that's when the heart attack occurred. The pain was incredible. Had I more sense, I would have checked into the hospital right then. But I didn't want to shake up the team. I didn't want to admit that at age forty, something could be seriously wrong with me. And besides, like I said, I never suspected anything, because of that stupid EKG. So I stood there, hanging on to a tree, wondering what the hell I had eaten to make me feel this sick, until the pain subsided enough to let me walk to the guest house. I introduced the president and sat down.

"What's the matter, Bo?" one of my coaches whispered.

"Nothing," I said. "I just feel a little . . . ah, nothing."

That night I went around and checked all the players in, and I went back to my room and lay down. God, I felt like hell. The coaches came in, as usual, to go over last minute things. "Look, guys, I'm tired," I said. "I'm knocking off for the night, OK?"

That kind of shocked them. The night before a game? Me? Not wanting to talk football? Apparently it was enough to make them call Dr. Anderson and Dr. O'Connor, our team physicians.

"There's something wrong with Bo," they said.

I had a terrible night. Barely slept. The morning of the game, the doctors came to my room while I was shaving and said, "Look, we know a couple days ago you took the EKG. We want to do another one. There's a hospital called St. Luke's at the bottom of the hill, and we'll run you down there right now."

"Right now?" I said.

Normally, I would have laughed in their faces. A few hours before the Rose Bowl? But I was a dead fish. I had no spark. I wasn't ready to coach that game. Oh, I *would* have. And I'm sure I would have collapsed on the sidelines somewhere in the third quarter.

Instead, we went to St. Luke's and they gave me another EKG. I can still remember when the results came back. I was lying on the table, reading my plays, and Dr. Haskell Weinstein, the chief cardiologist at the hospital, came in and said, "Coach, you've had a heart attack. We've got to sedate you right now."

"Oh, no," I said, "I can't do *that*."

I had a football game, I explained. My team was waiting. The Rose Bowl, for Pete's sake. A heart attack? Did he say a heart attack?

The next thing I knew I was in intensive care, and then everything went blank. The coaches returned to the team, which was just finishing the pre-game meal, and told some players what had happened. Word spread. By the time they boarded the busses, everyone knew. It was a terrible thing to have to spring on those kids, and they played, for the most part, like they were in a fog. We lost to the Trojans, 10–3 in a defensive battle. I don't know if we'd have won even if I was there. But it certainly would have helped our concentration. Dan Dierdorf says, to this day, he can't remember one thing about that game other than getting dressed for it.

Which is more than I can say. I didn't find out we had lost until the following day. Great. My first Rose Bowl defeat came while I was under sedation. I should have known right then this bowl business was going to be a problem.

When I awoke, Millie was in the room, and so was my mother. I was pretty groggy, and I kept sleeping, then waking up, then sleeping. I do remember some time that day, I opened my eyes, and there was Cecil Pryor, standing by my bed. That was kind of strange. Cecil was a linebacker, and I had always treated him a little rough during practices. Yelled at him. Worked on him. And here he was, in the room, with nobody else around.

"Uh-oh," I figured. "Old Cecil's finally come to get me back for all that abuse. He's gonna yank that tube and I'm a goner."

Actually, Cecil had just come to see how I was doing. He had stayed behind after the team flew home—he was a senior, so his football time was over. How he got into the room, I have no idea. But we talked a little about the game and how I felt, and then he left. I always appreciated that visit.

I appreciated him not pulling the plug, too.

And there I stayed, for three weeks. I had never been in a hospital before, and I guess I gave those St. Luke's nurses all they could handle. My mother says I left a few of them in tears, although she's probably exaggerating. I just didn't want to be treated like an invalid. I could get up and go to the bathroom by myself. Besides, there were so darn many of them around always, for blood tests or temperature or some stupid thing.

I was feeling pretty dejected, stuck in California while my team and coaches all went home. Shemy was only a few months old. Millie brought him to visit a couple of times. I got a ton of mail. And I accepted the National Coach of the Year award on the telephone from that hospital bed.

But I couldn't wait to get out. Larry Smith and his wife, Cheryl, had gone back to Ann Arbor and stayed in our house with our three boys. Took care of them. Made them meals. Sent them to school. They even slept in our bedroom. I though that was real nice of them.

The funny thing is, nine months later, Cheryl gave birth to their first son, Toby. We were sitting around one day, and suddenly, I figured it out.

"Wait a minute . . ." I said, ". . . nine months . . . you were staying at our house . . . . Damn it, Larry! That child *was conceived in my bed!*"

They laughed.

"I guess you're right, Bo," he said.

I laughed, too. "Well, I'll be damned."

At least my heart attack was good for somebody.

Six years later, the heart would strike again. I was playing racquet ball, having fully recovered and actually worked myself into decent shape. After the game, I took a shower, went up to my office, and suddenly I felt squeamish—a little like I did that week of the Rose Bowl.

"Uh-oh," I figured, "not this again."

I called Dr. Anderson, my team doctor, who took another EKG and sent me to Dr. Reichert, my cardiologist.

"Bo," he said, looking at the results, "I think you should have a catheterization."

"What's that?"

"Well, they stick this tube up through the groin and into the muscle and they take pictures."

"Sounds great."

What could I do? When the results came back, they showed where all my various arteries were occluded. "Bo," Dr. Reichert said, "in our judgment, you should have coronary bypass surgery. The sooner the better."

And I said, "Oh yeah?"

In football, when we come up with a radical idea, we bounce it off of everybody. And I had every intention of doing the same with this open-heart surgery business. I took that film, told the doctor I'd get back to him, and I started making calls. I went to the Cleveland Clinic. Finally, I went to Dr. Denton Cooley at the Texas Heart Institute. Famous guy. Ara Parseghian got me in there.

Of course, all this time, I'm avoiding the operation. That was the point. Dr. Cooley took that film, analyzed it, and said, "Coach, I'll tell you. On the basis of what I see here, I don't think I'd operate."

"Great," I said. "That's what I want to hear."

"However," he added, "do you have to get back right away?"

"Well, no, I can stay over at the hotel."

"Good. I have to fly to San Francisco. What I'd like to have you do is take a stress test, just in case."

I stayed over and took a stress test. I flew back home. One day passed; two days passed; three days passed. Finally, it was about ten-thirty or eleven at night. The phone rang. Millie answered.

"Western Union calling. We have a telegram for Bo Schembechler."

"You can read it to me," Millie said.

"I have examined the results of your stress test. I believe that you need surgery. I am available. Denton Cooley."

Well, Millie about died right there. "Oh my God!"

"What is it?" I said.

She told me. I went back to my doctor in Ann Arbor—by now, about six weeks had passed since that first meeting—and I said, "Well, Doc, based on everything I can gather, it looks like, you know, I should have this operation."

"Bo," he said, "I told you that six weeks ago."

Well, what do you want? I wasn't exactly thrilled about having open-heart surgery. As the hour approached, I tried to keep up a good front, but the fact is, I was scared. Heck, they're going to cut open my chest and play around with my heart? Wouldn't you be scared? From the hospital bed, just a few hours before surgery, I called up Joe Hayden, my best friend. He was in charge of my will and estate.

"Hey, Joe," I said.

"Bo, what the heck are you calling me for?" he said. "Aren't you supposed to be operated on today?"

"Yeah. They're just about to dope me up. Now, Joe, uh, listen. I want to know something."

"What?"

"Are all my papers and everything in order in case of, you know . . . stark disaster?"

"In case of *what?*"

"Stark disaster."

"What do you mean?"

I let him have it. "You dumb bleep! You never understood football talk! If these doctors go in there, and it's going ticky, ticky, ticky, and all of a sudden it stops going ticky, ticky, ticky—that's *stark disaster!*"

"Oh. I get it. Yeah. You're OK."

Good old Joe.

It didn't stop going ticky, ticky, ticky, of course. The operation was a success, and once again I had dodged my own heart-shaped bullet. And you know what? In the recovery room, right after the surgery, I opened my eyes and who do I see but Les Miles—a senior lineman! It was just like Cecil Pryor six years earlier. How that little son of a gun got in there I'll never know. But once again, I'm helpless, just lying there, this time with thirty-two tubes in my stomach. And once again, Les is a guy who I gave a hard time to, lots of yelling and insults. I'm starting to wonder if there's a society out there just trying to drive me crazy in the hospital.

"Hi, coach, how ya doing?" Les says.

I swore he was in there to cut those tubes. Maybe he just chickened out.

Anyhow, the effects of that operation lasted for a good eleven years. During that time I guess I fell into some bad old habits. Lousy eating, working too late, taking on too much. I knew I was headed for trouble during the Minnesota game in November of the '87 season. It was one of the toughest games I ever had to get through. I was feeling sick and squeamish, the crowd was unbelievably loud, and to make matters worse, Minnesota's Darrell Thompson ran ninety-eight yards for a touchdown right in front of me. Demetrious Brown, our quarterback, dislocated his thumb. Talk about stress! I felt like the whole stadium was spinning. We started to come back in the second half, but the noise was so bad, we sat on the ball for the longest time I've ever seen in a college game without snapping it, and meanwhile, my chest was killing me, my voice had gone froggy. I had to lean over a few times, just to catch my breath. We finally pulled it out, but afterwards I took Alex Agase aside.

"What's wrong?" he said.

"I think my heart's acting up again." Alex understood, because he had a heart problem, too.

Sure enough, five weeks later, I was in the hospital for another catheterization when I started to have that second heart attack, and a day that was supposed to be back-to-work turned into the day they cut my chest open and did my second open-heart surgery. That one, I thought, would be the clincher. *God, just let me live.* My heart was becoming like an old car; parts were hard to find. I really figured my life would change after that, and I'd be lucky to be walking, let alone coaching, again.

Yet here I am, as I write this, preparing for another season. What's that phrase—takes a licking and keeps on ticking? Maybe I'm meant to be like that. Who knows? I am sixty years old now, the same age my father was when he died of a stroke. And I guess I wonder when my time will come, although, as I said, I'm pretty sure how I'll go.

So what have I learned from my troubled heart? Well I figure it's God's way of keeping me in check. Just like my bowl record. Without that, I'd have nothing but success in football; my ego would go through the roof. Same thing with my heart. Without that, I might lose all sight of what life is really about. I might just coach myself into oblivion, let little things depress me, never have a good laugh or shoot the breeze with players. But because of all the times I've been in that damn hospital wondering if I'd ever get out, I've really come to enjoy life, as crazy as it is.

My heart has given me a certain perspective. I never get depressed. Little things don't upset me anymore. I'm a different guy than most people figure from watching the games or reading newspapers. All my screaming and carrying on is strictly in football—and most of that is for effect. Privately, I'm a fairly sensitive person, and I enjoy life, and I have a decent sense of humor. I like to laugh, I like people, and I'm pretty easy to please when it comes to doing things or going places. Why worry?

As long as I hear that ticky, ticky, ticky, I'm a happy guy.

☆ ☆ ☆

STRAIGHT TALK: COLLEGE FOOTBALL

The Recruiting War

RECRUITING is the worst part of college football. I no longer look forward to it. I can't wait until it's over. It makes me feel like a pimp.

You would be appalled at the things I have to do to recruit. A man my age. And you are listening to someone who does it cleanly, who doesn't cheat, who refuses to buy players. I am not the only one. There are plenty of honest coaches out there. But the need to win is so great now that certain coaches swallow their pride, certain administrations look the other way, certain payoffs are given—and a player's word doesn't mean a damn thing anymore.

I'm sick of it.

Back in the mid-seventies we recruited two kids out of Camden, New Jersey. One was Art Still, a defensive end who now plays for the Buffalo Bills. The other was Derrick Ramsey, then a quarterback, now a tight end for the New England Patriots. They came to visit Michigan. Looked over the campus. While they were riding with Tom Reed, my assistant coach, in his Ford Granada, one of them said, "Hey, is this the best kind of car we're gonna get at Michigan?"

Tom shrugged it off. But we knew something was up. Soon after I got a call from their high school coach.

"Are you interested in Still and Ramsey?" he asked.

"Well, yeah, they're great players," I said

"You understand that these boys both live with me," he said. "I've put a lot of money into them. We're going to have to take care of things if you want them at Michigan."

"What are you talking about?"

"They'll cost you five big ones apiece."

I paused. "Now, repeat that again. *Five big ones apiece?*"

"That's right."

"What do you mean by five big ones?"

"You know, five thousand dollars."

"You want five thousand dollars for two football players?"

"No five thousand dollars for each one. Ten thousand dollars. Coach, we're talking about two All-Americans."

"Well, let me ask you a question. Where do you think I would get ten thousand dollars?"

"Come on, coach. You're at Michigan. You can get all the money you want."

I made sure to repeat this again. "You want me to pay you ten thousand dollars for Art Still and Derrick Ramsey?"

"That's exactly right."

"And then you'll see to it that they choose Michigan?"

"Right."

"Well, I'll have to think about that. I'll get back to you."

"Okay. Bye."

He hung up. And I flicked off the tape recorder. I had taped the entire conversation. I couldn't believe the brashness of this guy. He's their coach! And he's asking for ten thousand dollars *on the phone!*

I gave that tape to the NCAA. I said, "I think you guys

might be interested in this." What happened after that, I cannot tell you. I don't know if Still and Ramsey were ever going to see any money from that little deal.

I do know both went to Kentucky.

And their coach is still in college ball today.

I'm going to state my position right at the start. I will not cheat. I will not buy football players. I find it demeaning enough to fly to some kid's home, a thousand miles from Ann Arbor, only to learn that he forgot about the meeting. Or to sit there, ready to offer a free educatioin at one of the finest schools in the country, and see the family refuse to turn off the TV set. I am sixty years old, and there's a certain amount of dignity I try to retain.

Besides, if a kid can't see the value of what we're offering at Michigan without having a car thrown in, the hell with him.

As a result, I end up walking out on some of the finest talent in the country. I've seen all kinds of payoffs, big and small. New clothes. New shoes. My assistant coaches have gone to visit houses, arrived just after other coaches have left, and seen five new sweat suits on the bed. Or a new car in the driveway, conveniently leased from a local businessman for one dollar a year.

Once, Elliot Uzelac and I were recruiting a star running back in Florida (he now plays in the NFL). On the first visit, he lived in a poor apartment in a poor neighborhood. A few months later, when we went back, he was suddenly living in a new house, in a nice surburb.

"What happened?" we asked the family.

"Oh . . . we just moved," they said.

Good-bye. He went to another major university. And I don't give a hoot if he can leap out of a building, I don't want that kind of kid in my program. If it means turning away the best running back in the nation, so be it. Once you pay a kid, he owns you. And pretty soon the rest of your star players expect the same treatment. And pretty soon someone is blabbing to the NCAA. And pretty soon you are history.

You can buy yourself a national championship if you want, but you better be prepared to get out of town as soon as the parade is over.

How did things get so crazy? How did recruiting grow into such a cutthroat business? Well, first, let's get a few things straight. I would say that 75 percent of recruiting today is still up-front and honest. The parents ask intelligent questions, the kid is bright enough to know what he wants, a decision is made, cleanly, and the athlete signs with the school.

The other 25 percent is a mess. Coaches make promises. Kids make demands. The competition is at a fever pitch and the whole process spirals out of control.

Who's at fault? First, consider the school and its administration. It wants the football program to be successful, because successful football means a ton of money—enough, in many cases, to fund the entire rest of the athletic program.

Next, consider the coach. He knows he has to win fast to please that administration—or else he loses his job. He might be able to build a solid program if they give him five full years to start from scratch and recruit cleanly. But they are too impatient. Ask Gary Moeller. He went to Illinios, tried to do it cleanly, and they fired him after three years—even though he was on the verge of turning that program around.

Now, in light of all that, consider the high school star —particularly a running back or quarterback. My God, how valuable he suddenly becomes! Coaches are drooling. He can help them *win*. So he begins hearing from colleges in his junior year. Not a little. A lot. Telephone calls. Letters. Pretty soon, he can't go anywhere without being asked "Made up your mind yet?"

People come to watch him play. Not just football. If he

wrestles or plays basketball, they are there, too. Coaches will fly from across the country to spend a few minutes with him. During the official recruiting period, the phone never stops ringing.

COACH: Hey, how you doing? Did you see our game on TV this weekend?

KID: Yeah. It was great.

COACH: Well that could be you out there next year. Just remember that. We sure would love to have you.

KID: Yeah, thanks.

Can you imagine that conversation thirty times a day? Forty? Fifty? That is how intense recruiting has become. The media keeps a daily tap of who's getting who. Heck. Nowadays, if you believe the media, there are two seasons: football season and recruiting season. You get ranked at the end of each one.

Against this backdrop, the athlete and his family often go from thankful to bossy. Early in December, I may call this kid on the phone and he'll say, "Oh, my God! Coach Schembechler. Oh, geez, this is great!"

I call him the end of January, two months later. "Yeah. Bo, how you doing? How's it goin', man?"

Last spring, I was visiting the home of Bryan Fortay, one of the top high school quarterbacks in the country. Lives in New Jersey. Nice home. Nice family. But his father was the type who gets real involved in the recruiting process. Not long after I arrived, he sat back in his chair and said, "Now, Bo, if Bryan agrees to Michigan, are you willing to issue a press release stating he is your quarterback and you will not recruit any other quarterback prospects?"

I was dumbfounded. "No," I said, "why should I do that?"

"Because the other schools did it."

"What other schools?"

"Miami and Alabama."

He pulled out two letters. Both were on school stationery. Both were signed by the offensive coordinators. Both said, in effect, "We've got the greatest prospect in the country. He's exactly what we were looking for. There is no other quarterback in the country we'd rather have, so we will not recruit any others."

It was all there. Miami and Alabama. I couldn't believe it. "Well," said the father, "what would you do?"

I took a deep breath. Then I told him. First of all, I don't give out press releases. Secondly, let's face it. If it's publicity you're looking for, you'll get it by signing with Michigan. Every newspaper in the country will run some mention of it.

"Well, what about other quarterback prospects?" asked the father.

"What about them?" I said. "If you think I'm withdrawing my offers to them, you're wrong."

"But you know two top quarterbacks won't choose the same school."

"Maybe not. But if another one wants to come, should I not take him?"

I was really getting annoyed. I mean, what's this all about, anyhow? A marketing campaign?

"You know what's really sad about those letters?" I said to Mr. Fortay. "I'll be damned if I want somebody to put that kind of pressure on my son. Every time he takes a snap, he's supposed to be great. Is that what you want for your child?"

I guess it was. He chose Miami.

Now, not every recruiting experience is like that. Some are genuinely enjoyable. You meet fine people, and you are encouraged when you see good kids growing up with the right values. But every year there is a knot of recruits that make the whole process miserable. And we coaches don't help. As long as recruiting has been around, we've been sub-scribing to a theory of "Tell Him What He Wants To Hear."

He wants to hear that he'll start as a freshman? Tell him

he'll start as a freshman. He wants to hear about his Heisman Trophy chances? Tell him his chances are great.

Let's face it. When I visit a home, this is the speech the player and family are looking for: "Son, you are the best. I can see you in Michigan Stadium with 105,000 people screaming your name, national television, the biggest game of the year. You throw a touchdown pass to win it. They carry us off the field and we're going to the Rose Bowl. You're voted All-American. Yes, sir. Sign with us."

What they don't want to hear is: "Son, you are a fine prospect. I want you to sign that paper. But once you do, you're coming in like all the other freshmen. You have to climb to the top. The demands will be great—in the classroom and the football field—and you're going to have to earn everything you get at Michigan."

That turns a lot of kids off. "Tell Him What He Wants To Hear." Like the "pro ball" speech: you'll hear that one if the family is not academically oriented. *"We'll get your son into the NFL. Just look at how many of our kids are in the NFL right now . . ."*

Or let's say the decision has come down to two schools. The rival coach will look for a way to cut down the other program. When Steve Everitt, who is on my team now, was being recruited by Jimmy Johnson of Miami, Johnson told him, "What do you want to go to Michigan for? You'll never play there. They already have the best lineman in the country."

I saw Johnson not long after Everitt signed with us. I teased him. "Hey, what's with telling Everitt that crap?"

"Well," he said sheepishly, "I thought it was true."

As a result of all this, the kids themselves have now adopted their own version of "Tell Him What He Wants To Hear." Used to be if a kid verbally committed to your school, that was enough. Now a kid will tell us, "Yes, I talked it over with my mother. I'm coming to Michigan." The next day he'll get a call from Penn State. "Yes, I talked it over with my dad. I'm coming to Penn State." What are we teaching them here? Before they ever leave high school, these kids are learning that their word means nothing.

This can get pretty depressing. Especially when you're flying from Ft. Lauderdale to Denver to Houston to Athens, Georgia, to Cincinnati, all in three days. That's the other lousy part of recruiting. The weather is bad, you're up late, you don't have time to eat, you're sleeping in strange hotels—all to chase after seventeen-year-old athletes. And the irony is, you *still* have no idea if the kid is going to pan out as a football player. Nobody does.

That's when you sit on the bed at 2 A.M., put your head in your hands, and say "What the hell am I doing?"

The real danger, of course, is when what you're *telling* the kid starts to become what you're *giving* the kid. It happens quite often. A coach will say to parents, "Your son shouldn't have to worry about money when he's playing for us. We'll see to it that he's taken care of." Or, "We want your son to be able to drive home and see you. We'll make sure he has transportation."

How can coaches get away with this? Cars? Money? In some cases, because their administrations not only put enormous pressure on them to win but are willing to look the other way when it comes to cheating. That, of course, is what happened at Southern Methodist University. People as high as the Board of Trustees knew what was going on with recruiting violations: One player was reportedly given twenty-five thousand dollars. Another was given a free apartment.

Who provides such payoffs? Usually the boosters and alumni. These are overzealous fans or graduates who will do anything to see that their team wins. I do not believe these people simply rise up where they are not wanted. But when the program has the attitude "Whatever It Takes," believe me, they crawl out of the woodwork. They are bad news. The worst. And if one of them pays off a player, only two things can happen:

1. The kid is highly successful, in which case, the booster will make sure everybody within earshot knows "I'm the reason he's playing for us. I got him. That's my guy."
2. The kid is a bust, and this booster is sitting there saying, "Son of a bitch! I paid that kid three thousand dollars because they said they had to have him, and, damn it, they don't even play him!" Sooner or later, that will come out, too.

The only answer to these people is to keep them as far from your program as possible. Early in my career at Michigan, I was disciplining Billy Taylor, our running back. I got a call from some doctor in Detroit.

"Bo, I don't think you're being fair to Billy."

I paused. "You don't? Well let me tell you something. I don't take outside advice on my program, and don't you ever call me about a discipline matter again."

"I don't think you understand," he said. "I'm a Victors Club member."

"Yeah? Not anymore you're not. I just threw you out."

And I hung up.

I have no sympathy for administrations that cheat. And I have no sympathy for boosters. I do not believe for one minute the coach who says, "I didn't want to cheat, but I couldn't control the alumni." That's hogwash. You can control the alumni. Right from the start you stand up and say, "By God, we're going to do it the way it's supposed to be done, and if I find out someone's doing it otherwise, I'm coming down hard on you."

They will accept that—*provided your administration ac-*

cepts it. If your administration, however, wants you to win so badly they don't care how you do it, then you better get out of town. You're in a bad place.

Because of all this, the NCAA has adopted enough recruiting rules to fill a hundred file cabinets. You are not allowed to give a prospect a ride to a game. You are not allowed to buy him a hot dog. You are not allowed in his house on signing day before 8 A.M.

They are a pain in the butt, these rules—and every one of them is necessary. The fact is, they were all created because somebody tried to get an edge; instead of just buying a hot dog, it was a meal for the family. Instead of a ride to a game, it was a limousine. Without those rules, there would be a lot of honest coaches who would be unemployed within three years.

So I am in favor of them. In fact, I would like to see a few more:

1. I'd like to reduce from five to three the number of paid visits allowed for the recruits. Five schools is too much. Make the kid do some thinking before he decides which campuses to visit. It'll cut down on costs and cut down some of the competition, too, since two less schools would be in the final consideration.
2. Let's forbid any head coach to recruit off campus. No visiting the home. He can meet with the recruit during the one visit to the school. That's enough. Now, coaches like myself or Joe Paterno and others might suffer more than most on this one. Having been around a while, we carry some weight in the home. But I just don't think we need to be out there. It's too much already.
3. I would like to see freshmen made ineligible. This would accomplish a number of things: it would make the transition from high school to college a lot easier.

It would also cut down on the media attention to recruiting, since the kid wouldn't even play a down for eighteen months from the time they write about him. No more of these "Instant Impact Player" headlines.

The whole process is a crapshoot anyhow. Like I said, you have no idea who's going to pan out. Jamie Morris, Michigan's all-time leading rusher, was a kid I didn't even want to take. I only took John Kolesar, one of the best receivers I ever coached, because he was a legacy and he could run fast.

In 1970, I was down to my last scholarship. I was going after a star wide-receiver out of Steubenville, Ohio. I thought this kid was great. But he was wavering between Michigan and Notre Dame.

At the same time, I had also been talking to a player named Dave Gallagher. Linebacker. Average speed. No superstar, but a good kid. And he really wanted Michigan.

"Coach, can you tell me anything yet?" he would ask when he called.

"Not yet, Dave. Hang in there."

I put him off, because I wanted this wide receiver in the worst way. But he couldn't make up his mind. On and on this went for a couple of weeks. Gallagher had been heavily recruited by Northwestern, and finally he told me he had to give them an answer.

So I called the kid in Steubenville. "Son, what are you thinking?"

"Geez, Coach, I don't know. I'm still in the same dilemma."

"Look, if you're leaning the least little bit one way or another—"

"Well . . . I might be leaning a little to Notre Dame, but I can't say no to Michigan."

That was all I needed to hear.

"Listen," I said, "you just said no to Michigan. You're going to Notre Dame."

"Gee, you really think I should?"

"Yeah," I said. "If you're leaning in that direction, I think you oughta go there. You'll do well there. Good luck." I hung up, and I called Gallagher. I said, "Dave, you've got a scholarship to Michigan."

"Great! Great!"

Dave Gallagher became an All-American defensive tackle and captain of our team. He was a first-round draft pick of the Chicago Bears. Today he is an orthopedic surgeon.

And the guy from Steubenville?

He went to Notre Dame and never played a down.

You would think, with recruits being so unpredictable, that it wouldn't mean so much for coaches to get this one or that one. But it does. Recruiting is a highly competitive thing, and sometimes I think coaches pursue athletes simply because they hear other coaches are after them. "Geez, he must be good," they say. "Let's get him."

I always joke if my son, Shemy, wanted to play football, he ought to get on a bus in early December and go to Lansing and see a movie. Then go down to South Bend and see a movie. Then go to Columbus and see a movie. Then go to Champaign and see a movie. And when some recruiter calls on the phone Shemy would say, "Well, I've been to Lansing and South Bend and Columbus," and immediately they're going to say, "Oh, my God, every top school in the country is after this kid!"

And he'd probably be recruited like crazy.

When I was younger, I took every recruiting effort personally. It was me against the other guy. And when I lost a kid, it hurt.

I'm not like that anymore. I recognize that Michigan will get its share. In fact, I tell my coaches, "We are not a great recruiting outfit. We will do the best we can with what we've got." That's all.

Speed will dazzle you, and so will strength. But what I look at most now is character. How will a guy fit into our program? Last season, there was a high school star named Mike Milia, from suburban Detroit. He played offensive guard. We didn't need offensive guards; we stopped recruiting him. Although he had been pursued by lots of schools, including UCLA and Michigan State, he applied to Michigan on his own and got accepted. He called our office and asked if he could come and meet with me.

"Well," the coaches told him, "you can come up if you like, but like we told you before, we don't need guards this season."

That kid walked into my office. He spoke well. He looked me in the eye. He said, "Coach, I could go elsewhere, but I want to come here. I want to play for Michigan. What do I have to do to get on this team?"

I grinned. "Not much, son. You just got on."

Barring injuries, Mike Milia will be a captain for me some day. I can see it. You bet I'll make room for a kid like that. Unfortunately, a number of the most talented players out there are blinding coaches with their talent, even if they have questionable backgrounds. Too many coaches are willing to say "Don't worry, I'll make him fit in; look at how fast he is!"

It sure seems to have happened at Oklahoma. Last year, in the course of a single month, one of their players was charged with shooting a teammate, three were charged with alleged gang rape, and the starting quarterback was charged with selling cocaine. The school was *already* on probation. The average citizen saw that and said, "My God. How did kids like that ever get on a college campus?"

It's a good question. One or two might slip into any program—but so many? There was obviously something shady with the kind of athletes they were recruiting down in Oklahoma. Critics, of course, blamed Coach Barry Switzer. "He's the guy who let them in!" they screamed. "Fire him, and you'll eliminate the problem!"

But he wasn't immediately fired (although he did resign in June), and I had to chuckle. Obviously, if nothing was done to Switzer, then there were people higher up who condoned the conduct of that program, right? And if the administration condoned such behavior, it's because football must bring in quite a bit of money and prestige for the university. It's like I said at the start. Everybody is at fault. And around and around it goes.

We have got to clean up recruiting. If we don't, we are going to sink our sport. Nothing we do is worth cheating over. Nothing we do is worth selling our souls. And nothing we do is worth feeling like a pimp. This may sound odd coming from a coach, but our game, as far as recruiting is concerned, is out of control. And we owe it to everyone involved to get it back.

Drugs, Steroids, and Alcohol

have never used drugs in my life. I have never tried cocaine. Never popped a pill. Never smoked marijuana. I
take two baby aspirin a day, and it ticks me off because
up to my first heart attack I swore I would never take
anything.

Because of that, I was once pretty naive about the whole
drug problem. Then one day in 1980, I started to get wind
of something. Some of my players had reportedly been involved with drugs. Not heavy. Not terrible. But still. I was
shocked. I never would have thought it, with *my* players, kids
I recruited, coached, loved.

I was furious. During a regular team meeting, I pulled
those kids out one by one. There were five of them.

"Now damn it, *what is going on here?* I have reports that
you guys have been using drugs. I want to know who, when,
and where! And I want to know NOW!"

One by one, they told me the stories. And it eventually
came out that the ringleader of this whole thing was a player

I never would have suspected: An All-American kid, smart, good-looking, cheerleader girlfriend—and a starter.

I sent for him. This was just before spring break. The word came back that he was in the Bahamas. We were able to get into his apartment (someone had a key), and we discovered all sort of drug paraphernalia, scales to weigh the stuff and so on. He was apparently selling drugs—including cocaine—all over campus.

The other players, who were all underclassmen, were thrown off the team for one year. Eventually, several cleaned up their act and were allowed back. And this All-American kid—who was a fifth-year senior and therefore done with football—never showed his face again.

I did hear about him, however. A few years later, he was up on a federal drug charge along with his brother. The judge on the case was from Ann Arbor. He came to me and said, "Bo, I want your opinion on this young man. I met his mother, a delightful woman, and it seems a shame such a nice family is torn apart by something like this."

I told him about what that kid had done. How he didn't have the courage to face me. How I, too, once thought no way he would do anything like that.

"You know what I'd like to see you do?" I said.

"What?" he said.

"Be as tough as you can. I have no sympathy for him."

And from that day on, I have been testing my players for everything.

You cannot be naive about drugs. You cannot be naive about steroids. And most of all, when it comes to college football, you cannot be naive about alcohol, because it is consumed more than any other substance.

Now I feel strongly about all three. None belong in a college football program. And the easiest and most effective way to eliminate them is to test.

"Hey, John. I've been hearing some disappointing things about you and cocaine."

"Oh, no, coach. They're making that up."

"Well, let's just test to make sure, OK?"

See how easy?

Schools should test. Schools must test. It is the only way to keep tabs on an athletic team that has nearly one hundred players, travels on the road, and is scattered all around campus. The coach who says, "I don't need to test, I know I don't have a problem" is the coach who has a problem. Guaranteed. Sometimes he doesn't *want* to know it—as is the case with steroids, which I'll get to in a moment—but the problem is there. Drugs and steroids are readily available. They are part of American life, and they cannot be ignored.

So we test. Randomly. Often. I got a laugh last spring, when "CBS Morning News" came out to Michigan for a show and asked to interview me. On national television, Kathleen Sullivan asked me why of all the schools in the Big Ten, only Michigan *did not* test its players.

I almost threw that microphone across the room.

"Young lady, your information is incorrect," I said.

"Well, uh . . ." she said.

"Not only do we test, but we have been at the forefront of testing in our conference. And anyone who knows me knows I *lead the way when it comes to drug testing!*"

"Well, uh . . ."

Somebody at CBS had better do his homework a little better. We test. Constantly. Which brings me into conflict with those people who say, "You are violating the players' civil rights by giving them drug tests." Yes. I've heard that a lot. And here's what I say: too bad.

When our athletes are recruited to Michigan, I tell them and their parents that there will be drug tests. I write the parents and tell them exactly what I'm doing. I promise there will be confidentiality. I promise if the player fails a test, he will be suspended from the team until the problem is cleared up.

And I have never had an objection.

Never. Not from a parent. Not from a player. When they come here, they know: this is going to be a drug-free operation. If you're worried about civil rights violations by drug testing, don't come to Michigan. If you're hell-bent on using drugs, don't come to Michigan. Believe me. You're going to get caught. You'd be better off someplace else. Got it?

The same goes for steroids. God, they make me angry. I want them abolished. I want them outlawed. The steroid problem hits me right in the gut, because unlike other drugs, they are taken to *increase* your athletic performance. To make you a meaner, faster, stronger football player. And with winning in football already as big as it is, the idea of what might be with steroids is absolutely terrifying.

Let's get a few things straight. Number one, steroids are dangerous. They are dangerous to the athletes who take them, and they are dangerous to the players who compete against them. Number two, we still don't know all the consequences of steroid use. But amongst the possible are cancer, liver problems, and perhaps even death. So a coach or parent who encourages a kid to use steroids might be, in a small way, killing him.

And number three, they are damn unfair.

I have coached against teams that used steroids. I lost a Rose Bowl in 1986 to an Arizona State team that, it was later reported, had a number of players who used steroids. When we went there I remember saying, "God, these guys are so big and aggressive." Then, a couple years later, one of their coaches was quoted in an Arizona newspaper as admitting the players were pumped up. We probably played an artificial team in that Rose Bowl. And we lost.

That wasn't the only time. I have seen opposing players throughout the years that I know are using steroids. After a while you can tell by the look, the size, the aggression, the hostility. You remember that last year the kid was half that size, and now, look, he's a monster! It infuriates me to lose to a team that is beefed up on steroids. And it absolutely kills me to learn that they are so widely used on the high school level.

Now some people point to such widespread use of steroids, particularly at the strength positions like linemen and linebackers, and they say the problem is beyond our control. Bull. I say to you right here, in this book, for the record, *any coach worth his salt can control steroids if he has the resources*—and at this level of competition, we have the resources. We can test. We can stop it.

Why, then, are steroids such a problem in college football? Well, for one thing, because there are plenty of coaches out there who don't *want* to catch their kids. They *like* the fact their players are bigger and stronger. They turn their backs. They let it happen. The truth is, if you want steroids in your program, you don't have to promote them. Just ignore them.

There are coaches today who know they have a problem and stand up before their squads and say, "Look, men, I've heard some of you are using steroids. I want you to know we don't want that here. It's no good for your health, and we're going to have to stop it . . . I must say, however, I'm really proud of the fact that you guys would sacrifice like that so that we can have a great team. I admire that spirit."

Now, how about that statement?

It stinks, that's what.

What do you think a kid will do after hearing that? He'll go right on using the steroids, because he thinks, deep down, his coach will be happier with him if he does. The college athlete is primarily concerned with his coach's opinion of him; he wants to make sure that he's liked and will get a chance to play. If he feels steroids will achieve that, he may run the risk.

Why would a coach permit such a thing? The same reason he might OK a cash payment to a player or overlook a player's woeful academic transcript: Winning. The coach wants to win. He needs to win to keep his job, and he is getting that message from the administration.

Sometimes it's not only the coach, it's the family. Larry Smith, the head coach at USC, told me that before the 1988 Rose Bowl against Michigan State, they tested the players twice. The first time they tested, about three weeks before the game, everyone knew when it was coming, and everyone passed. Then, about three days before the game, in a secret test, they random-sampled players, just to see if the previous testing was accurate.

Several of the players failed that second test. How did it happen? Hey. These kids aren't dumb. They cycled their steroid use to beat the first test. Since that second test did not affect the eligibility of the players, they got to play in the Rose Bowl with steroids in their system.

Now, I know Larry Smith like a brother. He was on my staff when we first arrived at Michigan. He stayed with my sons when I suffered my first heart attack. I said, "Larry, didn't you have any idea the kids were using steroids?"

He said, "Bo, I had no idea. I called this one kid in, an All-American offensive tackle, and he said, 'Coach, I don't want to get anybody in trouble. But yes, I admit that I am using steroids. I cycled it so that I'd pass the test.'

"I asked him why. He said, 'Coach, I want to be a professional football player. I want to be a top draft choice in the NFL, and I'm doing this with the advice and consent *of my father.*' "

Now, what are you going to say to that?

With the *consent of the father?*

I don't know how you combat parents like that. I do know if one of my players ever comes to me and says he's using steroids because he wants to make me proud of him,

I'll tell him right then and there: "Hey. Did I tell you to do that? Did I ever say you should do something that jeopardizes your health? Sure, we want to win. We'll work harder in the weight room. We'll outwork them in the off-season. But we are not going to kill ourselves to be football players or a football team! *We are not going to do that here! And if you do it, you will be gone!*"

That's the way I think you handle it.

Did you know the FBI is involved in the steroids issue? I haven't heard a lot of publicity on it, but it's now a felony to distribute steroids: three years in prison for distributing to people over eighteen, six years in prison for distributing to people under eighteen.

Good. I am working with the law authorities to make sure the penalties remain that harsh. The point is, steroids have no place in college football and I want them stamped out. I want fair competition. I don't want my players facing guys who are violent with the effects of steroids. And most of all, I don't want my players to take a health risk like that. I've always said my favorite part of this job is when your former players come back to visit, when they stop in the office unexpectedly and say "Hey, coach, I just wanted to say hi, tell you how I'm doing, that everything's OK."

I don't know how I would react if one of those times, the player came to tell me he had cancer because of steroids he took while trying to win for my team. It would kill me to hear that. It really would.

Let's talk about alcohol. As far as I'm concerned this is the biggest problem facing college sports today. The reasons are simple: it is legal, it is everywhere, and you can't test for it.

Unlike steroids, alcohol was around when I played college football, but it was almost never a problem. Oxford, Ohio, was a dry town, and all you could get was 3.2 beer—

remember that?—and you either drank that or nothing, unless you were some hotshot fraternity guy who managed to drive somewhere and get his hands on some liquor.

But even then, the attitude about drinking was somewhat the same: it's fun, relatively harmless, and sort of something you're expected to do as a college student.

That's the attitude that's getting us in trouble.

The biggest problem is beer. You'll probably think this is funny coming from me but it's that macho business about drinking beer that leads so many football players to it. They think they have to drink beer to be real men, real football guys. They also think it is harmless compared to hard liquor. It isn't. We spend a lot of time at Michigan talking about alcohol, I have speakers come in all the time to address the kids, and one thing they emphasize is how alcohol of any kind is a drug just like all the others. It can be addicting and hard to control. Even beer.

The problem is it is everywhere in sports. Events are sponsored by beer companies. TV sports commercials are about beer. We have created an environment where beer has a great image for fun, relaxation, and manliness—but we seem to forget that it is still an alcoholic beverage. And too much of it can get you killed.

We in Michigan don't have to look very far to see sports stars undone by alcohol. Last year alone, Reggie Rogers, the Detroit Lions defensive end, was charged with the deaths of three teenagers in an alleged drunk driving incident. Bob Probert, a star hockey player for the Red Wings, is an admitted alcoholic who had numerous drunk driving arrests and was caught at the Canadian–U.S. border with 14.3 grams of cocaine in his underwear.

I've had alcoholics in the Michigan program. I tried to get them treatment. They were all back-up players (you couldn't hack that problem and be a starter, not unless you were tremendously gifted), and sometimes we didn't find out until after their eligibility was up. In most of the cases, we found there was a history of alcoholism in the family. Unfortunately, life for those guys wasn't made any easier by the "let's have a drink" college environment.

"Was he drinking?" That's the first thing I ask these days when I hear about a player in any sort of trouble. "Was he drinking?" I have to ask—and rely on witnesses—because, as I said, there are no tests. And until there are, I think we are stuck with a major problem. It is impossible to police one hundred players every minute of the day. It is impossible to know what they are buying every time they enter a supermarket. We have to rely on the character of the kids, the influence of the coach, and the continued education of the team as to the dangers of excessive drinking.

That means beer as well, guys.

I am told there is a test on the way. A sort of litmus paper thing, where you can put a piece of paper in your mouth and it will turn a certan color if there's been any alcohol in the last twenty-four hours. I know. I know. You hate to think of having to ask college students to stick this piece of paper in their mouths. It's humiliating and embarrassing.

But it beats the alternative. If it deters drinking, great, I'm all for it. To heck with the critics. I learned my lesson and I want no more surprises. I will test even the most All-American guy, with the good grades and the nice family and the cheerleader girlfriend, because, I promise you, as long as I am here, Michigan will be clean. And we are not going to debate this.

Academics and
Football

I T'S one of the biggest problems we have in college football. Academics versus athletics. What is the answer?

The answer is to stop referring to it as "versus."

Take the case of Dominic Tedesco. Nice kid. Good family. I recruited him out of high school, and he wanted to come to Michigan. Then I ran into his father.

"I don't want my son going to your school," he said.

"Why not?" I said.

"Because I want him to be a doctor."

"He can be a doctor at Michigan."

"No he can't. Michigan is a big-time football school. I want him to be a student."

Here's what that father was thinking: once his son got to college, we'd ruin him. Make him take elementary courses and live in the weight room. When his football years were up, we'd cut him off, and he'd be left without a degree or a future. A doctor? Try a big, dumb, ex–football player. That's the stereotype, right?

I worked on that kid. Hard. And I finally convinced the

mother to let her son try—against the father's wishes. Dominic Tedesco became a starter for our football team. He was an excellent student. He went to medical school.

And today he is a heart surgeon.

Now everybody knows the horror stories about college athletics. How kids are being bumped along without the most basic academic skills, how some get out of college barely able to read. How coaches say, "Why don't you skip that biology class this semester and take the phys-ed class instead? It'll leave you more time for football."

And then along comes a kid like Mark Messner. You won't find a better player. I mean the kid would kick your butt if you lined up against him. But Mark was a class kid from the start; he went through school dividing his time between studying and football, had time for a girlfriend, had time to be the most interviewed player on our team, had time to get his degree in marketing *and* get drafted by the Los Angeles Rams. He's in a perfect position. He's got people interested in him in the sports world and in the private sector. And I promise you, the guy is no nerd. He's one of the most well-liked kids on the team.

The student-athlete system can work. It does work. More often than you think. But you have to have your priorities set right from the start. (1) Academics. (2) Football. And whatever is number three sure as hell better not interfere with the number one and number two. There is enough time. Football need not take up more than four hours a day—and that includes practice, film, weight lifting, and meetings. The rest of the day can be devoted to class and study; we have study table to encourage that. Remember, football is the only major collegiate sport where, thanks to the Saturday games, you *do not have to miss a single class*. Not if you schedule correctly. In most cases, the athlete has five years on scholarship, not four. So even a player who wants to make a go at the toughest of majors can do so.

And don't worry. They can find time for a social life. They always do.

Just the same, not every football player is going to be a heart surgeon. Not every one needs to be. Some players are just seeking an education that will help them make a good living when they are finished with sports. That is fine if the academic standards of a school are no different for athletes than they are for the everyday students. But schools like Michigan are faced with a tough dilemma. Admissions are usually reserved for some of the nation's brightest young men and women. And no matter how you slice it, some of the best football players out there are not the most gifted of students, any more than those gifted students are great football players.

What do you do? At Michigan—as with most major football programs—we occasionally have special admissions for athletes. And I don't have a problem with that. I believe that as a public institution, we have an obligation to educate a core of underprivileged kids who show special talents, be they music, physics—or football. You must understand, some of these kids have grown up poor, with ten brothers and sisters in the house. They went to high schools where it's a good day if no one gets shot. They didn't have the same chances as the private school kid whose transcript is gleaming with success.

But I can hear the critics now. "You only want to admit them because they're great football players." Well, hell, of course! But let's get a few things straight. First of all, we do have a minimum standard, based on Proposition 48, which requires at least a 700 on the college boards or a 15 on the ACT, and a C average in eleven core courses in high school. Secondly, even if he meets those minimums, we don't admit just any athlete, no matter how great. I walk away from a lot more than I take. There are some who wouldn't stand a chance of making it academically at Michigan. Good-bye to them. There are others who are looking for a payoff or an easy ride. Good-bye to them. Remember Still and Ramsey? *"Is this the best kind of car we're gonna get if we come to Michigan?"*

Good-bye to them.

I believe a coach should recruit academically the same way he recruits for his team: look for character. I also believe critics should be more concerned with what the kid does once he arrives than with the digits on his application.

I'll give you an example. Gil Chapman. High school running back from Elizabeth, New Jersey. Tough neighborhood, but a great kid. I knew that after meeting him and his family. He wanted to come to Michigan.

The admissions department said no.

"Why not?" I said.

"His test scores aren't high enough. And look at this: he wants to attend the business school. He won't make it in the business school."

"How do you know? His grades are good. Maybe his school didn't prepare him well for the college boards. Come on. Give him a chance."

Eventually they did. Gil Chapman had a great football career at Michigan. He also graduated from the business school, got an MBA in finance from Rutgers, bought a Ford franchise in Staten Island, and paid it off quicker than anybody in Ford's history.

I wasn't surprised. I knew he had the right stuff. But my argument with the admissions people over Gil was not unique. I have those battles *every single year!* They look at the transcript, they look at the test scores, and they say, "This kid is a dummy. We're not letting him in." And I have to beg to get the kid a chance.

Those admissions people never leave the damn office. I've been to the kid's home, his school, I have talked with his coach, his principal, his guidance counselor, and his community leaders. That should count for something. If you look for character and use a little common sense, I think you can make a decent guess at whether a kid stands a chance at your school. Check the way he speaks to his parents. Check the way he acts in the classroom. Check with neighbors, see what kind of friends he has. Dig a little. And when you find someone, go to bat for him, and be willing to stick with him all five years.

I wasn't wrong about guys like Gil Chapman. I wasn't wrong about Mike Harden. Mike came out of Detroit Central High School. Great kid. Defensive back.

Admissions didn't want him either.

"Forget it, Bo," they said. "We can't get him in."

The hell they couldn't. I got him an interview, and the people were so impressed they offered him a spot. Mike Harden got a degree from Michigan—in political science— and he's still playing in the NFL for the Denver Broncos.

Now, I don't mean to rattle off names of success stories. But here is my beef: There is enormous pressure by administrations on college coaches to produce winning football programs. They must fill the stadium, generate revenue, or in very short time, they will be fired.

That's a fact. But to produce winning programs, you need excellent players; that is also a fact. And many of those excellent players are not at the top of the academic pile; that is also a fact.

A recent NCAA study shows that 37 percent of Division I college football players are black—58 percent for basketball—and that, in general, those blacks come from lower socioeconomic backgrounds than their white counterparts. Their grades in high school are also lower. But many of these kids are not learning in warm, safe, productive school systems. Their potential can't really be judged by matching their transcripts with the best and the brightest. Here's where— if you're going to pressure the coach for both championships *and* diplomas—you must give him a little credit for judgment. There is *not an admissions officer in America* who knows more about a recruit than a coach does.

In the early eighties, I went to see a recruit in urban Detroit. It was the middle of winter. The electricity had been turned off. There was an old fireplace filled with wood from the houses that were falling apart next door, and in the middle of the wood was a huge boulder that took at least three people to carry. During the day the family burned the wood, so this boulder would get red hot, and at night they slept around the boulder, on cots, trying to stay warm.

The kid's name was Thomas Wilcher. A great kid. Quiet. Sensitive. I knew right away he had the desire to make it. I also knew his transcript wasn't going to read like an MIT sophomore's. But when you get a feeling for a kid like that, your back bristles and you say, "God damn it, I'm going to get him in. I want this kid." I had to fight. But he got in. He was a great player. He earned a Michigan degree. And he came back to get a teaching certification.

Now doesn't a public institution have an obligation to students like that, just as it has to scholars from Cambridge and Palo Alto? Sure, we're making exceptions. Yes, it's because of football. But that's not necessarily bad, is it? With something to excel in, like sports, the kid doesn't have to feel inferior every time he goes into a classroom. He feels proud. And maybe he realizes that these smart, privileged kids are no better or worse than him. When that happens, you'll be amazed at the change.

OK. This whole theory falls apart if a coach takes advantage of it. And there are many that do. Coaches who could care less if the kid graduates once he finishes football. Coaches who are happy as long as the kid's grade point average keeps him eligible—never mind that he's taking nothing but "cake" classes.

How can we avoid that? Here are some suggestions. I

propose that every football coach be required to graduate *more* than the school average. If 75 percent of the students on campus end up with degrees, the football team must graduate at least 76 percent. If it's a 90 percent average, the football team must graduate at least 91 percent. And if it fails, it should be docked scholarships.

I also suggest giving a flat twenty-four scholarships a year, no ceiling, versus twenty-five scholarships a year and a ninety-five athletes-on-scholarship ceiling, the way it is now. This way, if you lose a kid to drugs, crime, or academic problems, then you lose his scholarship—and you could wind up playing with a roster of eighty-seven or eighty-eight players. But if you're smart and pick good-character kids, you could have as many as ninety-seven or ninety-eight.

It would also eliminate the following scenario: say you are a scholarship football player, and the coach calls you in after your sophomore year. "Hey, John," he says, "sit down. Listen, you're a nice kid. But you are not gonna make our football team. You're just not good enough."

"Now, what I suggest you do is transfer to another school where you have a better chance to play, OK?"

That stuff goes on *every season*. And a lot of times the kid transfers because he's ashamed or he feels like a failure. The coach gets his scholarship back and gives it to someone more promising. I'm sorry. That's just wrong.

Under the system I propose, that wouldn't happen. If the coach made a mistake and recruited a kid that wasn't good enough to play, that would be *the coach's problem*. Why should the kid be denied his education? That is not to say if the kid is a disciplinary nightmare, you must look the other way. But cutting him off just because he's not a good enough player? I don't believe in that.

The point of this whole chapter is simple: school and football don't have to be at war with each other. Yes, it is hard to do both. Yes, you may have to bend on admissions —at least in premier universities like Michigan—to recruit the topflight athletes. But if the coach is smart, he can find the ones who want to learn, create an environment where learning is the norm, and give those kids the chance that athletic scholarship is supposed to be about.

No, he won't be 100 percent successful. But is any admissions department 100 percent successful? Not even close. Remember that every kid they allow in who doesn't cut it could be considered a failure on their part. I believe holding football coaches to a slightly higher standard than the university norm is fair and acceptable.

And possible. The phrase is *student athlete*. I don't believe it should be a contradiction in terms.

Get Those Agents
Off My Campus

THE agent problem is simple: anyone can be one.
That's the problem.

There are no qualifications, no degree necessary.
You simply declare yourself an agent. "I am an agent."
Now, that's the easiest way to get a title I've ever heard.

Even so, probably 90 percent of the agents out there are halfway reputable guys trying to earn a buck. What concerns me is the 10 percent who will stop at nothing, lie, cheat, steal, just to entice a college athlete to sign with them.

Here's the way they generally work. First they hire some ex-athletes to be their pimps, and I use that word because that's what they really are, pimps, talent collectors, front men. These men make the initial contacts with the kids, using their football background as means of introduction. Usually they zero in on the most vulnerable prospects—talented players from poor backgrounds.

They learn the kid's likes and dislikes. He's a music lover? Get him some concert tickets. He's a car guy? Give him a ride in something fancy. Eventually they bring him to their offices—which may be in New York, Chicago, Los Angeles. Just by flying him there, they've already violated the NCAA rules. But it doesn't stop. They pick him up at the airport in a limousine. They set him up in a nice hotel suite, maybe send a girl up there, maybe make some drugs available. And then, when he's relaxed and enjoying this sudden dose of the good life, they hit him with the bait.

"Hey, man, you're going to make big money in the NFL. You should hire us as your representatives now, and we'll provide you with a little walking-around money until draft time, because a future star like you shouldn't have to eat in the dormitories like other college kids."

The next thing you know, they've got his signature on a contract.

And that's when everything changes.

I know about this stuff, unfortunately, because two of my players fell victim to it not very long ago. I consider that the single biggest off-field disappointment of my football career. These were good kids, solid kids, terrific players. And their heads were turned by agents who saw them, and others, as available pieces of meat.

The players names are Rob Perryman, an outstanding fullback who now plays with the New England Patriots, and Garland Rivers, an All-American defensive back who did not succeed in pro ball. Both of them played for me from 1983 to 1986. Several months before their senior season, unbeknownst to me, they were wooed by sports agents Norby Walters and Lloyd Bloom, whom I consider two of the lowest guys on earth. I am not sure of the exact time, but I believe there was a party in New York that summer, a celebrity thing with a lot of entertainers. The players from around the country were flown in, and that's where the big pitch was made.

Now, I knew Rivers had talent. As early as *six months* before his senior season, I began to talk to him.

"Garland, I want you to know something. You're the kind

of guy that agents will come after. They see you're from a modest background, they see your mother is out of work, and they see you have talent. They'll work on you."

"Don't worry, coach," he said. "I won't listen."

"They'll tempt you with money."

"Don't worry, coach."

"You know that's against the rules, right? You've got another year of football. If you take any money, you would be ineligible and we might have to forfeit any games we played with you."

"I know. I won't do anything like that."

We had these discussions *at least five times* between February and September. "Don't worry," he always said. I had every reason to believe him. Like I said, he was a good kid. Besides, he had been at Michigan three years, and before every season, we go over certain dangers with the *whole team:* drugs, alcohol, steroids, gambling, *and* agents. I bring in speakers from law enforcement agencies. I even post names on the bulletin board of people who have been known to prey on college athletes. "STAY AWAY FROM THESE MEN."

Just before the 1986 season, I posted the names Norby Walters and Lloyd Bloom.

We played the 1986 season. Went to the Rose Bowl. Rivers did not have a particularly good game. A few weeks later, I was coaching the Hula Bowl in Hawaii and Rivers was one of the senior players. He missed the plane out there. Then he missed one of the practices. It wasn't like him. I came down to breakfast one morning and I saw him sitting with a man in the hotel restaurant.

"Hey, coach," Rivers said, "I want you to meet Lloyd Bloom."

"Hello, Coach Schembechler," Bloom said, sticking out his hand.

It was all I could do to keep from yanking that hand and throwing that guy across the room. I could tell by looking at him he was bad news. Real slick. Tried to dress young, talk fast. Hey. After thirty years of recruiting, I can smell a guy on the prowl, and this guy was on the prowl. He was the pimp. Norby Walters's pimp.

By this point, I had no control over Rivers. He had finished his eligibility with Michigan. He could eat with whomever he wanted. But I began to suspect that Garland, whom I had trusted implicitly, had not been telling me the truth.

When we got back to Michigan, I began to hear rumors about Perryman as well. I sent for him, and it took a while before he showed up.

"Perryman, I want to know something," I asked when I finally got him in my office. "Did you sign a contract with Norby Walters and Lloyd Bloom, the sports agents?"

"Well, yeah. But not until after this season was over."

"You didn't sign it last year?"

"Nuh-uh. After the season was over, coach. I promise. I'll get Mr. Bloom to call you."

"Don't bother, son. You made a tragic mistake if you signed with those guys, no matter when you did it. I only hope you aren't ruined by it."

The next day, Lloyd Bloom called. I told my secretary to give him a message: "I don't talk to people like you." It would turn out, of course, that Perryman had indeed signed illegally with Bloom and Walters that summer before— as had a number of college athletes around the country— and that Bloom had told Perryman to lie to me, promising he would call and back him up. I did not know that at the time.

Shortly thereafter, the FBI came around. They were investigating the agents. They wanted to talk to Perryman, but, as a fifth year senior with no further ties to the program, he had suddenly disappeared. The FBI men then called Rivers for a meeting in my office.

They began by asking him general things. A few dates and times. Then came the big question.

"Did you sign a contract with Norby Walters and Lloyd Bloom?"

He lowered his head. "Yes," he mumbled.

"Before your senior season?"

"Yes."

I felt like someone hit me with a ton of bricks. I was shocked—not so much that this could happen, but that Rivers had lied to my face so many times. He admitted that he, like Perryman, had taken money the previous summer, some ridiculously low amount, maybe fifteen hundred dollars. When the FBI guys left, I shut the door and sat down behind my desk.

"Garland," I said, doing all I could to control myself, "why?"

No answer.

"For the money?"

No answer.

I took a deep breath. "Son, you sold us down the river. You lied to me. You lied to this program. You risked the integrity of all the games we played this season. There will be no more grant-in-aid for you. Your locker is cleaned out. You are through here."

He got up and left. And I have not seen him—nor Perryman—since.

Now I want this understood. For three years, Garland Rivers was a great player. He was a good human being. He worked hard in school. He was liked by everyone. Garland Rivers was one fine kid, he was one of those kids that you were going to be very proud of, and these men bought him away from me. They changed him—changed his personality and his ideas. The values we had been drumming into this kid went right down the drain.

When I first questioned him (and Perryman), I gave them the benefit of the doubt. It bothers me that I was fooled. It also bothers me that, for all the pre-season talks and speeches, all the personal warnings I gave those guys, they were apparently willing—for a relatively small sum of money—to say "the hell with coach, we'll do it anyway."

And that is why this agent problem is so dangerous and has to be stamped out.

How do you protect your players? The first thing you do is make your campus off-limits. Don't let agents (or their pimps) anywhere near the place. Nobody at practice. Nobody at the weight room. Nobody at training table. Post their names, post their pictures. This, unfortunately, will not help in bowl games or All-Star games, which agents treat like meat markets. But at least the players should be safe in their own backyard.

The next thing is to make sure these agents are registered with an NCAA agency as well as an NFL agency. Maybe this would help weed out the sleazy ones. It would at least give the college athlete a stamp of approval to look for before signing.

And these agents, by being registered, would understand the rules: no signing of players before the completion of their eligibility. In many states that is now a felony. Good. Sophomore and junior players, only nineteen and twenty years old, do not understand what they might need for representation in the NFL—*if* they even make it. They can (and sometimes do) wind up signing away 5 or 10 percent of *everything*.

Today, an agent is considered a status symbol. Players walk around bragging about how they have one. The truth is, many of the players good enough to "need" an agent probably don't need one at all.

How about this scenario: let's say I'm a college senior, and I'm drafted by the NFL. First question: what is my status? Am I first-round or tenth-round? Having determined that, I then make an appointment with the team that drafted me, go down there, perhaps with my parents or a close friend, and meet with the personnel people.

"What do you have in mind for me?" I ask.

"Well," they say, "for a guy like you, in your position, and your round in the draft, figuring bonus and a three-year deal, this is what we would offer you."

And I say, "Would you put that in writing?"

"Sure, we'll put it in writing."

I take that paper, say thanks, and walk out.

Now, pretty soon, the agent comes around. And he says "I can do this for you, I can do that, I can get you this much money, blah, blah, blah."

And I pull out that paper and say, "Look, before I even met you, I was able to get this offer from the team. Now, if you want to negotiate my contract, I'll give you 10 percent of everything you can get me above this, but I'm not going to pay you anything more."

Now how about that?

Oh sure, if you're a first-round pick with a huge contract and lots of perks, you obviously could use a little help. But if you are a second-, third-, or even lower-round pick, that, right there, is the way I'd do it.

And if the agent doesn't like it, let him take a hike.

During the trial—and subsequent conviction—of Walters and Bloom last April, several issues were raised that are worth mentioning. The first has to do with paying players.

The defense in that case (in which I was called as a witness) argued that college football players are merely performers paid with scholarships. I disagree. They are college students who play football. Yes, some may choose to make a pro career out of it later, the same way a physics major may make a career out of physics after graduation. And yes, universities make a good deal of money off their athletic programs—but that money is *put back into the school to fund other programs*. It's not like somebody's taking it and buying a fleet of fancy sports cars. The money from football will fund the tennis team and the gymnastics equipment and the swimming pool. If for some reason, a hundred thousand people came out to watch the swim team instead, then that money would go to help fund football.

The athletes play for the school, and while they do they must play under the school's rules; they are amateurs, and amateurs do not take money from agents, they do not take cars, they do not take apartments. They are given housing, food, and an education—which is the most any college gives any student. Maybe I'm naive. But when I look at my team I don't only see the guys with NFL potential. I see the guys who are third-string, too. Guys who play for the fun of the sport. If we were to pay the players, how much should they get paid? Would a star earn more than a second-stringer? Do I pay Demetrius Brown twice as much because he passed for a touchdown in the Rose Bowl?

Joe Holland came to visit me recently. Joe was on the team in the mid-80's. He was a backup player and a good student. He never had a prayer of playing NFL football. But he said, "You know, coach, the nice thing about coming out of this program is that I can use it later in life. I tell people I played football at Michigan. That's impressive. Almost as much as my degree."

Now, I honestly believe Joe felt a part of the team as much as Mark Messner or Jamie Morris, even though he wasn't a starter. And if you were to ask him whether he should have been paid for his time, I think he'd tell you he's been amply paid. He got a great education—free of charge—and had a great experience. Critics say the athletes don't care about the education, they're only there to play football. Tell that to Stefan Humphries, with his honors degree in biomedical engineering. Tell it to the dozens of doctors and lawyers and now-millionaire businessmen who have come out of the Michigan football program.

Hey, if you've got a class full of players who don't give a hoot about academics then maybe you recruited wrong.

But don't tell *me* we might as well throw them a paycheck and let the agents chew them up.

Many of these agents try to persuade the kids by saying "Hey, this Coach Schembechler doesn't care about you, you're just a piece of meat to him." And then they fleece the kid. "Oh, we'll only take 4 percent." Yeah. Four percent of everything. Bonus. Salary. Endorsement. Outside income. Future earnings. And almost inevitably, the athlete winds up dumping the guy after a few years—or vice versa.

Now, who's a piece of meat?

So call me old-fashioned. I still believe in college athletics—without agents, without paychecks—but with classes and standards and fun. I think about Joe Holland, the back-up, who's got a lot to show for his time at Michigan, and then I think about Garland Rivers, who is out there somewhere, having failed at pro ball, trying to get by, ordered by the court to pay back the free tuition he used after he'd accepted the money from the agents. Had Garland not taken that money, he could have tried the NFL, not made it, and come back to Michigan to complete his degree—free of charge.

You tell me which is better. I read recently where some people are thinking about unionizing the college players. Demanding fair play. Fair hours. Breaking down this so-called "exploitative" system.

Maybe I'm just getting old. But if it ever comes to that, I'll quit the next day. I really will.

The Game the Way It Should Be

COLLEGE football coaches today are being asked to do just five simple things:

1. Fill the stadium
2. Don't break any NCAA rules
3. Graduate every player they recruit
4. Be morally better than anyone else on campus
5. Win all their games

Hey. No problem. And then I'll flap my wings and fly to the moon.

Until administrations stop making ridiculous demands, college football will keep swelling out of control, coaches will continue to cheat, players will continue to rebel, and we will all continue to miss the point.

This is what college football should be: the most rewarding experience in a young man's life. A time he looks back on, years later, and says, "You know, for all the things

I've done and seen, that was still the best time I ever had. It was tough, it was hard, and the old coach could be a son of a bitch. But everything was fair. Everything was honest. He never asked us to use steroids, never asked us to cheat, never brought kids in and paid them. And when it was all said and done, we played some great games, I made some lifelong friends, and it was a hell of an experience."

If the player can't say that, then, folks, we cannot justify the game as it is today.

Do you know the most significant lesson I ever learned in football? It did not come in a showdown with Ohio State. It came in my own house, from my son Chip, who, at the time, was on his high school football team. He was a backup, one of the last guys on the squad. But he loved to play and he was happy to be out there.

One day the phone rang. Chip went in the other room to answer it. He didn't come back.

I walked into the kitchen and saw him there, crying.

"Hey," I said. "What's wrong? Who called?"

"Aw, nothing."

"Hey, I want to know."

"Aw, that was this kid, Joe. He said he talked to the coach and he's going to return punts in tomorrow night's game. His game pants don't fit him, so the coach said he could have mine."

"HE SAID WHAT?"

"Dad," Chip said, wiping away the tears, "I don't mind so much, except that I'm already the only guy on the team who doesn't have a warm-up jacket. So when we go to warm-up, I'm the only one who stands out. And now, this guy gets to wear my game pants."

I could have killed that coach. I tried to explain to Chip that not all sports are handled that way. Eventually, he got it straightened out. But I'll never forget his face, seeing the tears, knowing how it felt to be the last guy on the team.

If you watch my teams at Michigan, you will notice they all dress alike: full uniform, name across the back. All 125 of them. I've got guys out there I wouldn't put in a *high school* game, guys who can't even catch the ball. You watch them in warm-up drills and you say, "Look at that guy, he's awful."

Yes, but he's a part of the team. And he's warming up alongside the Anthony Carters and Mark Messners. Do you know why? Because somewhere, up in the stands, there's a mother and father watching. And that is this kid's reward for busting his butt all week.

Everybody equal. That's what the college football program should be about. You can't do that if you bribed some kid with a car. You can't do that if one player becomes the reason your fans buy tickets.

Call me old-fashioned, I don't give a crap. I believe in the concept of a *team*. None of this big-names-first, little-names-second stuff. Sure, you spend more time with the regulars, but those other guys, hey, don't just kick them in the face.

We used to have these two running backs we called "Super Sid" and "Super Cede." Super Sid was a walk-on named Ron Szydlowski. And Super Cede was a walk-on named John Cederberg, the slowest son of a gun that ever lived. Nice kid, tougher than hell, but couldn't run a lick. Toward the end of his freshman year he was drinking, and he got in a big fight at the dorm and rammed his hand through a glass.

"Damn you," I said. "How could you do something like that? You're out of football for a year, and if you don't get your act together, you will never play here!"

Well, he stayed out a year. He could have become a full-time screw-off. But he wanted back on the team, so he straightened up. We took him back, and he rode the bench for three years. By his senior season, he and Sydlowski had become sort of cult celebrities. Whenever we were beating a team by twenty-five points or more, the cry would go up. "Hey, Super Sid! Hey, Super Cede! Time for you to go in!"

I'd throw those two in there, and they were like two peas in a pod. If they got back to the *line of scrimmage* it was a miracle. But we gave them the ball, and the rest of the team loved it, because they knew walk-ons work just as hard as the regulars. And at the end of four years, they get the M letter jacket and the M ring just like every other scholarship player.

Super Sid and Super Cede. I still hear from them. In fact, Cederberg—the one who got in trouble—is now a successful lawyer. And I promise you, those two enjoyed the heck out of their college years, even if they never played a down of football that mattered.

I think that's great.

I loved my time playing college football. And since the day I became coach, I've been trying to recreate it for my players. I wanted them to learn the way I learned under Woody and Ara. I wanted them to work that hard, to sweat that much, to feel that bad and to feel that good, and to make the kind of friends you can still call, even in your sixties, and say, "Remember that game when we played in a snowstorm . . ."

Maybe that's not possible these days. When I played at Miami of Ohio, we had a medium-sized crowd and no television. At Michigan, it's 105,000 fans and network TV. At Miami, almost none of us expected a shot at the NFL. At Michigan, four or five a year may get there. Professional football has strongly influenced college in areas like money, steroids, and lack of interest in academics. It consumes these kids, making the pros. And that's sad.

I've never had a guy in the NFL who didn't swear he had more fun in college. Jim Mandich has a handful of Super Bowl rings, and he always tells me, "Coach, it just didn't compare." Dan Dierdorf was about as good as you can get in the NFL, but when I see him he still talks about that locker room after the Iowa game in 1969. "Coach, I've still never felt anything like that, before or since."

Why do you think I've never coached in the NFL? Because I'd have coached them like a college team and it wouldn't have worked. You can't ask players to win for pride and teamwork when you're pink-slipping and trading them.

The NFL is a business. But college football, *real* college football, shouldn't be. And there's the problem. For all the emphasis on academics, the bottom line with many administrations is still filling the stadium, producing revenue, keeping that program in the black.

And the pressure grows. Everyone wants to win—but not everyone can. Schools must recognize a mission impossible when they see one. You don't hire a coach at Northwestern, then say, "Go get Ohio State and Michigan." You don't hire a coach at Vanderbilt and say, "You must win the Southeast Conference." You don't go to the coach at Kansas State and say "When are we going to beat *Oklahoma and Nebraska?*"

Not unless you want him to cheat, bend, and look the other way.

You know what you get if you put that pressure on a coach? You get a coach who knows he won't be there long. He plays the "face man" game, tries to look good while he's collecting his paycheck, and sees how much he can get away with, waiting for the inevitable ax to fall.

I have one question.

What about the kids?

There's a guy on my team right now, Allen Jefferson, a highly touted running back from Detroit. Under normal circumstances, he might be a starter; he has that much talent. But he got injured in the middle of his sophomore year, a shin injury, and for the last year and a half he has been unable to run. His leg just wouldn't heal.

This kid suffered terribly. He wrote me a ten-page letter saying how much he felt left out. He'd always fantasized about what college would be like—"Local Kid Makes Good for Michigan"—and all of a sudden, he was watching Tony Boles and Leroy Hoard run for glory while he sat. People wondered why it took him so long to recover from a fairly simple injury. It broke his spirit.

"Allen," I would tell him, over and over, "it's not your fault, son. Don't torture yourself."

Then in March, the doctors operated on him again. They removed a calcium growth between his bones that I swear was almost two inches wide. This poor kid busted his ass for a year and a half trying to play with that thing in his leg. I ran to the hospital the day after the operation.

"Hey, Allen," I said, "I saw it! I SAW IT!"

"Saw what, coach?"

"I saw the growth they removed. Son, it was THAT BIG! It was as hard *as any bone in your body!* You tried to play with that thing in your leg? Son, you are the gutsiest damn football player I've ever run into.

"I'm gonna tell you, you're gonna be all right. We've got two years of eligibility left for you. And we're gonna play some *football!*"

The reality is, there's a fifty-fifty chance that calcium deposit could grow back. But when I left Allen, he was ecstatic. And I swear, I am going to save the college experience for that kid. If I can just get him a big moment, one game, something he can look back on years from now. You can't forget about guys like Allen Jefferson. If you do, you're not running a program, you're running an All-Star team.

The temptation today is to grow cynical. Many people have. "The whole college sports system is a joke," they say. "The schools are just using the players to make money and the players are just training to go to the NFL."

Well. That's one person's opinion. I'm here to tell you otherwise. The system can work. Take a look at Stefan Humphries. Now there was a kid who got everything out of every minute of college *and* football. He studied biomedical engineering, got mostly A's, some A-pluses—they even printed his transcript in *Sports Illustrated*. Yet Humphries was one of the toughest guards you'd ever want to meet. Made All-American in 1983. Played with the Chicago Bears and now the Denver Broncos. He used to kid me whenever he had a lab that conflicted with practice. "Bo, you're not going to like what I have to tell you, but there's nothing we can do about it . . ."

Now, my point is you didn't have to tell Stefan Humphries that being a student athlete could be a great thing. And there are plenty of guys out there like him.

How about Kenny Higgins? He was as brilliant as they come. After four years at Michigan he was accepted at Stanford, Harvard, Yale, and Michigan law schools. My problem was, he was my leading receiver, and he had a fifth year of eligibility.

"Sorry, Bo," he told me, "but I'm finished here academically, so I'm going on to law school."

"Where are you gonna go?" I asked.

"Harvard. It's the best."

"But, Higgins, you're my top guy. Why not go to Michigan and play another year of football?"

"Bo, Harvard is the number one law school. It's rated a little better than Michigan's. I had a great four years playing for you, but it's time to move on."

He grinned at me. How could you not be proud of this kid?

"You're right," I said, "get your butt out of here."

"Thanks, Bo."

"Higgins?"

"Yeah?"

"Harvard Law School is *not* better than Michigan's."

* * *

Back in April, we had a big weekend celebrating my twenty years with the Wolverines. The highlight was a Saturday night banquet for players and coaches—everyone who had ever played since 1969 was invited.

Do you know that out of 640 players who wore the uniforms, nearly 400 showed up? Some traveled from Seattle, Florida, San Diego. There were guys from that 1981 Rose Bowl team that finally beat the jinx, and from the 1973 team that was denied a trip to Pasadena, from Jim Harbaugh's year, when he "guaranteed" a win over Ohio State, and Tom Slade's year, when our quarterback was really a pulling guard, and from that 1984 team that went 6–6 (they got the most teasing), and, of course, from the 1969 group, which year after year keeps coming back, even though I was harder on them than any other team.

That banquet started around 6 P.M. and did not end until the wee hours of the morning. It was laughter and insults and bad jokes and cigars. And it was more. It was doctors and lawyers and businessmen and fathers with sons in college. It was good men with decent values—not all, but most —who were reliving some great years not because those years were the only highlights of their lives, but because those years prepared for the years that followed, taught them how to work hard, to endure adversity, to keep plugging away even if an old man with a whistle or an old man called "the boss" was making life miserable. None of these guys ever won a national championship or a Heisman Trophy. But you should have heard them talk, and laugh, and cry, and throw their arms around each other as if they were all related, blood to blood. I think that's what some of these other coaches are missing when they focus on themselves, their money, their fame.

"Time of my life," the guys said over and over that night. "Time of my life."

That's what college football should be.

* * *

As for me, well, I've read a lot about how I've mellowed as a result of my health. If I've mellowed—and I'm not sure what the word means—it's because I'm coming to the end of the road. I have no ambition to be a coach at the age of sixty-five, so I've got a few years left, and it could be anytime. Next year. This year. Soon.

There are lots of things I'd love to do. What worries me is doing *without* the Saturday afternoons on the field. Heck, I've been involved with football since I was a kid. And I flat-out love being with the players. I always have an empty feeling when the last game of the season ends and they disperse back to campus. That's when the fun goes out of the job, for me anyhow.

Last year, on the final day of recruiting, the phone was ringing off the hook. "This one's changed his mind, Bo . . ." "This one's coming, Bo . . ." "I think this kid's been bought off, Bo . . ." I sat in that damn office from 7:30 A.M. until late afternoon, and I was going out of my mind. Finally I grabbed my coat.

"Bo, where are you going?" my secretary asked.

"Out."

I marched down to the football building, saw a bunch of my players in the weight room, took off my coat, and sat down. And I stayed there the rest of the day, talking, shooting the bull, teasing them about their girlfriends and their classes. Maybe it wasn't the most responsible thing to do, but the hell with it.

That's why I don't know about this athletic director business. There's talk about me just doing that after football, but I'm really not sure if I could handle being around and not coaching. I was never a desk guy. Maybe I should just disappear when I take the black sneakers off.

As for being remembered, well, I always thought that was an odd question. I don't want to be remembered for anything other than what I'm trying to do right now: be a person of some honesty and integrity and reasonable intelligence, who loves his work, makes a lot of friends, and maybe does some good with young people. Football? Hey. Whatever. Why worry about going down in history as a great coach? People are gonna argue you weren't, anyhow.

I began this book with the story of a heart attack. I'll end it with less drama, a nothing story, really, it just happened to take place today, the last day I'm working on this final chapter.

It was a cool spring afternoon. We were finishing practice. And we always close out with a one-on-one scrimmage. I was coaching the offense. And we suckered them with a trick play. Leroy Howard took a handoff and threw twenty yards to Derrick Walker in the end zone. Touchdown! Against the first defense.

"No fair," they grumbled.

"OK, FINE!" I yelled, grinning. "WE WON'T COUNT THAT. WE'LL DO IT AGAIN FROM THE TWENTY-YARD LINE. AND THIS TIME . . . NO TRICK PLAYS! WE'RE JUST COMING AFTER YOUR ASS!"

They cheered. OK. Great. Another chance. We lined up again. We handed off, nice and simple—and they stuffed us.

"ONE MORE TIME," I demanded, laughing.

The players whooped it up. Here we go. Last play of the day. We want to score. They want to stop us. I called the most beautiful screen pass you ever saw. It was supposed to go to Leroy. But damn if Michael Taylor, our quarterback, who was rushed, didn't throw it clear back in the other direction!

"Look out!" someone yelled, laughing.

"FUMBLE!" someone else yelled.

Leroy had no chance to catch it—but he went back and scooped that ball off the ground anyway, one-handed, and headed up field. We threw a few blocks, like sandlot ball;

guys were yelling "This way! This way!" He was gonna go
. . . and they stopped him at the five-yard line!

Everyone got up laughing—call it a draw—and the horn
sounded and practice was over. The players took off their
helmets and walked lazily off the field, slapping each other,
smiling as if they didn't want to leave, because it had been
fun, like it was supposed to be. The sun was setting, the air
was cool, and God, if every day could be like that, just football
and laughter and a bunch of good kids. That's what it's all
about, you know. The kids, the memories, the wonder of
growing up.

Me? I'm just the guy with the whistle.

And that's all I ever wanted to be.